PEPPER TIME

REWIRE YOUR BRAIN, FUEL YOUR GUT, AND LIVE THE LIFE YOU WANT

Jolien Demeyer

For my rockstars, Gisèle & George.

Add the peppers that make life yours.

Credits:

Interior Design: Annemarie Lamprecht

Cover Design: Elenor

First Printing, 2026

ISBN Print: 978-1-7356897-1-5

ISBN eBook: 978-1-7356897-2-2

Library of Congress Control Number: 2025922499

Table Of Contents

Summary

Consider what your life would look like if you lived more loyal to your dreams and less influenced by your fears.

What started as a side hobby has grown to a global community and a meaningful movement.

Dig in to explore how to begin playing bigger in the ways that matter most to you.

You're NOT stuck.
You're under-seasoned.
Add pepper.

Preface

You Already Know. Now Dare.

From the outside my life looked impressive. But inside, something was quietly slipping away. Fine looks stable. But fine is not alive. Fine is settling. And here's the truth: Fine is expensive. It costs you your joy, health, creativity, and relationships. For years, I paid that cost without realizing it. Then my body whispered what my brain refused to hear: *This isn't the life you promised yourself.* I tried to ignore it. I told myself to be grateful. To work harder. But the whisper grew louder. Pregnancy turned the volume up. My head screamed, Run faster, prove more, don't stop. My gut whispered, *Listen*.

That moment cracked me open. It forced me to choose between the life that looked good and the life that felt good.

I made a choice. And that choice changed everything.

I swapped proving for presence. Hustle for alignment. I began building with a new compass—**brain to execute, gut to guide.**

Who This Book Is For

This is for the Scaleurs who look successful but feel something missing. For founders chasing one more investor call even though deep down, they've been ready for years. For mothers who think they must choose between power and presence when they were built for both. For women waiting for one more degree. For ambitious builders who are done shrinking themselves to fit the room—who feel the fire but keep dimming it to match what others expect.

I keep meeting the same Scaleur in different industries and stages of growth. On paper, they are unstoppable: smart, hardworking, compassionate, visionary. Their companies are growing, their teams expanding, their highlight reels sparkling. But behind the scenes, they carry a heavy belief: *Maybe I'm not a real leader*.

And alongside that belief lives another ache: *Is this really it?*

These women want more than fine. They want freedom in their time, choices, bodies, and businesses. But they feel stuck inside systems that praise their polish while draining their voice.

I became obsessed with one question:

"What does it take for Scaleurs to stop performing for approval and start building from their gut— to build a life on their own terms?"

That question is the heartbeat of this book.

Years of coaching sessions—celebrating daily wins, learning from setbacks—taught me what truly makes the difference. From that work, and from my own path, I shaped the GutScaleurs approach: **ideas, practices, and tools to play bigger your way—plus the pepper you need when hesitation gets loud.**

Why Pepper, And Why Now?

This isn't just another self-help book. This is a manual for survival in a world that quietly trains us to shrink.

Too many of us live trapped in patterns shaped by pain—our own, our family's, even our ancestors'. These stories are not just in your head. They're embedded in your body, your energy, your nervous system.

Your brain, brilliant as it is, was designed to keep you alive, not to keep you fulfilled. In every millisecond, your brain's 86 billion neurons are interpreting signals from your body, gut, and environment. And it files those signals not by truth, but by habit: *What does this mean, based on yesterday?*

This is why you get stuck.
This is why you sabotage yourself.
This is why change feels so hard.

The lies sound familiar:

- *This is just the way I am.*
- *Later will be better.*
- *If I just work harder, it will click.*
- *Everyone else seems to manage; it must be me.*

These are not truths. These are loops, survival shortcuts your brain learned long ago. And here's the catch: Your brain hates change. It tags new as unsafe and familiar as safe—even when the familiar is making you miserable. That's why so many of us live on autopilot. From taking the same route to work to repeating old relationship patterns and telling the same stories about what we can and can't do. Autopilot is efficient. But efficiency without awareness kills aliveness.

This book is urgent because if you don't take back control of your brain, your autopilot will keep flying you to destinations you no longer want.

Gut leadership is the answer. Your gut sends signals to your brain before your brain has even formed a thought. It knows when you're aligned and when you're betraying yourself. This book will teach you to listen to those signals—and then train your brain to back them up with action. That's the shift: **gut to guide, brain to build.** Pepper matters because breaking free from the lies is uncomfortable. Without a spark, you'll stay stuck in "fine." Pepper is the spark that moves you. And the sooner you begin, the sooner you can break free.

A Living Field Guide

This is not a book to keep clean. Books are houses meant to be lived in. Underline what hits. Write in the margins. Fold corners. Let it get messy. I'll often ask you to pause. To put the book down, do an exercise in your journal, stretch, breathe, take a short walk, or simply sit still. Because this is not a race. There's no medal for speed. The real trophy is a lifestyle shift that leaves you happier, steadier, and more you.

Think of this book like an operating-system upgrade. Together, we'll keep installing happier, stronger versions of how your brain runs your day. Not by pushing harder, but by practicing differently. The tools are simple on purpose. They're not here to impress you. They're here to rewire you.

This book is both a hand on your back and a spark under your seat—the pepper in your ass. It's science and soul, story and system. You'll see how your survival wiring keeps you looping. You'll learn why your gut often knows before your head catches up. And you'll discover how to stack small, simple Pepper Reps until your identity matches your ambition. Playing bigger isn't about doing more. It's about doing what matters—with alignment, courage, and gut-led clarity.

Building The Framework

Our goal is to help you feel good while you build. Because if you don't feel good, nothing you build will feel good either.

Everything in this book comes back to three pillars:

- **Relationships:** Navigating conflict without losing connection, maintaining healthier bonds, being more present as a parent and partner.
- **Performance:** Being more productive, making better decisions, unlocking creativity and resilience, persuading without selling yourself out.
- **Well-being:** Reducing stress, feeling happier, taking care of your body in ways that fit your life.

It sounds ambitious because it is. But it's possible—because we'll go to the root of the problem: the loops that sabotage you and the Brain Powers that replace them. Your brain loves efficiency. It tags the familiar as safe and runs you on autopilot to save energy. That's useful when you're brushing your teeth or driving to the store. But it's dangerous when the patterns you've automated are making you small, tired, or stuck. And here's the truth: Insight alone doesn't beat a pattern. You can't think your way out of it. Muscle counters muscle.

That's why this book will help you build Pepper Reps—tiny, daily practices that rewire your brain while you live your real life. You'll learn how to quiet the Judge (the loud voice that magnifies what's wrong). You'll learn how to trust your Future Self (the wiser version of you who already lives your vision). And you'll learn how to pair that guidance with action—so your identity can finally catch up with your behavior. And here's the best part: Lasting change isn't about punishment or discipline. It's about design.

1. Make it easy to start. Break change into steps so small you can't fail.
2. Reward the small steps. Celebrate Pepper Wins so your brain wants to repeat them.

That's how you Design Your Default. We don't fight autopilot. We train it.

My Turning Points

I didn't learn this from theory. I lived it.

Nine years into my corporate career, I wanted to expand, innovate, build something bigger with the team. My gut buzzed with possibility, but every bold idea I brought forward was met with the same answer: "Stay in your lane." I realized I couldn't keep shrinking myself. So in 2018, I started my first marketing agency in Chicago. The Judge screamed: *You're not ready. You don't know enough. Wait a little longer.* But my gut said: *Go.* So I did. One pitch. One contract. One small Pepper Rep at a time. And once I moved, momentum came.

But life tested me in ways business never could. Miscarriages. Losing my mother. The weight of grief that productivity can't erase. Abuse. Days when my head said *Push harder* while my body whispered *Rest.* These valleys brought clarity and taught me that resilience is about aligning.

Today, I'm a mom of two living in Switzerland with my partner of two decades. I juggle like you do—work calls, little hands tugging at me, dreams, deadlines, and sometimes spit-up on my shirt. Motherhood taught me endurance, patience, and the daily choice to turn myself into love.

My mission now is simple: **Help one million Scaleurs build the life and business they want with #gutleadership.**

Let's start practicing right now.

PEPPER ASK:

- *What would be the most inspiring change you want to create in your life this year?*

Don't search for the perfect answer. Pick what feels alive. Write it down. Then choose one goal in each pillar:

- Well-being: less stress, more peace, a body that feels good.
- Performance: better decisions, visible progress, more of the work that matters.
- Relationships: clearer boundaries, kinder conflicts, more presence with the people you love.

Now close your eyes for sixty seconds. Imagine one ordinary Tuesday shaped by those changes. Just a simple day where you feel different. That scene belongs to your Future Self. We'll return to it later.

Our Journey Ahead

This book is a journey. One that will take you from the quiet drain of "fine" to the fire of alignment, energy, and courage.

Along the way, you'll meet the cast inside you:

- **The Judge:** That loud, sabotaging voice in your head that keeps you small.
- **Your Power Brain:** The rewired circuits you'll train to flip fear into courage.
- **Your Gut:** Your built-in compass that always knows faster than logic.
- **Your Future Self:** The wiser version of you who already lives the life you're building.

You'll also encounter plenty of **Pepper Experiments (GutScaleurs.com/bookexperiments)**—fiery Pepper Time challenges that move you from knowing to doing. You'll just need a quiet space, your journal, and a pen for most of these.

We'll begin in **Part I: Being**. This is your wake-up call. Most of us don't crash because of one big disaster. We leak slowly, stay in jobs that don't light us up, relationships that drain more than they give, routines that keep us comfortably stuck. In these opening chapters, you'll see the cost of comfort. You'll meet the Judge—that loud, sabotaging voice in your head—and realize how it keeps you small. And you'll remember what your gut has known all along: Joy is your default. By the end of this part, you won't be lulled by fine anymore. You'll be restless for fire.

But waking up isn't enough. Awareness without action fades. That's why **Part II: Rewiring** exists. You'll learn how to catch the Judge in the act, flip sabotaging thoughts, and start stacking Pepper Reps—tiny, repeatable practices that rewire your brain and gut to work for you instead of against you. The reps may look simple—one breath, one sentence, one pause—but repeated daily, they change your identity. And you'll meet your Future Self, the wiser version of you who already lives the life you're building. This part is about reps, rhythm, and consistency. Day by day. Choice by choice.

Once the noise quiets and your new muscles strengthen, something shifts. That's **Part III: Flow**. Flow is when you stop forcing and start aligning. When your energy fuels you instead of draining you. Here you'll learn to protect your fire, set non-negotiables, and build boundaries that let you thrive instead of leaking energy everywhere. You'll see why joy isn't an extra; it's a strategy. And you'll discover the paradox that doing less creates more. Flow is when you stop fighting yourself and finally start moving with yourself.

Then we'll zoom out in **Part IV: Revolution.** Your rebellion—saying no to autopilot, yes to alignment—is powerful on its own, but when joined with others it becomes a movement. This is where you'll learn to turn private fire into public impact. You'll learn the GutScaleur Code: the principles that turn individual boldness into collective rise. And you'll finish by understanding that you don't need more degrees, more time, or more permission. What you need is the courage to go all in.

All In is daring to put everything you've built—your presence, your rewiring, your flow—into what matters most. To stop waiting. To stop shrinking. To put the pepper where it belongs and finally play big on your own terms.

Each chapter will give you the science to explain, stories to inspire, and an experiment, we'll call them Pepper Times, to practice. Transformation isn't something you highlight; it's something you live. So let's circle back to this question I asked you in the preface: *What would be the most inspiring change you want to create in your life this year?*

This journey is how you answer it.

It's time to move from fine to fire. From being, to rewiring, to flow, to revolution. Until finally—you dare to go all in.

Change the game within. Add the pepper you need. Start installing the happier code.

You already know. Now dare. It's Pepper Time!

Let's Play!

"The greatest danger in life is not that we aim too high and miss, but that we aim too low and hit."

— Michelangelo

From Fine To Fire

Most people don't dream of a mediocre life. Yet that's where so many end up. Not broken. Not in crisis. Just... fine.

Fine is the quiet thief. It convinces you to tolerate the draining job, the lukewarm relationship, the routine that looks okay on Instagram but feels hollow when you're alone. Fine whispers, *Don't rock the boat. It's not that bad. Others have it worse.* But fine is expensive. It costs you joy, creativity, intimacy, money, energy—and most of all, time. And once time is gone, you don't get it back.

This part of the book is your wake-up call. Together, we'll price the real cost of comfort, unmask the elegant lies that keep you small, and explore why your gut already knows the truth your brain keeps dodging. You'll see how autopilot runs your days, how fear disguises itself as logic, and how "fine" has been draining more than you ever realized. By the end of part 1, "fine" won't feel safe anymore. And from that fire, you'll finally be ready to move.

Chapter 1:

Comfort Has A Cost - From Fine To Fire

This is not a polite chapter. This is the match. The sting. The pepper in your ass. And if you feel a little offended, a little called out—good. That means your gut is awake.

Comfort sneaks in wearing a suit of "maturity," "stability," "respectability." It looks like a paycheck that never bounces, a nice house, a fancy LinkedIn title. Everyone's impressed. Meanwhile, something small but vital in you starts to dim. You stop asking questions that might rock the boat. You tell yourself this is fine—not thrilling, not fulfilling, but not bad. That's the trap. We trade aliveness for predictability. Dreams for routine. Joy for safety. And the cruel thing about comfort is that it feels easier than daring—until the invoice lands.

I know because I paid it. I spent nine years in corporate, climbing, delivering, mastering my role so deeply I could run it in my sleep. But my gut wanted more—bold moves that stitched people and possibilities together. My boss didn't want fire; he wanted a thermostat. When I offered bigger, he tightened the reins. More than once I heard, "You like to color outside the lines," and not as a compliment. Stay in the box. Don't disrupt. Don't dare.

I stayed anyway—for a while. It was comfortable, the salary was steady, I was able to travel. The praise of others drowned the ache in my gut. I told myself it wasn't that bad. Then the whisper got louder: Move. One day the gut out-shouted the paycheck, and I walked. That choice became the seed of my marketing agency in Chicago. Looking back, I shudder at how easy it would've been to keep "winning" on paper while losing myself one beige Tuesday at a time.

And it isn't just me. I see this pattern in Scaleurs again and again. On the outside: steady, reliable, respectable; on the inside: quietly suffocating. Lindsay is a composite you'll recognize: mid-40s, razor-sharp, known in her community as the steady hand who grew a modest family business into a serious real estate operation. She inherited a portfolio from her parents and, brick by brick, built it further. For years, she thrived on the chase. But something shifted. The spark in her eyes that used to ignite when she described a new project began to dim. Instead of building something alive, she was maintaining a machine.

She told herself she had too much to lose to take new risks. So she kept the business running. Sunday nights became heavy. Even her reflection grew tired—not from age, but from the quiet erosion of passion. She whispered, *I should be grateful.* And she was, partly. But "should-gratitude" is fear in a fancy dress. It's what convinces us to stay quiet, to stay safe, to trade joy for respectability. That's the cruelty of comfort. It slowly convinces you that safety is the same as purpose. That steady is the same as alive. And the longer Lindsay obeyed it, the heavier life became.

Then there was Any, a mid-30s Scaleur with a laugh that could fill a room and ideas that made people lean forward. Before kids, she dreamed out loud. She wanted to write, speak, build a social enterprise that had teeth. And then the script dropped on her shoulders: "Be everything for everyone;" "Good mothers put themselves last." Her family pressed her to stay home more. Daycare was scarce. So, she swallowed her hunger. One idea shelved. Then another. Until the shelf was full and she was empty. She became the supermom and smiled while people clapped. But inside, she was vanishing.

This is where culture betrays women most. Society demands that mothers juggle everything—work, caregiving, health, relationships—and then shames them whichever way they lean. The impossible burden of "shoulds" turns love into self-erasure. Comfort steals not in disasters but in degrees. Lindsay didn't fail. She just stopped daring. And that was the slowest death of all.

What most women don't see until it's too late is that *constant sacrifice is not love; it's abandonment of self.* And you cannot build a thriving family, career, or life from an abandoned self. Sometimes, gratitude is just fear in polite clothes. "Should" is comfort's favorite weapon. It keeps you tolerating a life that isn't truly yours. And the cost? You'll find it bleeding into the three areas where we most crave aliveness:

- **Relationships.** You smile, but the people closest to you feel your absence. You avoid conflict to keep the peace, but connection suffers. You're sitting at the table, but your kids feel your stress more than your joy. Your partner feels the distance. This is how intimacy erodes—not with explosions, but with polite silence.
- **Performance.** On paper, you're doing fine. You check the boxes, deliver on time, keep up the image. But inside, creativity dries up. Conviction fades. You keep saying yes to projects that make you look good but drain you. Work stops being about possibility and becomes about maintenance. Your fire becomes obligation.
- **Well-being.** You normalize exhaustion as adulthood. You numb yourself with endless to-do lists, scrolling, and busyness. You forget what vitality feels like. You can't remember the last time you belly-laughed or felt fully present in your own body. You confuse survival for living.

Comfort drains you. And the spark it takes is the very fuel you need to build the life, business, and relationships that feel truly yours. It might sound almost too good to be true that you could reclaim energy, joy, intimacy, and creativity without adding more to your already overflowing plate. But it is possible. Not by juggling harder or layering on more hacks but by going to the root and stripping away the lies that keep you small. That's what this book is about.

#PEPPER ASK: So let me ask you:

- *What's the most inspiring change you want to create in your life right now?* 

Don't overthink it. Just feel into it. Picture an ordinary Tuesday where it's already true. That's your compass. See yourself living it. That's your starting point. That's the scene your gut is already pulling you toward. Grab a fresh page in your journal and answer the question. No editing, no perfection—just honesty.

Just Fine Is Not Fine

You've probably seen women like Any. They juggle everything—family, work, community—and society claps. But if you look past the applause, you see the shame in their eyes, the fatigue in their bones. Because no one can be all things for all people forever. You've probably seen men too, praised as steady providers, admired for their responsibility, but lying awake at night whispering, *"Is this really it?"* I've seen successful entrepreneurs shrink inside until they dreaded waking up to face the business they'd built. Nobody stages an intervention for "fine." Society claps for it, but your gut knows better. If you've been so busy being responsible that you've forgotten what happiness feels like, that's the cost. And most of us don't even notice the slide into fine until we're numb.

And because it isn't a crisis, you stay. Nobody posts *#JustFine* on Instagram. Nobody pulls you aside and says, *"Careful,* *you're suffocating."* But your gut knows the truth: Fine is where dreams go to suffocate quietly.

Take Gwyn in Michigan. Mid-30s, running a profitable food manufacturing business. Inside, she was brittle, anxious, burned out. She stayed in leadership for a decade, convincing herself stability was worth the price—until she realized she had sacrificed ten years to a version of success that never felt like her own. She told herself she'd get back to her dreams "once the kids were older." But the years passed, and so did her sense of self. Fine robs you of the one currency you can never get back: time.

Both comfort and fine drain your well-being, your relationships, your performance. That's why we start this book here—at the gut punch of fine. But here's the hope: Just as your brain can learn fine, it can unlearn it. Science confirms what your gut already knows: The brain is wired for efficiency. Eighty-six billion neurons fire constantly, scanning for patterns. From childhood, the brain learns to equate familiarity with safety.

Growing up with two teacher-parents, I was raised with the pattern: *"Study hard, get the degree, get the stable job."* That narrative carried me to three master's degrees. But inside, I knew I wasn't fully alive yet. Fine masquerades as safety because it's familiar. Add the stress response to the mix, and the trap tightens. The moment you consider leaving the job, ending the relationship, or launching the idea, your brain interprets it as danger. Cortisol spikes. Fear whispers: *"Don't risk it. Comfort is safer."* And once again, you trade fire for fine.

But here's the breakthrough: Neuroscience proves we can rewire these patterns. Pathways can be reshaped. New defaults can be created. Courage can become familiar. Boldness can become automatic. This is what gut leadership is about—letting your gut lead and retraining your brain to follow. Building the mental muscles that make courage less of a performance and more of a habit.

Think back to childhood again. Rules about thing like respecting authority and playing it safe carved a groove in your brain. Over time, those grooves became highways—thoughts on autopilot. By adulthood, you don't even question them. That's why so many of us stay in jobs we've outgrown, relationships that have expired, or routines that suffocate us. Because the brain has mislabeled *familiar as safe*. But familiarity isn't the same as aliveness. And when your brain loops on old predictions, you lose touch with your natural state. You forget that joy is baseline. That happiness is your birthright.

Over 95 percent of serotonin—the neurotransmitter most linked to joy—is produced in the gut, not the brain. Your body is literally wired for happiness. It's not a prize you unlock at the end of success; it's your default. You just have to strip away what's blocking it.

And this is where Pepper Reps come in. Pepper Reps aren't about brute force or pretending to be bold. They're about mental stillness. Think of them as micro-trainings for your brain, kind of a mental fitness: Before a hard conversation, you pause, breathe, and listen to the gut signal beneath the panic. When procrastination hits, instead of scrolling, you sit in stillness until the next true action emerges. When fear screams "Stay safe," you choose one small act of fire instead. (We'll explore Pepper Reps more deeply in part 2.)

Each time you do this, you're carving a new groove in your brain. You're teaching your system that courage is safe, stillness is power, and joy can be trusted. At first it stings—like lifting weights at the gym. But that sting is growth. With repetition, the pathway strengthens. Eventually, your default isn't fear. It's boldness, clarity, and alignment.

Comfort doesn't just rob you abstractly; it bills you in real ways:

- **Time:** Years you can't get back, like staying a decade in a role you've outgrown.
- **Energy:** Afternoons you'll never remember because they were numbed by busyness.
- **Money:** Projects that paid the bills but never compounded into meaning or legacy.
- **Intimacy:** Silences with your partner that felt polite but hollow.
- **Creativity:** Ideas you never tested because you were too busy being respectable.

Every invoice comes due. But neuroscience shows us that you can build new pathways where courage feels familiar, boldness is the baseline, and happiness isn't something you chase but something you uncover. That's the essence of gut leadership. It's about listening to the whisper in your gut, retraining your brain to follow it, and building the mental fitness to keep doing it—even when fear shows up in polite clothes.

#PEPPER ASK: So let me ask you:

- *Where in your life have you been telling yourself "fine"? Where have you been tolerating, shrinking, settling?*

Write it down. See it clearly.

Opting Out Of Old Systems

Comfort is baked into the systems that shaped us. Inherited rules. Corporate dogmas. Family codes passed down like heirlooms even when they don't fit. Systems disguise themselves as values when they're really cages. But your gut knows when a rule doesn't fit. When you live by someone else's version of normal, you perpetually feel like you're failing because the rulebook was never designed for you.

Some new mothers feel pressure to return to work quickly after birth. Others feel pressure to stay home as long as possible. Many feel pulled in both directions at once. The only way to win is to do what feels right for you and your family regardless of the system around you. My daughter, Gisele, started daycare at three and a half months, five days a week. In 2023 and 2024, during my pregnancy and early motherhood, I cut my working hours roughly in half. My business didn't skyrocket—but it didn't tank either. Our real-estate portfolio grew steadily. And I learned two things that shook me:

1. Much of the "busy" I carried before pregnancy was unnecessary noise.
2. My worth had never been the sum of tasks completed by 6 p.m.

That year became one of the most productive of my life in the only currency that matters: presence. I made a human being, learned to work differently, stopped worshipping the grind, and started honoring my biology. I started to learn about gut leadership and the brain. That was a pepper moment—a sting of truth I couldn't ignore: The system will not give you permission to live aligned. You must give it to yourself. Motherhood taught me the beauty and value of the unknown, the seasons, the spiral.

Culturally, we still treat life as a ledger: Men go make money, women hold the world, and anyone who deviates is measured and found wanting. But real life isn't a spreadsheet; it's a tide. And when you move with it, you discover a deeper, steadier power than the one you get from forcing yourself into someone else's timetable.

Let's also tell the truth about gendered bodies and expectations. Men don't carry pregnancy fatigue. Many want to help and do—but the system applauds quick return, uninterrupted output, endless availability. Women feel that gravity too. We get praised for juggling it all and then judged whichever way we lean. Pour into work? *"Cold."* Devote to family? *"Lazy."* Attempt both? *"Do it flawlessly, and smile."* It's not just parents either. Quietly, a huge share of adults act as unpaid caregivers for aging parents, partners, or friends. Most are women. So what do we do besides rage?

We build what we need. We create environments—homes, teams, companies—where people can earn what they need *and* still have the time and energy to care for themselves and their people. Not someday. Now. I applaud the ones who reform from within—truly. Stay in the system and bend it better if that is your path. But there is also a legitimate lean-out strategy. That path isn't always supported by policy or praised by culture, and it might look unruly from the outside. It is still holy work.

For me, opting out meant running my own show from any-where. It meant letting my body set the pace during pregnancy and postpartum and trusting that depth would beat volume. I realized I'd been propping up an identity that confused busy-ness with worth. Letting that identity die was terrifying—and freeing. Also, let's retire the fantasy of "work–life balance." The real question isn't, *How do I balance these two enemies?* It's, *What rhythms let me feel alive while I contribute at my highest?* Most companies still reward constant availability. Your job is to stop confusing their comfort with your calling.

To reimagine anything, you start by subtracting what's not work-ing. Remove the obligations that are actually performances, the roles you never chose, the "shoulds" you inherited. When you strip away what suffocates you, joy returns—like breath when the pressure lifts.

Because here's the truth: the only way to create a new system is to *be* it. Don't wait for others to understand your reality. Start now. Choose the rhythm that works for you. Build the habits that sustain you. Let your gut be the compass even when cul-ture calls you reckless. That is gut leadership in practice. It's pepper in the ass—not because it's comfortable, but because it wakes you up to the life that is yours to claim. And once you feel that click of alignment—the moment your choices match your truth—you can't unfeel it. Comfort will try to negotiate.

You're not breaking the rules to be rebellious. You're breaking the cage to breathe.

Happiness Is Your Default

We've seen the tax of comfort. But here's the part most people miss—beneath the stress, the obligations, the "shoulds," your natural state has never left you. That state is your happiness state because happiness isn't something to earn or achieve. Happiness is your born default.

If you doubt it, look at a child. Gisele at two years old radiates joy with no reason at all. She laughs from her belly when the wind ruffles her hair. She squeals with delight at the sight of a balloon, a puddle, or a simple tickle game. George, only weeks old, shows it too. When his basic needs are met—warmth, food, love—his face melts into a peace so complete it stops me in my tracks. Children don't wake up asking, "Am I worthy of happiness today?" or compare themselves to the toddler in the next stroller. Happiness is built in.

And when discomfort interrupts? They let the world know something's wrong. But the moment the irritation is removed, happiness returns instantly. They don't have to strive their way back to joy—it was waiting underneath all along.

That same childlike happiness is still inside you. But over the years, it gets smothered under layers of expectation, cultural conditioning, and achievement-based worth. You start to believe the illusion that more money, titles, or recognition will finally make you feel what once came naturally. But here's the gut truth: **Happiness isn't about adding. It's about removing.**

When a baby cries, you don't try to "motivate" them into joy. You don't hand them a checklist of affirmations or a shiny new toy and say, "This will fix you." You remove the discomfort, and joy resurfaces. The same is true for us. Instead of looking for more, we need to strip away the toxic beliefs, suffocating routines, and false obligations that interrupt our joy.

And yet, most of us grow up learning the opposite. We're told that happiness is something we must earn. That you'll be happy when you graduate, land the job, find the partner, buy the house. Always one step away, always conditional. And because it's always in the future, you normalize unhappiness now.

I've lived this trap too. And my valleys were dark. I went through seasons of loss that hollowed me out so deeply I wondered if joy would ever return. Six miscarriages. Each one a storm in my body leaving me raw, ashamed, whispering to myself in the dark: *Maybe I deserve this. Maybe I am not enough.* And it didn't stop there. In the space of seven years, I lost my mom, my aunt, a close friend of the family, and all of my grandparents. Every year brought another funeral, another empty chair at the table. Each time, I thought: *This is too much. This is the year joy won't come back.* Was I being punished? Was I too ambitious, too reckless, too selfish for wanting more than what life was giving me?

Those seasons nearly broke me. And yet—underneath all of it—something essential remained. Happiness hadn't disappeared. It was buried. Under the grief, the shame, the endless "should," it was waiting. The turning point came when I finally stopped listening to the voice in my head that kept saying I was the problem. When I allowed myself to do the things that sparked me—to write, to create, to sit in stillness, to breathe deeply, to be present in the smallest good moments. Slowly, joy crept back in. Not because life was perfect—it wasn't—but because joy had always been the baseline.

That rock bottom gave me new clarity. I realized that from those moments, I had to progress on my own to fulfil my potential and return to my happy state. Not as a reward, but as a starting point. And that required awareness of the patterns I had learned. We all carry these patterns. Negative thoughts that loop. Behaviors that once protected us but now keep us small. Habits that made life easier but stole our joy. You don't bulldoze over them or ignore them—you meet them, work with them, and then move past them.

I saw this same rediscovery in Sarah from Belgium. She looked unstoppable. A powerful entrepreneur who had built her business fast, sold it within 18 months, hit the revenue goals everyone else envied. And yet, every morning she woke up heavy. Irritated. Already behind before her day began. She carried a secret ache. And one day, with tears streaming, she said to me: "I don't even know what joy feels like anymore. I just want to feel light again. I want to laugh without needing a reason."

That was her gut speaking. She didn't need another strategy. She needed to remove what was suffocating her. So we started stripping away—one false "should" at a time. You don't rewire decades of habits, beliefs, and "shoulds" in a week. You don't replace exhaustion with joy by downloading one more productivity app. You do it slowly, patiently, like peeling layers off an onion—sometimes with tears, sometimes with relief.

Sarah and I spent months peeling back what didn't belong to her. The "shoulds" that ran her calendar like a dictator. The meetings she said yes to because she didn't want to look weak.

The roles she played because she thought that's what a "good leader" or a "good mother" should do. Slowly, we replaced "should" with "would." Would I actually want this? Would I choose this if no one was watching? That small shift opened space she hadn't felt in years.

One of the hardest battles was with her Judge—that relentless inner critic we all carry. Sarah's Judge told her she wasn't enough. That unless she added another degree, another award, another sacrifice, she hadn't "earned" the right to breathe.

She began listening to her gut instead—the voice that whispered, *"You already are enough."* And slowly, joy returned. Not in one grand breakthrough, but in the quiet details of her days. She laughed with her kids without needing a reason. She hummed while making coffee. She started to feel light again, not because her circumstances had drastically changed, but because the weight she carried no longer crushed her.

Joy comes from removing what blocks it. Sarah didn't need a new strategy. She needed space breathe, to feel, to remember what was already inside her. And once those false obligations fell away, she discovered something profound: Happiness had never left. It had only been buried. It's biology. When your thinking brain and your emotional brain align with your gut, your whole system shifts into ease. Flow. Aliveness. That's what happens when you stop forcing yourself into comfort zones that don't fit and start listening to what your body has been telling you all along.

And here's where I bring it back to you. Maybe you've been telling yourself, "It's not that bad." Maybe you've been performing, producing, pleasing—while a quiet ache whispers, *Is this it?*

That ache is not a flaw. It's a signal. It's your gut reminding you that you were built for more. That happiness is your default. That you don't need to add—you need to strip away. So here's the pepper in this chapter: Stop waiting. Stop convincing yourself that joy is a prize you'll earn later. Take one step—just one—to remove what suffocates you. That's how you find your way back to default. Because at the end of the day, this isn't about building a new life from scratch. It's about remembering the one you were born with. The one where happiness was natural, ease was normal, and aliveness was the only metric that mattered.

To be happy is a human drive as basic as the need to take the next breath. To reach happiness, you need to remove those rocks, one by one, starting with some of your most fundamental beliefs. And once we reach our happiness, something else opens up: a flow that leads us into joy. Those who reach joy are not only accepting of life as it truly is but are utterly immersed in it. They live in harmony with the present moment, entering a realm of timeless flow. They move with every tiny thing life throws their way. The state of uninterrupted happiness—that is joy.

Unfortunately, the English language isn't equipped with a term that fully captures this state. Inner peace, stillness, calm—those words come close. Perhaps a mixture of all of them is the closest we can get. But none of them alone conveys the essence. True joy is to be in harmony with life exactly as it is.

Rewiring your brain toward joy only happens when you take action. So let's begin. We'll keep it simple and light—something anyone can do right away. Grab your journal, and let's try this together.

PEPPER TIME 1:
YOUR HAPPY LIST

Timing: 3 minutes, anytime today.

What you'll need: Your journal and a pen.

What it's about: Happiness isn't something to chase—it's your default. This exercise makes it visible by surfacing everyday moments that already light you up.

How to do it:

1. **Write the starter sentence:** "I feel happy when..."
2. **Complete it as many times as you can.** Don't censor yourself—small things count. (For example: "I feel happy when I sip coffee in silence," "when my child laughs," "when the sun hits my face.")
3. **Keep writing** until you feel you've emptied your mind for now.

What to expect: You'll create your personal Happiness Map—a list you can return to when life feels heavy. You'll notice that joy often hides in ordinary moments, and writing them down trains your brain to spot even more.

Reflection

____

____

____

____

____

____

____

*   *   *

That's the invitation of this first chapter, to see comfort for what it is: the quiet killer of big lives. To see "fine" for what it is: the most dangerous place you can be. And to remember what your gut already knows: Happiness is your default, fire is your truth, and comfort has a cost too high to keep paying.

Chapter 2:

Our Amazing Brain

Your brain's number-one job is survival. Everything else—goals, storytelling, strategy, growth—comes second unless you train the system. That one fact explains so much: why a single raised eyebrow can crush a pitch, why "This is just the way I am" feels true on hard days, why scrolling wins over sleep, and why we sometimes choose harmony over truth in rooms that matter.

To keep you alive, your brain runs five jobs all the time:

- First, it reads the body—fuel, rest, touch, protection, temperature—so it knows what the organism needs.
- Second, it keeps a map of the world so you can find what you need and avoid harm.
- Third, it mobilizes energy and action to move you toward your goals.
- Fourth, it flags dangers and opportunities as they appear.
- Fifth, it updates the plan as conditions change.

Because we are social mammals, all five jobs are relational: We steady each other, learn by watching, and thrive in safe groups. When signals are muffled, maps are outdated, action is paralyzed, alarms get stuck on high, or relationships fray, the whole system suffers. Here's the miracle: The same brain built for protection can be trained for expansion. The brain is plastic. It rewires with experience. **Train your brain, and the engine that once kept you small becomes your engine for clarity, courage, creativity, and joy.** This chapter shows you how amazing that organ is.

Your Brain Map

If you want to understand why we behave the way we do, start with the driver of the day: the brain. Most of the reasons you feel calm or spun-out live inside this three-pound city. A little science makes the rest of the book click. As a daily-life map, picture three systems sharing one steering wheel:

1. A survival system
2. An emotional-social system
3. A planning system

When they cooperate, you feel like yourself. When one grabs the wheel, life feels off. Your brain's first mandate is to keep you safe. That devotion is so strong that—even when your basic needs are met and no physical threat is present—it can still talk you out of contentment. Worry, second-guessing, peo-ple-pleasing, over-prepping: They're all safety plays. In other words, much of your unhappiness (or puzzling behavior) is gen-erated inside your own head by systems doing their job a bit too well. In the pages that follow, we'll use this three-system map to decode reactions and choices. Once you can see who's driving, everything else starts to make sense.

#1 SURVIVAL SYSTEM (the "reptilian" layer): the vigilant bodyguard. Rooted in the brainstem and hypothalamus, this is your oldest wiring. It keeps the lights on—heartbeat, breath, temperature, sleep-wake cycles—and scans for threat long before conscious thought arrives. In simple terms, it avoids pain and grabs quick relief. Like a frightened lizard, it would rather run from the slightest possibility of danger than risk being wrong. That's why it fills your head with "what if" stories that sound protective but shrink your life: *What if I stay with my partner even though it's unhealthy—being alone might be worse. What if I leave this job I hate and fail at the next one. What if the train derails—today of all days.* Statistically, most of those scenarios live in fantasy; they're your bodyguard overperforming. Seeing that matters. A lot of stuckness is overprotection.

#2 EMOTIONAL-SOCIAL SYSTEM (the mammalian layer): the color and the compass. This limbic network (amygdala, hippocampus, striatum and friends) assigns meaning. It tags people and places as nourishing or draining, burns memories in with feeling, and learns reward loops—what to seek, what to avoid. It loves belonging and the familiar, which is why yesterday's patterns can masquerade as "good" simply because they're known. Left to itself, it can escalate quickly—catastrophizing from a single cue, replaying slights, or chasing short hits that never satisfy (the same doom-scroll, the same "yes" you don't mean). Pleasure seeking and pain avoidance keep us alive. But when this system drives without the others, you get drama without direction: big feelings steering old loops.

#3 PLANNING SYSTEM (the rational layer): the strategist and narrator. Prefrontal and cortical networks let you imagine futures, hold ideas in working memory, weigh trade-offs, use language, and choose on purpose. This is the part that builds a plan and sequences steps. Its shadow is the all-pervasive "not enough." It compares, tallies, optimizes, and moves the goalposts so satisfaction never lands—*I should look like them; I should live like them; one more purchase, upgrade, or perfect fix.* Dopamine's "wanting" circuit fuels exploration here, but wanting and liking are different; you can chase forever and rarely feel arrived. When the strategist hogs the wheel, life becomes a spreadsheet: rumination, analysis paralysis, self-trial with no verdict.

All three systems are you—and they trade control all day. Under alarm, the survival system pulls rank and the other two dim. Under strong emotion, the planner blinks. Under chronic overthinking, the body's signals are ignored. Knowing who's driving explains why you said yes when you meant no, why you snapped, or why you couldn't decide. It also clarifies the central tension of modern life: A brain built to keep you safe will routinely overprotect you from the very growth you want. Part 2 is about rebalancing the wheel. For now, understand the map.

Cracking The Brain Code

Picture is a city that never sleeps. Billions of neurons are lights in high-rises, passing messages along shimmering bridges called synapses. Each time you repeat a thought or action, you cast a vote for a route. Traffic thickens. Bridges widen. Over time, a narrow street becomes a highway. That's how habits form—pavement, not fate.

The survival district is all sirens and floodlights; Social Square is music and cafés where belonging lives; the Planning Quarter is whiteboards and labs. Which district controls rush hour depends on what your senses, memories, and body state report. The hopeful part: City maps change. Old roads grass over; new ones can be built. Repetition lays asphalt; different repetition lays it somewhere else.

The brainstem links brain and spinal cord and keeps you alive— the Survival command center. The cerebellum, tucked at the back, fine-tunes movement and timing (a pianist's fingers "thinking for themselves," a child who suddenly gets the bike). The limbic system sits in the middle—our Emotional–Social engine. The folded outer cortex handles much of the planning, language, and sequencing.

Experience rides on neurons talking across tiny gaps—synapses. The more a circuit fires, the stronger the bridge; busy routes get wrapped in myelin (think fresh asphalt) so signals travel faster. That's why habits feel automatic: They're highways in your nervous system. Neuroplasticity—your city's zoning board—never retires. Watch a baby learn to walk, and you're seeing it in real time. Wiring is real—and changeable.

If the city is roads and buildings, neurotransmitters are the traffic lights and weather. They don't make moral judgments; they set conditions:

- Dopamine powers exploration and progress in the Planning Quarter—that little lift when a tiny win lands—but untethered, it keeps you circling the "more" roundabout.

- Serotonin steadies mood in Social Square; because much is made in the gut, a rattled belly can thin your patience.
- Oxytocin deepens bonding and trust—eye contact with someone safe, a baby's snuggle, honest teamwork—telling the Emotional-Social system, *You belong here.*
- Endorphins blunt pain and give brief euphoria after exertion, a Survival message of *We made it.*
- Norepinephrine flips Survival into high alert under challenge—attention sharpens, view narrows.
- Acetylcholine helps the Planner lock in and learn; glutamate drives change; GABA is the brake that lets the whole network settle.

Knowing the chemistry explains why states feel different and why "safety" isn't just an idea; it's a bodily climate that decides which driver grabs the wheel.

Two Dialects Of One Mind

Your brain speaks two languages. The left hemisphere loves words, logic, and sequence—it narrates, labels, and plans. The right hemisphere is sensory and holistic—it reads faces and tone, tracks rhythm, and holds the "music" of life. In a hard conversation, the left side maps the steps—*name the goal, share one example, propose a path*—while the right side reads the person—*jaw tight, shoulders lifted: Slow down; add warmth.*

Under pressure, the right can flood with feeling and the left goes offline; that "I can't talk about this" moment is literally a brief language dip. When the left dominates, life can feel thin—you can explain the story and feel nothing. Integration is safety: When both hemispheres cooperate with the three systems, calm returns faster and you can choose cleanly.

One last truth before we move on: Loops aren't identity; they're just wiring you've rehearsed. Habits aren't fate; they're highways you can reroute. And so-called "negative" emotions aren't enemies—they're one-second alerts, like the pain that pulls your hand from a hot stove. The alert is useful; camping in it is not. The Survival system keeps you circling the smallest, "safest" block.

This book's promise is simple: Once you can see *which system and which hemisphere* has the wheel, you can steer—body first, then brain—so your inner city runs on steadiness, not sirens. Your brain is built to keep you safe. That's good—until safety-first becomes *safety-only.* Then the mind starts exaggerating threats, spinning worst-case stories, and talking you out of the very growth you want.

Don't let an overprotective system run the show. If your mind runs you, performance, well-being, and relationships all pay.

A negative emotion is an alert, not a home. Pain means *something needs attention now.* But once the message is delivered, staying in stress, anger, or shame stops helping. Your brain shifts to tunnel vision, and the part that solves problems goes dim. That's why this book pairs gut leadership (listening to the body's signal) with brain skills (rebalancing the systems).

In part 2, you'll learn quick, repeatable moves for handing the wheel back to the right driver—so you can act with clarity, protect what matters, and build a life you don't need to escape.

Brain Self-Care

We've been picturing your brain as a city, and cities need clean streets and steady power. Your brain is the most energy-hungry thing you own—about 2 percent of your weight yet roughly a quarter of the fuel you eat—and it can't stockpile energy for later. Run it on four hours of sleep, a double espresso, and a train-station croissant and of course you feel foggy, jumpy, or overwhelmed. The "boring" basics—breathing, eating, sleeping, moving, hydrating, even a tidy corner—aren't luxuries. They're maintenance for the organ that runs your life.

 # SLEEP. Sleep isn't a treat; it's strategy. For most adults, seven to eight hours a night is the sweet spot. When you sleep well, your brain files memories, clears waste, and resets reward sensitivity so tomorrow's work actually feels worth doing. Skimp and mood dips, focus scatters, and impulse control tanks; staying awake for around twenty hours can impair decisions like being legally drunk. Enough sleep also makes it easier to manage emotions and choose cleanly. Some seasons don't allow textbook nights—pregnancy, newborn life, caregiving. In those chapters, think recovery: Catch morning light to anchor your clock, nap for around fifteen minutes when possible, reduce optional decisions, batch similar tasks, and be kind to yourself.

MOVEMENT. Your brain runs on oxygen and rhythm. Every time you move—walk fast, dance in the kitchen, take the stairs—you pump more blood upstairs and release a growth signal that tells neurons to build and strengthen connections. That's why a brisk ten-minute walk can turn frustration into clarity: The alarm center cools, and the planner comes back online. Keep it human-sized: two or three "exercise snacks" of five to ten minutes, a lunchtime loop, squats while the kettle boils, a short yoga flow between meetings. In late pregnancy, when strangers guessed my due date twelve weeks early, I still walked gently most days and did three short yoga sessions a week—not to win a badge, but because it helped keep my head clear and my mood steady.

HYDRATION. Your brain is mostly water. A small drop in hydration—just 1 to 3 percent—can dull focus, attention, and memory. Start your morning with water before caffeine. Keep a bottle in sight. Swap one soda for still or sparkling water. Add a pinch of salt or a squeeze of citrus if you need help drinking more. Headaches and brain fog often improve with a glass.

BREATH. Breath is the remote control for your state. Stress shortens and speeds it up, which your survival layer reads as "danger." Slow it down and lengthen the exhale, and your body gets a different message: "safe." Try simple box breathing—inhale for four seconds, hold for four, exhale for four, hold for four—for a minute before you speak, hit "send," or step on stage. Even one long sigh (a full inhale, a tiny top-up, then a long exhale) can reset your system. I've used these in high-pressure moments—before a keynote, in hard conversations, anytime my head yelled, *Too much.* The shift wasn't magic. It was biology.

 # FUEL. Food is information. Your brain's messengers—dopamine for drive, serotonin for steadiness, acetylcholine for focus—are built from what you eat. Your brain burns 25 to 30 percent of your intake and can't store fuel; hunger degrades decisions (hello, "hangry"). Aim for a simple rhythm that feeds your gut and steadies your mood:

- Get protein at breakfast (eggs, Greek yogurt, tofu scramble, smoked fish, beans) so motivation and appetite regulate.
- Pack your meals with fiber and color from vegetables, berries, beans, and whole grains to nourish your gut ecosystem and smooth energy.
- Include healthy fats like olive oil, nuts, seeds, and avocado for satiety and cell health.
- Add fermented foods—yogurt, kefir, kimchi, sauerkraut—to diversify gut flora.
- Bring in omega-3s from fatty fish, algae oil, or walnuts to support mood and thinking.
- Treat caffeine as a tool—after water and food, earlier in the day.
- Keep sugar low-drama by pairing sweets with protein or eating them after meals so blood sugar rises gently.

In real life, that might look like an omelet with greens and feta for breakfast; a handful of nuts midmorning; a lunch grain bowl with salmon, beans, mixed veggies, and a spoon of sauerkraut; an afternoon walk and water; and pasta with olive oil, tomatoes, and a big side salad for dinner. That's leadership fuel.

 # ENVIRONMENT. Messy desks, overflowing countertops, and relentless notifications siphon attention. You don't need Pinterest perfection; you need less static. Try a daily "one surface reset" (desk, sink, or nightstand), a "single-tab rule" for deep work, and a "notification fast" for one hour. Light matters too: Open blinds in the morning, step outside if you can, and protect dark at night. Tiny environmental shifts buy you clarity for free.

When the power is steady (sleep), the roads are maintained (movement), the cooling system works (breath), the battery is charged (food and water), and the workspace is clear (environment), the whole system runs quietly. That's when you can hear your gut, tell the difference between growth and danger, and choose boldly. When the city is under-resourced—sleep-starved, dehydrated, under-fueled—the inner Judge gets louder, autopilot clings to "fine," and fear masquerades as data. Brain self-care is the precondition for the life you're building.

Building Your Mental Fitness

We've tuned the hardware—sleep, light, movement, food. Now we upgrade the software. Think of your mind as an operating system that sometimes runs outdated code and, on tough weeks, picks up a few bugs. Old loops—*"I'm not ready," "I'm a fraud," "Keep everyone happy"*—hijack your bandwidth, and suddenly the day is running you. Mental fitness is how your scaling brain learns to lead while your gut takes its rightful place as compass.

You don't build a new life at a weekend retreat. You don't rewire years of "fine" with a single journal entry or a fresh planner. Change sticks the way muscle does—through repetition. The body you want is built by daily reps. The calm home you crave is built by daily resets. The mind you can trust is built by small, repeatable mental moves that etch new pathways until they become your autopilot. Every thought, reaction, and belief travels a pathway—a route your neurons use to talk to each other. Picture a hiking trail. The more you walk it, the clearer and faster it becomes. Stop walking it and the weeds creep back.

Repetition wraps myelin—a fatty insulation—around busy circuits so signals travel faster. Practice doesn't make perfect; practice makes *automatic*. In Chapter 5 we'll go deeper into how to redesign these pathways on purpose; for now, remember: Every day you are choosing which trails to widen. Willpower is a sprint—useful for a moment, exhausting if you rely on it. Mental fitness is endurance training.

Pepper Reps are mental push-ups, tiny, spicy, ten-second or longer practices that train attention, steady your state, and install better defaults. They're the mental equivalent of push-ups—small on their own, transformative in sets. Each rep moves you from threat-driven autopilot to your wiser brain; from the inner Judge to the inner Guide; from "fine" to fire. Most bad days aren't caused by real danger; they're caused by a brain stuck in protection mode—spinning "what ifs," chasing "not enough," or replaying old stories.

Pepper Reps lower the survival noise so your wiser brain and your gut can take the wheel. Brief, repeated shifts are how the brain rewires. Each rep is a micro-vote for calm over panic, clarity over clutter, choice over autopilot. Stack enough votes, and your baseline changes: You notice sooner when you're spiraling, and you spend more time in the part of your brain that solves, creates, and connects. Under a brain scanner you'd see survival chemistry settle and planning circuits come back online.

Do one rep, you feel a notch calmer, more present in the moment. Do sets through the day, you build a new default—clearer, steadier, braver. Link new reps to habits you already have. We'll talk more about this in part 2. For now, the idea is to uplift yourself in each of the three main pillars: relationships, performance, and well-being.

- **Relationships:** Got a tough conversation? Do a couple of quick reps before you walk in. You carry your own weather, so you respond instead of catching the other person's storm.
- **Performance:** Facing a task you've been dodging? Use a rep to ground, then begin. It cuts through hesitation and protects momentum.
- **Well-being:** When thoughts start to spiral, a rep interrupts the loop so the inner Judge doesn't run the dashboard.

Negative emotions are alerts, not homes. They're the hot-stove signal. Pepper Reps train the shift after the signal—out of tunnel vision and back into the present, where judgment improves and courage lives. That shift is a skill, and like any skill, it grows with practice. In part 2, I'll show you the exact Pepper Reps and how to stack them until they become your autopilot for relationships, performance, and well-being. For now, hold the master law of mental fitness: What you use grows; what you ignore fades. Keep casting tiny votes for the mind you want to live in.

Chapter 3

The Lies That Keep You Small

Listen. Can you hear that voice? The one right there inside your head?

Stop reading for a minute and try to enjoy a moment of silence. See how long it lasts before that voice barges back in—reminding you of all the things you still need to do, replaying the rude person you encountered earlier, or worrying if you'll ever get that promotion you've been waiting for. That voice rarely rests. It belittles us, disciplines us, argues, fights, worries, debates, critiques, and compares—hardly ever stopping to take a breath. Day after day we listen as it talks and talks, shaping the rhythm of our inner world.

And this is where the trap begins. That voice isn't random—it comes from the same machine that keeps you alive.

Your Brain Under Attack

Your brain is the most astonishing and loyal machine you'll ever own. It wakes you every morning, keeps your heart beating without asking, and runs thousands of programs before your first coffee. Miraculous, yes—and, as you know, stubbornly biased toward comfort and safety. Not greatness. Not wild aliveness. Comfort. The tax for that bias—paid in muffled truth, missed chances, and the quiet ache of "I'm fine"—is higher than most of us admit. In Chapter 2 we mapped this miracle: a three-system brain that rewires with repetition.

In this chapter, you'll see how a brilliant machine can hijack its owner in today's world. Algorithms farm your attention. Notifications spike your survival chemistry. Comparison feeds whisper "not enough." Ultra-busy schedules steal sleep, and the whole system drifts toward threat mode. When that happens, tiny, fearful thoughts start running the day. Negativity scales. A single sigh at the dinner table becomes silence in the meeting; silence in the meeting becomes a culture of "don't rock the boat."

But courage scales, too. One person treating themselves as valuable—clear, kind, aligned rather than anxious and performative—changes the temperature in a room. Families breathe. Teams unlock. Communities warm. That wave starts inside you, with the biggest driver of everyday unhappiness: unquestioned thoughts. In the pages ahead, we'll expose the common hijacks, name the patterns, and show you how to take the wheel back. You need to understand your brain—and use it on purpose.

I saw the hijack happen in public. Web Summit, Lisbon. A brilliant founder stepped onto the stage with twelve minutes to pitch a product that could change how remote teams build trust. She had done the work: numbers at her fingertips, story clean and compelling. For the first three minutes, she was a current you wanted to step into. Then a ripple: a raised eyebrow in the front row, a quick glance at a phone in the second. Her survival brain translated it as danger. Her inner narration grabbed the mic: *This is your shot. Everyone is judging.* Her rhythm stuttered. Her voice softened. She began to over-explain, to apologize. She fought to the end, but the power she opened with was gone.

Later, in a backstage interview, she said, "I don't know what happened. I was ready—then I was overwhelmed."

I knew. Her brain had been attacked from the inside—the static of a thousand moments where approval equaled oxygen. Her scaling brain—the part that plots, decides, dares—still knew exactly what to do. But her survival brain—wired to keep the tribe from rejecting her—had taken the wheel. We've already named the cost of comfort; this is how it charges interest.

Grumpy Brain Mode

Think of a beloved, battered car you keep meaning to trade in. You fix one thing, another slips. The paint looks fine, but the alignment is off and the ride never feels steady. That's the Grumpy Brain: a system with small internal faults that skew every trip. When those inner mechanics wobble, thinking tilts negative. Tiny, defensive programs amplify small signals into alarms. A raised eyebrow, a phone glance—the brain reads these as threats and spins stories: *"They're judging me," "I'll be exposed," "I'm not enough."*

Those stories feel urgent because the survival brain is wired to prioritize threat. Today it looks less like survival and more like a constant drip of pessimism, self-critique, and hesitation.

Here's the twist most people never learn: It isn't you sabotaging you. It's your brain's automatic narrator—the Judge—humming in the background so steadily you stop noticing. Because it borrows your voice and memories, it sounds like truth. But it's just a patchwork of predictions, half-remembered rules, and old fears passed down from parents, culture, and hard moments. It believes it's protecting you, but it keeps you small. It whispers: *"Don't post that. Don't ask for more. Don't admit what you really want."* And because it speaks in your voice, you confuse it with truth.

In the pages ahead we'll get to know that narrator by its proper name—the Judge—and learn to catch the exact moments it seizes control: when your chest tightens before a bold sentence, when you soften a clear no into a polite maybe, when you swap action for more preparation and call it "professional."

Part 2 will show you how to retrain the system. For now, just see your patterns. The first step is inspection. We're not throwing the car away. We're opening the hood, listing faults, and prioritizing repairs. That's what the next chapters do for your brain: Map the faults, name the circuits, and give you the tools to tighten the bolts where it matters.

PEPPER TIME 2:
TRACK YOUR GRUMPY BRAIN

Timing: Ongoing for 1 day.

What you'll need: A sheet of paper and a pen.

What it's about: Catching your inner narrator in the act. This test reveals how your brain tilts toward survival bias by tracking the tone of your thoughts.

How to do it:

1. **Fold a sheet of paper in half.** Mark one side with a plus sign (+) and the other with a minus sign (–).
2. **Observe the dialogue inside your head.**
3. **Each time you notice a thought,** add a quick tick mark on the appropriate side.
   . "Life is good, she loves me, I am capable." → + side
   . "I hate my job, I'm not enough, he's such an idiot." → – side
4. **Don't judge the tally—just record.**

What to expect: Most people will see more ticks on the minus side. That's not a character flaw; it's your survival bias at work. Seeing the pattern is the first step in changing it.

Reflection

____

____

____

____

____

____

* * *

Don't be discouraged. The human brain gives more weight to negative signals than positive ones. Self-critical, pessimistic, and fearful thoughts appear more often because, historically, noticing threats kept us alive. We also lean on negatives and discount positives because they offer no obvious survival benefit. That's the Grumpy Brain doing its job—protective, but often misleading. Remember: These are assumptions, not facts. They feel convincing, but they're not true. **Your Grumpy Brain means well—but it lies.**

 # Survival first. Long before you dreamed of purpose, your ancestors dreamed of surviving the night. Their brains evolved to scan constantly for threat, conserve energy, and stay close to the familiar. A rustle in the bushes could mean predator; a wrong glance from the tribe could mean exile. That wiring still runs the show. It's why your body reacts the same way to pressing "publish" on a vulnerable post as it would to that ancient rustle. Sweaty palms. Racing heart. Shallow breath. To your survival brain, rejection equals extinction.

Habit economy / autopilot. Your brain is an efficiency machine. Anything repeated—thoughts, emotions, actions— gets automated to save energy. This is autopilot. Autopilot will just as easily run loops of procrastination as loops of produc- tivity. If you've rehearsed self-doubt, autopilot will make *"I'm not ready"* your default identity. That's why your thumb unlocks your phone before you realize it or your hand finds the cookie jar under stress.

Fear as data. Your brain mislabels growth as danger. The racing heart before a keynote? Same chemistry as meeting a wild animal. Your wiring flags both as *"Don't go there."* Without awareness, you treat fear as a stop sign when, in fact, it's often the arrow pointing to your next level.

The seduction of praise and fear of criticism. Your brain craves belonging. Approval once meant survival. Criticism meant risk. That's why an offhand remark can still send you spiraling. Your north star shifts from impact to applause. You stop building what matters and start performing for claps—or hiding to avoid critique.

Hiding. Hiding looks like diligence and feels like preparation. But it's fear disguised as productivity. You polish slides for the fifth time, collect "just one more" certification, or perfect a plan no one ever sees. It's not laziness. It's autopilot keeping you "safe."

Negativity bias and the Judge. Your nervous system is tuned to notice what's wrong three to five times more than what's right. That bias once kept our ancestors alive. Today it means one nasty email outweighs a hundred thank-yous. The Judge— the harshest version of your brain's narrator—thrives here. It

magnifies flaws, replays failures, and convinces you those loops are your identity.

This is how your brain attacks you. Not by breaking, but by over-protecting. By confusing safety with smallness. The task is not to silence the brain or fight it into submission but to recognize the game it's built to play—so you can choose a different one. That is what this chapter is about: shining light on these attacks so you can see them for what they are. Because the moment you can name the voice, you can separate from it. And once you separate, you can lead.

If you don't understand how your brain works, you'll keep feeding it programs you never chose—family scripts, cultural codes, survival patterns. **I wrote this book to show you how to run the machine differently, to sync it with your gut—your built-in compass.** Your gut feels the truth before your brain can argue. Gut leadership means putting that compass back in the driver's seat and retraining the machine to serve it.

Remember: **YOU ARE IN CHARGE.**

Who's talking most of the time in your head? I can tell you with certainty—it's not you. And while I wish I could impress you with the story of some dramatic epiphany, the truth is, my realization came slowly, through lived moments. Let me show you, across the three main areas of my life: well-being, relationships, and performance:

 # Well-being. When I was pregnant and beginning what would later become GutScaleurs, my head kept telling me: Stay in the lane of marketing and scaling companies. Safe. Predictable. Familiar. But my gut whispered something else: *Bring the gut* *in. Add the practices you're learning. Test presence, not just performance.*

I thought it was nonsense. But when I tried it, clarity came. Clients shifted. And something in me shifted, too. That's when I started to accept a startling truth: There's someone in my head that isn't me. And so, I began to dig. Why do I hear the angel and devil of cartoons, whispering opposites in each ear? If the voice in my head is not me, then who is it?

Relationships. The same battle showed up in my marriage. Tobias and I were carrying the weight of miscarriages and unspoken grief. He had grown up in a household where success was survival: Perform, or you're a failure. His father escaped into work instead of conversations. His mother laughed things away rather than confronting them. That wiring lived in him. And my wiring? Autopilot had me overexplaining, begging for connection, repeating myself like a broken cassette recorder: *"Communication is important."* I tried new strategies, new seductions, new arguments. The truth I finally faced was painful but freeing: I cannot rewire Tobias's autopilot. I can only rewire mine. My choice was not to force change on him but to shift myself—to accept, to influence, or, if needed, to let go. That realization gave me my power back.

Performance. Then came the investor room in Belgium. Jelloow, my data-AI company, was ready to shine. Ninety-five percent of the room was men, most over fifty. I wore a yellow dress and spoke about hyper-personalized marketing. And what did they ask? *"What about family, you are mid-30's?"* and, *"Why do you think you can do this?"* In that moment, my autopilot screamed: *Shrink. Smile more. Prove harder. Perform until*

they believe you. But my gut whispered: *You belong here. Their questions are not your truth.* That whisper didn't erase the sting of bias, but it gave me ground to stand on.

These moments left me restless. Why was I being hijacked by a voice that was supposed to protect me? Why did autopilot hand me fear, doubt, and silence when I wanted courage, clarity, and presence? I devoured books and dove into deeper work: Neuro-Emotional Integration, somatic training. I followed what pulled me, because I needed to know why.

I learned the most liberating truth: **Your thoughts do not define you.** Your brain is your inner narrator. It's the stream that tells you what's happening and suggests how to respond. But your thoughts are not you. For years, I carried hidden shame: the fear that I was the reason my babies didn't make it, that I was somehow at fault for the abuse I endured, that my mother's death was tied to me not being enough. Those were not truths. They were loops my brain had stitched from grief and trauma. When I realized that, the relief was enormous.

This is the pivot I want you to feel: If you aren't the voice in your head, then you don't have to obey it. You don't have to listen. With practice, you can even learn to quiet it completely. And when you do, you discover something extraordinary: The brain is the greatest gift humanity has been given. We just never learned how to use it properly.

The power isn't in fighting your brain. It's in learning to run it. To feed it gold instead of garbage. To link it with your gut—the compass that already knows the truth. Because the stakes are real.

If you don't consciously decide who leads—your compass or your default loops—you'll set inspiring goals and watch in frustration as your days are steered by the part of you terrified to be seen. You'll long for intimacy but replay the same conflicts, because your nervous system prefers predictability over closeness. You'll build a business that looks impressive but feels hollow. Not because you're weak or untalented, but because the machine outran the compass.

Again: **YOU ARE IN CHARGE.**

Gut leadership in one sentence? Put the compass back in charge, and train the machine to serve it. That's the pepper—the sting that wakes you when old software tries to tuck you back into bed. Awareness cracks the loop. Once you see a program running, you don't have to treat it as truth. You can pause. You can choose differently. You can add pepper—a micro-sting that disrupts inertia and points you back to alignment. That's how habits are built. That's how you return to happiness.

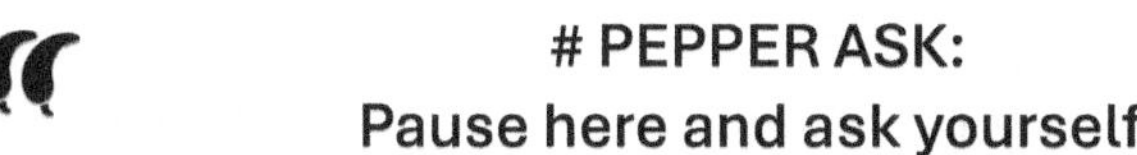

PEPPER ASK:
Pause here and ask yourself:

- *Who is talking in your head most of the day? Is it the Judge, protecting you from embarrassment at any cost? Or your gut, inviting you into the life you actually want?* 

If it's the first—good. You've spotted your starting line. If it's the second—good. You've already felt the compass. Either way, you're ready.

Next, we'll open the hood and look at exactly where autopilot hijacks your brain—and how to reclaim the wheel.

Your brain is under pressure every day, and when you don't realize which layer is steering, you end up sabotaging performance, well-being, and relationships. Negative emotions themselves aren't the problem. Like pain, they're critical alarms—sensations designed to say, *"Look here."* But once the message is delivered, lingering in anger, shame, or fear narrows attention, locks you into tunnel vision, and blocks the creative networks you need to solve the very problem you're facing.

Feel the signal, then switch systems. The goal of this book is to help you build self-command so you can do exactly that— move from autopilot to choice, from hijack to clarity.

The bad news: Most of us are doing far more self-sabotage than we realize—thousands of automatic thoughts, most unexamined, many unhelpful.

The good news: The shifts you'll learn are simple, repeatable, and powerful.

In part 2, we'll train your "Power Brain"—the networks that steady the body, clear the story, and make courageous action easier—so that safety, emotion, and reason all serve you instead of running you.

Autopilot Exposed

Here's the uncomfortable truth: Most of your life isn't being lived by conscious choice but by autopilot. You *think* you're steering, but most of the time, the machine is driving. We convince ourselves we're making choices—how to spend our mornings, how to answer emails, how to respond to our partners. But zoom in. Do you *really* decide to check your phone the second your eyes open, or does your thumb move before you're awake enough to stop it? Do you choose the sharpness in your voice when your partner asks an innocent question after a long day? Do you consciously decide to push your big dream project off until "tomorrow"?

That's autopilot at work. It conserves energy. But efficiency comes with a hidden cost: It keeps you in the familiar, even when the familiar is suffocating your spark. Autopilot was designed for survival, not greatness. It saves energy in the short term, but in doing so, it robs you of aliveness. The danger is not that autopilot exists—it's that you don't notice it running, so you mistake its programs for "truth."

And here's where it gets dangerous: The more we give in to these unconscious loops, the more they shape us and ripple outward. Negativity breeds negativity. Rooms catch that energy. Teams mirror it. Cultures form around it. Possibility drains.

But the opposite is equally true. One spark of courage—one person choosing kindness, clarity, honesty—shifts the entire space. A partner who interrupts the loop of irritation and chooses tenderness changes a whole evening. Aligned action sends ripples further than fear ever could. The world doesn't change "out there." It begins inside you.

The biggest reason for unhappiness isn't circumstance—it's the unchecked loop of negative thoughts. Autopilot isn't quiet.

And the main voice it uses is the Judge. Left alone, autopilot will happily run every program you've practiced: hesitation, perfectionism, avoidance, overwork. It doesn't ask if this loop is serving you. It just repeats it. Garbage in, garbage out. Gold in, gold out. That's the economy of the brain. Autopilot will drive you in circles for decades if you never grab the wheel. It will whisper, *"This is just who you are,"* and you'll believe it.

Self-awareness is the crack in the loop. The moment you notice *"Oh, this isn't me. This is autopilot,"* you create a gap. And in that gap, you can choose. You can reset. You can clear thought patterns that were never truly yours. You can install new beliefs.

 **# PEPPER ASK: Ask yourself:**

- *When was the last time you cleared out your mental files?*
- *When did you last delete a program that said, "You're not ready," or "You don't deserve it"?*
- *When did you last upgrade the system you're running your life on?* 

Most people just keep living yesterday's code. That's why autopilot is the silent thief of joy, courage, and freedom. Autopilot is a machine that learned to run without your permission. Your gut—the quiet compass inside you—is the part that notices when the machine is wrong. Autopilot keeps you alive. Your gut is here to help you live.

This Is Just The Way I Am

We've all said it. And every time I hear those words, I get goose-bumps—not the good kind, but the kind that rise when you watch someone quietly hand their freedom away. Because on the surface, it sounds like self-knowledge, confidence, accep-tance. But most of the time, it's the white flag we raise to the brain's hijack after it has run the same loops so many times that we mistake them for truth. And the danger is subtle but lethal: The moment you decide you are fixed, you stop trying to change. But you can absolutely change yourself—if you want to.

We'll talk about the gut in the next chapter. For now, accept what your gut already knows: You are not your wiring. You are not the patterns that your family, culture, early bosses, or old heartbreaks installed in you. Identity isn't stone; it's clay. Your brain isn't a truth-teller but a prediction engine. It takes old data and assumes the future will be the same: Last time you froze in a meeting; you'll freeze again. Last time you loved and were hurt; better not risk it now.

It feels like identity, but until you overwrite the formula with new reps, new experiences, new truths, the program runs unchecked.

Picture this: It's late evening. A man sits on the sofa, his body heavy from another long day. The TV hums in the background. His partner is running late. He sighs, checks his phone, then reaches for the app he knows so well—pizza delivery. Within seconds, the order is placed. A large pepperoni, a bottle of cola. Relief washes over him. The thought of preparing something fresh feels like an impossible mountain. His brain has already decided: This is comfort, this is familiar, this is me.

But is that really who he is? Or is that a loop his brain has rehearsed so many times that it now sells it back to him as identity? In that moment on the sofa, it feels true. The short-term motivation is powerful: comfort, ease, instant gratification. And because the body loves immediacy, the brain reinforces it. And yet—somewhere deeper, quieter—another truth hums. He knows that the long-term win would be different. That if he had fed his body something nourishing, maybe even earned the peace of a late stroll afterwards, over weeks, those small reps would build energy, clarity, confidence.

But the loop doesn't care about long-term. The loop only cares about familiar. And so it throws up that line like a shield: "This is just who I am." It's comfort masquerading as destiny. And it's dangerous because once you believe that sentence, you stop questioning it. But here's the opening: Motivation doesn't just come from willpower. It comes from awareness. Motivation grows when you see that every rep teaches your brain something new. That even if the first night you chop vegetables feels clumsy, or the walk feels pointless, your brain is watching, recording, learning. The loop is weakening.

This is where gut leadership comes in. The gut knows the difference between contraction and expansion. Contraction feels like collapse into the sofa, that dull ache of giving up. Expansion feels like the small sting of pulling yourself up, of stretching into a new habit. Expansion isn't easy, but it feels alive. And that is the compass. So the real question is *"Am I willing to act one inch beyond the loop?"* One inch to cook instead of order. One inch to walk instead of collapse.

Because the moment you reinterpret "This is just who I am" as data, not destiny, you find the motivation to change. You stop mistaking wiring for truth. And that's the pepper in your ass: the sting that pulls you off the sofa, out of the old loop, and into the life your gut already knows you want.

Identity is rewriteable. Who you are is not fixed. Your brain is plastic. That means it changes—constantly. It builds new pathways when you do something different. It strengthens old ones when you repeat them. You're only stuck if you keep feeding the same loop and calling it "just me." Every time you try something new—taking a class you'd never normally pick, walking a different route to work, traveling somewhere that bends your map—you're literally stimulating the growth of new neurons. Novelty doesn't just make life interesting; it rewires your brain.

Aerobic movement does the same. Those ten thousand daily steps, those 150 minutes of heart-pumping effort each week—they flood your brain with oxygen. I call it brain fertilizer. It's what allows new learning to stick.

Emotional intensity matters too. The moments you never forget—joy, grief, awe, the trembling honesty when you finally speak your truth—etch themselves into your brain more deeply than logic ever could. That's why a breakup, a birth, a loss, or a moment of courage can change you forever. Those emotional surges are your system saying: Pay attention. This matters.

And unlearning is just as powerful as learning. If you stop speaking a language, those neural pathways wither. The same happens with identity. If you stop repeating *"I'm just this way,"* the loop begins to starve, making room to feed something new. Replace *"I'm not very active"* with *"I'm becoming someone who moves."* Bit by bit, the brain updates its files.

So, let's make this practical. Take one "It's just the way I am" belief—the one that feels heavy, limiting, suffocating. Write it down. Then cross it out. Beneath it, write the upgrade your gut has been whispering all along. And then—this is the crucial part—take one small, uncomfortable, honest action that favors the upgrade over the old loop. Send the email you've been avoiding. Walk around the block instead of sinking into the sofa. Say the sentence you've been afraid to say.

It will sting. You'll feel the pinch in your chest, the flutter in your stomach, the wobble in your voice. That sting is the pepper— your nervous system receiving new data. And the more you repeat it, day after day, the more the loop rewires. The identity shifts. Because the moment you dare to see *"It's just the way I am"* as wiring rather than truth, everything changes. Your brain begins to shift. Your gut breathes again. You realize you are not your wiring or your patterns, You are not stuck. You are rewritable. And the power to rewrite begins in this moment—with one choice, one rep, one pepper sting of courage.

 **# PEPPER ASK: So I'll ask you:**

- *Which habits are you ready to make, and which addictions or labels are you finally ready to let go of?* 

Write them down. Don't let them live unchallenged in your head. Because neuroplasticity is on your side. The compass in your gut is on your side. And the pepper in your ass is there to jolt you out of autopilot and into alignment.

Fear Is Data

Fear has been misunderstood for far too long. We grew up thinking it was weakness, that if we felt it, we had to stop. Don't risk. Don't stretch. Stay safe. But the truth is far more interesting, and far more liberating. Fear isn't weakness. Fear is data. Your brain is wired to produce fear because it was built for survival, not for scaling.

Deep inside your skull sits the amygdala, a small almond-shaped cluster of neurons that acts like an overprotective bodyguard. Its only mission is to keep you alive. It scans constantly for threats, and the second it senses something unfamiliar, it slams the alarm. A rustle in the bushes? Fear spike. Your boss's tone dipping half a note? Fear spike. The idea of pressing "publish" on a bold new post? Fear spike.

The bodyguard doesn't care about your dreams, your growth, or your happiness. It only cares that you stay alive. And so, fear hijacks you. Your body reacts the same way whether you are stepping into traffic or stepping onto a stage: sweaty palms, racing heart, clenched stomach, shallow breath. Unless you learn to decode those signals, you confuse growth with danger. You back away from the very expansion your gut is pulling you toward, because the voice in your head shouts, *"Don't go there!"*

This is exactly what happened to Sofia. On the outside, she was thriving. Early forties, from Barcelona, she had built a consultancy with a solid reputation. She was confident in meetings, her clients loved her, her company was profitable. She had the credentials, the clients, the numbers. But each time she thought about raising her prices, her heart raced, her stomach clenched, her throat tightened. Her amygdala was reading growth as danger. The whisper that followed was relentless: *"Don't do it. Stay safe. This is just the way you are."* That whisper wasn't truth. It was wiring.

When Sofia learned to see fear as data instead of danger, she began asking a new question: *"Is this fear telling me I'm in real danger—or is it signaling that I'm about to grow?"* That one shift cracked the loop. Within six months, she doubled her rates. She didn't wait for the fear to go away—it never does. She acted while the fear was still in her body, but with a new interpretation. Same signals. New meaning. Different outcome.

That's the shift I want you to feel. Fear doesn't always mean stop. Sometimes it means go. Sometimes it's the signpost at the edge of your next expansion.

Children show us this truth in its rawest form. Toddlers fall, bruise, cry—and then stand up again. They don't sit down and declare, *"I guess I'm just not a walker."* They don't overthink the risk of falling again. They don't worry about who's watching. They simply rise, wobble forward, and fall until balance comes. For them, fear isn't danger—it's part of learning. But somewhere on the road to adulthood, we started treating fear as a stop sign instead of as the natural companion of growth.

We began filtering every move through judgment—what if I fail, what if I look stupid, what if it doesn't work?

The child in us remembers: Joy is the default, mistakes are data, and trying is how you learn.

That's why this next Pepper Time matters. It asks you to borrow wisdom from both ends of your life—your bold 7-year-old self and your no-nonsense 70-year-old self. Together they form a compass that cuts through hesitation. One shows you how to act without overthinking. The other reminds you what you'll remember in the end. Between the two, you'll see clearly: The leap is always smaller than the regret of not trying.

PEPPER TIME 3: 7-YEAR-OLD vs. 70-YEAR-OLD SELF 

Timing: 5 minutes.

What you'll need: Your journal, a pen, and a quiet spot (optional: timer).

What it's about: Borrow courage from two versions of you—your bold 7-year-old and your wise 70-year-old—to cut through overthinking and choose your next brave step today.

How to do it:

1. **Meet 7-year-old you.** Picture your wild, curious, fearless self. They don't overthink—they play, try, explore. Failure isn't a thing; it's recess. Write exactly what

they'd do next: Knock on the door. DM them. Post it. Press "go."

2. **Meet 70-year-old you.** Picture your wiser, no-BS future self. They remember the leaps, not the almost. Write a one-line postcard from them: "Dear me, you'll be proud you [told the truth / pitched / booked it / launched it]."

3. **Choose the micro leap.** Overlay both answers, and pick one bold action you can do in 24 hours. Keep it tiny and real: Say yes to the opportunity. Book the flight. Pitch the client. Launch the offer. Make the move. Write it as a commitment: "Tomorrow at 10:30 a.m., I will ____."

What to expect: A clear, doable action that feels both playful and wise. Your 7-year-old cuts the fear. Your 70-year-old keeps perspective. Together, they point you toward courage.

Reflection

____

____

____

____

____

____

*   *   *

When you face something new, your brain predicts danger because it hasn't filed the experience as safe yet. The amygdala fires, cortisol floods your system, narrowing your focus. Your prefrontal cortex—the part responsible for decision-making, creativity, and vision—goes offline. That's why fear makes you tunnel-visioned, reactive, sometimes even panicked. But here's the breakthrough: When you teach your brain through experience that the situation is safe, the wiring changes. The alarms quiet. The cortex comes back online. You regain access to creativity and choice.

This is exactly what I saw with David, a 29-year-old founder I met in a co-working space in Tel Aviv. He was brilliant—clear, polite, full of vision for his tech startup. When he talked to me one-on-one about his idea, his eyes lit up. He spoke with conviction, mapped out his model like a pro, and I found myself nodding along, convinced by his clarity. But when he told me about pitching to investors, his entire body shifted. He described sweating through his shirt, stumbling over words, avoiding eye contact, feeling like his brain went blank. "I'm just not a salesperson," he said, almost ashamed. But it was just his fear hijacking his system.

I was devouring books on neuroscience and gut intelligence, testing theories on myself, trying to connect the dots between science, coaching, and lived experience. I gave him small hints, simple tasks that came more from my gut than from any polished framework. "Try sharing your idea with a friend," I suggested. "Then with a small group. Don't think of it as selling—just as sharing what excites you." I wasn't entirely sure how far it would take him, but I trusted the principle: Small reps rewire big fears.

And he did it. First with friends over coffee, then with peers in the coworking space, then with smaller investors. Each time he practiced, his brain learned: this is safe. This is growth. The fear still showed up, but instead of spiraling into shutdown, he started to anchor himself in presence. And then the breakthrough came: Within a month, he wrote me an email saying he had pitched to a group of investors, landed serious interest, and—for the first time—actually enjoyed the experience.

Watching him take those little steps, hearing the gratitude in his voice, I felt something shift in me. With each small compliment he gave me—"That tip really worked," "I felt different this time"—he was helping me dig deeper into what I was studying. His lived proof was stitching my research into real, tangible practice. It gave me validation I didn't even know I was seeking, that extra pepper for myself: the sting that said, Keep going. *You're on the right track. What you're building here matters.*

That's the beauty of these moments: The learning is never one-sided. As David rewired his brain to see pitching as growth instead of danger, I was rewiring mine too—learning to trust my gut, to believe that this marriage of science and intuition had real power. His courage fed mine. And together, without planning it, we both walked out of fear and into growth.

Fear always shows up when you stretch. The bigger the stage, the bolder the dream, the louder the alarm. Fear doesn't disappear as you scale; if anything, it grows with you. The work is not to get rid of fear but to learn to read it—to recognize when the alarm means danger, and when it means you're about to grow.

There are two kinds of fear. Real danger fear, the kind that protects you when your physical safety or deepest values are under attack, and growth fear, the kind that shows up when you're safe but stretching. Real danger fear says, *"Don't step into the oncoming car."* Growth fear says, *"Don't raise your rates. Don't say what you feel. Don't stand on stage."* One keeps you alive. The other keeps you small.

Think of your own life. In performance, real danger fear is walking into a workplace that violates your ethics; growth fear is asking for the raise. In relationships, real danger fear is staying in abuse; growth fear is saying the hard truth instead of people-pleasing. In well-being, real danger fear is ignoring chest pain because *"I'm tough;"* growth fear is getting off the sofa when your brain insists, *"I'm not a gym person."* The body feels both as alarm, but only one is true danger. The other is expansion disguised.

PEPPER ASK: So here's my ask for you:

- *Where in your life right now is fear whispering "stop," while your gut is nudging "go"?*

Write it down. Feel it in your body. And the next time fear shows up, remember—sometimes it's danger. But many times, it's data. Sometimes it's the pepper in your ass, the sting that jolts you out of autopilot and into fire.

Praise & Criticism

I once knew a kid who loved to write. Words poured out of him—messy, alive—whole worlds tumbling onto the page before dinner. In primary school, teachers smiled, parents bragged, every poem made it to the fridge. Applause was oxygen; joy multiplied. Then he got older. The stickers disappeared. Rubrics arrived. One teacher—brilliant, exacting, and not his audience—disliked his style. Another required a voice that wasn't his.

What had felt like play became performance. Each sentence stopped being a door into discovery and turned into a test he might fail. The desk that had been a playground became a prison. He stopped returning—not because he had nothing to say, but because fear and the hunger for praise had hijacked his art.

Challenge the assumption that one opinion equals truth. We learn early to scan the teacher's face and treat it as reality. But swap teachers and you often swap verdicts. Everyone carries different focus, bias, and history. Yes, take what helps. But if one teacher loves minimalism and another loves lyricism, should the kid amputate his voice to please both? Or keep writing, learn the craft, and find his readers?

The moment you begin writing, selling, or leading for claps instead of clarity, you've entered the performance trap. Applause is a lovely drug. It looks harmless. You do good work, you get a nod, a repost, an invitation, and your nervous system hums, *Yes, this is safe.* The problem is that when approval becomes your GPS, your decisions wobble with the room.

I hear versions of this constantly—especially from Scaleur women: *People won't like what I have to say. My colleagues will think I don't know enough. My family will disapprove.* The goal is bold, free motion. Praise-seeking and criticism-avoidance tie sandbags to that kite. **We care too much what people think** because our brain, trying to keep us safe, lies about the stakes. Here are six reasons why that is:

Relational focus. Many women (and plenty of men, too) are raised to prioritize relationships, harmony, and care. It's beautiful—families stay connected, teams bond, communities thrive. It's also why the overwhelming majority of unpaid caregivers are women. Numbers vary by country, but across Europe and the US, around 62 to 70 percent of unpaid caregiving—whether for children, elderly parents, or relatives with disabilities—falls on women's shoulders. This is not just about cooking meals or folding laundry; it's about the invisible mental load of remembering birthdays, noticing moods, smoothing over conflicts, and anticipating needs before they're spoken.

The muscle for harmony is strong. But here's the shadow: When harmony is preserved at the expense of truth, you lose yourself. The radical idea stays unsaid. The innovation remains unborn. You smile instead of speaking because you don't want to rock the boat. You tell yourself you're being considerate, but you're really betraying your own gut. The project moves on without your idea, and no one knows what was lost.

Children learn this pattern early. Picture a little girl on the playground. She builds a tall, lopsided tower in the sandbox. Another child laughs, calls it "ugly," and instead of defending her creation, she kicks it down and joins in the laughter to stay included. The lesson burrows in: Belonging is safer than standing by your own design. These are not dramatic betrayals; they are small, daily edits. But stacked over time, they leave a quiet ache of unlived truth, of brilliance kept on mute.

Here's the paradox: The very muscle that helps us nurture and connect—the gift of relational focus—becomes the leash that keeps us small when we let it rule unchecked. And your gut knows the difference. When you hold back to avoid rocking the boat, your gut feels contraction: a tightening in your chest, a lump in your throat. When you speak the uncomfortable truth, even if the room bristles, your gut feels expansion: shaky, yes, but alive. That is the compass pointing toward fire instead of "fine."

Hyper-awareness of others' reactions. Walk into a room, and your radar hums. You clock who's tense, who's open, who holds power. You hear the shift in someone's tone and know there's a history under it. This sensitivity is a superpower. You can connect, adapt, bring people with you. The hijack comes when it never turns off. A single flat face in the audience becomes the entire verdict on your talk. One short email from your boss launches an evening of spiral.

Recall the founder on stage at the Web Summit, crushing the first half of a pitch. Then she noticed a couple of investors fidgeting and took it as a sign that she was bombing. Her voice shrank. She sped up. She edited out the boldest part of the plan. Her survival brain had made a few micro-gestures more important than the work.

We learn this early. On the playground, you quickly figure out who's influential and what earns entry. As adults we upgrade the tactic: Soften your certainty, pad the hard truth, bring ten backup slides "just in case." Not because the idea needs it— because your nervous system wants proof it won't be rejected.

 # Likability as safety. For generations, approval was currency. Many women couldn't rely on law, income, or status to protect them; they relied on being likable. Nonthreatening. That contract hums in our bodies even if our lives look different now. You'll see it in subtle ways. A manager stays late to rewrite a colleague's work rather than give direct feedback. A founder keeps the product generic because niches feel risky. A consultant fills her deck with industry buzzwords not because they help, but because they sound "safe."

The survival brain whispers, *If you're easy to like, you won't be left.* The gut counters, *If you're easy to like at the expense of what's true, you'll leave yourself.* There's a cultural layer too: some rooms reward polish over substance. The slickest talker wins the budget. The tidy narrative beats the messy truth. If you lead people, you can shift this. Praise the teammate who killed a feature to ship faster. Celebrate thoughtful dissent. When impact—not performance—gets rewarded, everyone's nervous system relaxes and the real work gets done.

 # Fear of personal attacks. Step into visible power, and you'll meet criticism that sticks to your skin. Suddenly you're "too much," "too direct," "not feminine enough," "not warm enough." The message: *Your existence needs sanding.* That's not feedback; that's policing. It's tempting to make yourself smaller to avoid it.

Liyana, a head of sales in Dublin, was told in a 360 that she was "too direct." Some colleagues were threatened by her clarity; sometimes she truly bulldozed. The performance trap would have her dim herself. Instead, we built a simple practice: Ask one genuine question before offering a conclusion. Not to appease—to learn. Her close rates rose. Respect rose. She kept the blade and learned when to sheathe it. The survival brain hears an attack and screams *danger.* Your body floods. You want to fix everyone's perception. Meanwhile, the work that would help people never sees daylight.

Especially for women in corporate life: The more visible you are, the more commentary you attract—on your tone, your clothes, your timing, your face. WOMEN GET CRITICIZED. PERIOD. That isn't proof you're doing it wrong; it's proof you're visible. Part of the work (we'll practice it later) is learning to let criticism exist without letting it run you. If they want to gossip—fine. Your job is not to micromanage every opinion. Your job is to stay with the work.

Appearance as currency. From toys to TV to office dress codes, girls are taught early that being looked at is part of the job. Entire industries profit from keeping women small—in body and in ambition. You can feel it when you hesitate to film a video because you "don't look perfect," or when a leader spends more energy on keynote outfits than on the keynote. This isn't vanity. It's an old safety code: *Look right and you'll belong; belong and you'll survive.* The hijack is that your work gets scheduled around your reflection.

Gwyn from Michigan delayed a launch until she "felt camera-ready" after having a baby. Her product was ready three months before her self-image was. When she finally recorded, the thing that landed wasn't contour—it was conviction. Gut leadership flips the lens: Presence and purpose beat polish.

Good girl rules. *Be small, be nice, be modest, don't rock the boat, don't be angry, don't shine too bright.* Those rules

don't evaporate when you get a title; they whisper under big moments. For men, the box is different—don't cry, don't falter—but it's still a box. Your survival brain loves rules because they promise belonging. *Break them and you'll be alone,* it warns. So when you're about to name the real problem, a voice says, *Don't be difficult.* When you're about to ask for the number that reflects your value, it says, *Don't be greedy.* When your idea catches light, it says, *Don't outshine.* This compliance also feeds perfectionism—another form of hiding. You keep polishing because *nice people don't inconvenience others with messy drafts.*

Criticism lands three to five times heavier than praise because your survival brain is yelling, *"Notice the threat!"* A hundred people love your keynote and one stranger posts a snide line; your body wants to pitch a tent in that one line and live there. "Ignore the haters" rarely works—your physiology just heard a tiger. Public figures receive an endless stream of comments about their hair, their clothes, their bodies, their performance. The ones who keep creating build a filter. They know whose voices are customers, collaborators, and true peers—and whose are just noise. The move is body-first: longer exhales, feet grounded, shoulders down; label it—threat response, not truth. Then ask the scaling questions: Is *there signal here? What improves the work? What stays because it's my voice?*

This conditioning starts early. Someone praised you for being reliable, polished, drama-free. Your brain learned that belonging equals survival. So, when stakes rise, you simply read the room and edit yourself to keep the temperature down. You speak softer. You gather "evidence" to soothe your nerves, not to serve the work. The part of you built to scale—the part that values clarity and moves you toward what matters—gets out-voted by a committee of habits.

It isn't *"I don't care what anyone thinks."* It's *"I know which opinions matter."* I've seen leaders run this update in their lives. One phoned her parents after a launch and said, "It didn't go as planned," and survived the silence. Another renegotiated roles at home so the measure of a good week wasn't who did more but whether both felt seen. A third politely declined a "great opportunity" that was actually a detour—and sat in the discomfort long enough to realize the world didn't end; her world began. Praise still lands as a warm pat on the back. Criticism still shows up. But neither owns her.

Appreciation is beautiful—when it lands as confirmation, not as a leash. And criticism can be a mirror—sometimes clean, sometimes warped. Use what's true.

If the performance trap had a slogan, it would be: *Make yourself smaller to be acceptable.* Gut leadership flips it: *Make your work truer to be useful.* The more useful your work, the more it will be loved by the right people and disliked by the wrong ones. So, when the old heat rises—heart quickening, breath shortening, mind racing to please—remember: That's just the survival brain running last year's play. Drop your shoulders. Lengthen your exhale. Return to the promise you made in these pages: Impact over approval, truth over performance, aliveness over "fine." That's how you stop acting and start leading.

Hiding In Plain Sight

Another way your brain lies to you is through hiding. It whispers, "Not yet." It puts on the costume of diligence, responsibility, even maturity. You get applause for being "thorough," admiration for being "polished," relief from people who like you predictable. And meanwhile the real work—the bold, messy, gut-led thing you're here to do—waits in the corner like a kid not picked for the game.

 # Hiding in perfectionism: Sometimes hiding looks like excellence. You polish the slides a fifth time, tweak commas no one will notice, reorganize your Trello until it gleams. It feels productive; it's delay in disguise. Anna, 42, a Berlin founder, lived this loop. Her SaaS customers kept asking for an AI feature. Investors were excited. She said, "Almost ready—give me two more weeks," then, "Let's re-record the demo; the voiceover isn't warm enough," then, "We should tighten the onboarding copy—people might get confused," then, "I want benchmarks against three more competitors."

Every time someone asked for a date, her chest tightened and she said, "Soon." While she was polishing, a competitor pushed a rough beta and took the conversation. When Anna finally told herself the truth, it wasn't "quality" holding her back; it was fear—fear of criticism, fear of not being enough. She had chosen the polished prison of hiding. Once she saw the hijack, she stopped measuring "ready" by flawlessness and started measuring by contact with reality.

She invited twenty power users into a messy beta, killed two shiny features nobody touched, doubled down on the one that made people's eyes light up, and set a hard launch date. Three months later, she was back pitching—clear, specific, alive—not because it was perfect, but because it was real.

 # Hiding in "one more degree": Sometimes a credential is the bridge. Often it's your brain saying, *"I'll be worthy when someone stamps me."* Elena in Zurich—brilliant designer, strong track record—wanted to lead a sustainability hub. "I need a second master's or no one will take me seriously," she said. Translation: *If I build and stumble, they'll see me.* She paused the application and hosted a lunch-and-learn on circular design for twelve people in a borrowed room. Two sessions later, a city office asked to partner. The door that opened wasn't stamped by a university; it opened because she stepped into the arena.

 # Hiding in gathering opinions: Instead of writing your truth, you curate quotes. Instead of sharing your take, you link to experts. It looks smart and feels safe; it's also a way of saying, "Don't look at me, look over there." Experts should inform you; they cannot replace your voice. Risk a sentence that begins, "My view is...," ship it, and let the world meet your thinking unmediated.

Here's the sting: Hiding gets rewarded. Your boss praises your "thoroughness." Peers admire your "dedication." Family relaxes because you look stable. But applause isn't alignment. You can be celebrated for the exact behaviors that bury your brilliance. Gut leadership asks for the opposite. Not recklessness—honesty. Honesty about what you're here to build. Honesty about what matters enough to risk critique. Honesty that your aliveness doesn't live on the whiteboard, in the extra degree, or in the pristine draft; it lives in the arena, in the scrappy experiment, in the moment you dare to share the imperfect version.

How to spot hiding fast:

- If you keep telling yourself, "I'll do it once X is ready."
- If you plan in private but never test in public.
- If you stack credentials but rarely use your voice.
- If you're endlessly polishing instead of pressing "send."

PEPPER ASK: Do the check-in and ask:

- *Is this action moving me closer to impact, or buffering me from risk?*

So—what are you hiding right now? Your inbox? A spotless house? Another course? A plan no one has seen? Your gut already knows. Will you keep playing safe—or let the pepper in push you into the light? Hiding feels safe, but it suffocates you. Exposure feels risky, but it's the only path back to fire.

Meet Your Judge

It's time to meet the main voice in your head that's been running the hijacks. This voice parks itself between you and the life you picture when the house is quiet. It's reasonable, almost kind. *Not yet*, it whispers when you're about to raise your price. *Play it safe*, when you finally want to speak truth. Don't embarrass yourself, when your finger hovers over "send." Because it borrows your tone and your memories, you mistake it for truth. But it's a protection program—your inner narrator trying to keep you safe—and in this book we call it the Judge (the saboteur, the voice of "not enough").

"Negative" emotions are useful alarms for about a second—they highlight something to notice. After that, camping in them becomes self-sabotage. Stress, anxiety, frustration, anger, disappointment, regret, blame, guilt: Feel them long enough to get the message; then you need your creative, solution-making system back online. And remember: Humans amplify and remember the negative three to five times more than the positive. That bias is the Judge's fuel. So if you're feeling bad for more than a breath or two, assume the Judge has the wheel.

The Judge has three favorite targets—you, other people, and your circumstances. Here's how you can spot each mode so you can stop confusing protection with truth and reclaim your power to choose.

 # When the Judge turns on you. You feel the Judge most clearly when it turns on you. It spots a plain fact and stamps it on your forehead as identity. *"I missed a deadline"* quietly mutates into "I am unreliable." *"The launch was bumpy"* becomes *"I'm not a real founder."* That's how impostor syndrome grows—not from facts, but from repeated verdicts. Your body joins the trial: chest tight, breath shallow, shoulders up, stomach buzzing.

A client says, "Great work," and you file it under luck. One sharp comment from a stranger and you replay it in HD for three days. You become busy without being bold, productive without moving. I've watched a brilliant designer stare at her pricing page for months, convinced a tiny increase would expose her as a fraud. The Judge spoke softly—*"Be considerate; don't be greedy"*—and she nodded as if it were wisdom. It wasn't. It was fear wearing a nice jacket.

When the Judge turns on others. The judge issues character verdicts you don't say out loud but carry like stones in your pocket. *"She's just better than me." "He doesn't deserve that role." "They don't care."* Meetings stiffen. Partners shut down. You keep score in silence—who contributed, who flaked, who got credit—while the real conversation never happens.

Bryan, head of marketing at a Chicago agency, watched a high-performing team start to slip. Deadlines wobbled, and Charlotte, the lead designer, was late on a critical launch. His old move would have been to call her out in the Monday stand-up and push for harder deadlines. He knew exactly how it would go: Charlotte would offer something too late —too many priorities, not enough time—and everyone would leave tighter and more defensive. After learning about the Judge, he tried a different approach. He asked Charlotte for a one-on-one, softened his voice, and got curious. No accusations. Just open questions and real listening.

What came out surprised him: Charlotte felt she had only one shot to get each concept "perfect" because time was scarce, so she kept polishing in private and missing share-outs. The fear of wasting time was making her waste time. Together they changed the process—rough drafts early, short daily check-ins, permission to show imperfect work. Output picked up almost immediately, and so did trust.

That's the trap of the Judge when it turns on others: It gives you a flash of superiority while draining your influence. It's contagious, too. Judge someone, and they judge back; soon everyone is performing, defending, or ghosting the hard conversation that would have moved the work forward.

When the Judge turns on your circumstances. "It's not the right time." "The market is hostile." "If I had more support, I'd start." A moving moment gets treated like a fixed verdict and used to justify delay. A setback becomes proof that you should stop. Your mind camps in yesterday's regret or tomorrow's catastrophe and you lose the only place you can act—now.

It's like the story of the old farmer and the stallion. On market day the horse wins the village race. Neighbors pour in with wine and congratulations. "What good fortune!" they say. The farmer wipes the sweat from the horse's neck and shrugs: "Who knows what's good or bad?" That night, thieves cut the rope and the stallion is gone. "Terrible!" the neighbors gasp. Again, the farmer: "Who knows?" A week later the stallion returns, mane wild, driving three untamed horses into the paddock. Cheers all around. "Who knows?" the farmer says, smiling this time. The farmer's son tries to break one of the new horses, is thrown, and shatters his leg. Wails from the neighbors. "Who knows?" says the farmer, now quiet.

Days later the army comes through conscripting every able-bodied young man. They leave the son in his bed. The neighbors finally understand the refrain. What looked like blessing or curse kept changing shape. The only constant was the farmer's refusal to stamp the moment with a permanent label.

That is the precise move the Judge can't stand. It demands certainty today. I've watched a founder read one flat investor face and, by evening, rewrite the whole product roadmap. Parents mistake a slammed teenage door for a broken bond when it was just a bad Tuesday. When the Judge narrates your circumstances, you don't see data; you see destiny. And destiny, conveniently, says wait. The work that would move things forward is almost always smaller and nearer than the Judge admits.

The stallion story isn't about passivity; it's about refusing premature endings. Keep the refrain handy—*Who knows?*—and you'll keep enough space to do the one thing you can do now.

All of this is universal. I haven't met a Scaleur, CEO, artist, or parent who doesn't wrestle with the Judge. In fact, the more ambitious you are, the louder it barks—like a guard dog pacing the edge of your comfort zone. Stay in the middle and it sleeps. Walk toward the edge—launch, speak, ask, step into visibility—and it wakes. That spike of doubt isn't a stop sign; it's a proximity alarm. It means you're close to the work that matters.

So this is the Judge: a risk-averse narrator that shrinks your world, swaps impact for approval, and keeps you looping where it feels familiar but not alive. It wears your voice so well that you trust it without checking whether it's working for you. You'll keep hearing it in three places—inside your skin, across your relationships, and in the way you read the world. Your job in this chapter is simply to notice. Name it—Judge—and feel how that tiny bit of distance lets your chest loosen and your breath come back. We're not trying to delete this voice; it was built to protect you, and sometimes it still does. We're going to retrain its influence.

In part 2 you'll learn how to quiet the alarm in your body and hand the microphone to the wiser system that can see clearly and act cleanly. For now, remember this: The Judge will always have something to say. Don't let it have the final word.

Other Saboteurs

The Judge rarely works alone. Once it stirs, it calls in its accomplices—other saboteurs you built long ago to stay safe, loved, or accepted. They began as real strengths. A child who needed harmony learned to soothe; a teen who had to perform learned to push; a young adult who felt safer with facts learned to live in the head. Those strengths can still serve you. The trouble starts when stress wakes them and they take the wheel. They look helpful from the outside—responsible, diligent, caring—but inside they quietly trade aliveness for control, connection for approval, progress for perfection. Think of them as characters in a cast; you'll recognize their voices as we go.

 # Controller. At its best, the Controller is your get-it-done muscle. You decide, you move. That's a gift. Under pressure, it tightens. You correct small things, jump in midsentence, and think, *"If I don't drive this, it won't happen."* Rooms go quiet—not from agreement, but from retreat. People nod, then disengage. Work boomerangs back to you and you end the week carrying everything. You can feel the shift in your body: jaw tight, breath shallow, sentences short and clipped. It protects you from chaos, but it chokes trust. The harder you grip, the less control you have.

Turn control into gravity. State the outcome and the why, set a few guardrails, then ask first and speak last. Name an owner. Match work to strengths. Let people learn out loud instead of correcting every move.

That's what Bryan did on a team project. In past years he would've assigned tasks in minute one. This time he opened with, "What would great look like?" He drew out the quiet classmate, shared his view last, and aligned roles to what each person did best. The deadline didn't move. The energy did. People leaned in, and the load didn't land back on his shoulders.

Avoider. The Avoider looks kind and easygoing. You keep the peace, smooth rough edges, and tell yourself you're "flexible." But when something has teeth—a tricky email, a money talk, a tough decision—you slip out the side door. You answer simple messages, tidy the desk, reorganize files. The one task you're dodging grows claws. Your chest tightens, your stomach buzzes, and by late afternoon the thing feels ten times bigger. Avoidance gives a quick hit of relief, but it's a slow leak—energy drains all day and confidence goes with it.

Elena in Zurich lived this for weeks with a beloved client. Prices had to go up. She drafted paragraphs, deleted them, told herself she'd send it "after lunch." One morning she tried a different move and sent a single line: "Can we talk pricing on Thursday?" Sixty seconds, send. The dread evaporated into a calm, adult conversation and a fair agreement. That's the Avoider's lesson: Relief doesn't come from *not* acting; it comes from a small, clean action that faces the thing.

Hyper-Achiever. The world loves the Hyper-Achiever. You're fast, focused, tireless—the person who can move a mountain. That drive is a gift. But when achievement becomes your identity, the joy drains from the journey. Each win buys ten minutes of relief before the next climb. The finish line moves, so you move faster. You start setting safer goals—impressive enough to post, low-risk enough to keep the streak. Quietly, you under-reach.

This was one of my strongest saboteurs. People kept saying, "Enjoy the view," "Take a breath," and I would nod while lacing up for the next sprint. Pregnancy finally slowed me down long enough to notice my default setting: Earn peace by achieving. The pause made something obvious—my worth and my output had fused. No wonder rest felt like failure. You feel hollow because the goalposts keep moving.

Here's the paradox that frees you: Detaching your worth from results doesn't blunt your edge; it sharpens it. When you stop proving and start creating, pressure loosens, attention widens, and performance improves. You make braver choices, ask for help sooner, learn faster, and—sometimes for the first time— actually enjoy the work while you're doing it.

 # Hyper-Rational. In a storm, the Hyper-Rational sees the map. You cut through noise, weigh trade-offs, and make clean decisions while everyone else spirals. That clarity saves teams. When it overreaches, feelings get treated like bugs in the system and people like spreadsheets. Influence drops because humans decide with feeling and justify with logic.

A CEO once told his wife that missing her birthday "didn't matter strategically." Arms crossed; case closed. He believed he was solving the problem; she felt invisible. The shift came when he learned to name what was in the room: "You felt hurt and unimportant." He didn't abandon reason; he added humanity. Their conversations opened, and his leadership did too.

The fix isn't to stop thinking; it's to think *with* feeling. Ask, "What matters here besides the numbers?" Label the emotion once—"angry," "disappointed," "excited"—and then return to the facts. Pair a crisp plan with a human check-in. Your logic lands *more* when people feel seen first.

Hyper-Vigilant. The Hyper-Vigilant wears the guardian's uniform. You spot the loose step, the short runway, the clause in tiny print. That talent saves teams from preventable pain—recalls avoided, launches de-risked, money not wasted. When it overreaches, you start looking for tigers in every rustling tree, sending long "what-if" threads, hedging every decision. People stop listening—not because risk isn't real, but because the alarm is constant.

I watched Maya, a COO, check Slack at 2:07 a.m., add five new contingencies, and nudge the deadline "just in case." The team went quiet, real momentum died, and when an actual threat landed—a vendor collapse—everyone was too numb to respond fast.

The shift isn't to stop caring; it's to calibrate: Is this a real threat? *If so, what should we do in the next twenty-four hours?* Pair every worry with one concrete check or contingency, then close the scanner and return to build mode. Share one top risk so people know where to place attention. Vigilance, done well, buys you calm presence—the kind that can tell noise from danger and put focus where it has leverage.

Pleaser. The Pleaser wears a warm smile. You read rooms fast, anticipate needs, and offer help before anyone asks. Teams feel seen and cared for. The trouble begins when your yes becomes a way to earn approval. You agree when your gut says no, you pad feedback so it lands soft instead of true, and you push your own needs to the back of the line. Kindness stays on the surface while quiet resentment builds underneath.

Anna, the SaaS founder in Berlin, was famous for being "always available." Investors loved her responsiveness, her team pinged her day and night, customers got instant fixes. Her sleep thinned, her workouts vanished, and at home every conversation started with "Sorry." She thought boundaries would make her selfish. Instead, they made her clear. He began saying honest no's—"I can't take this today; here's who can"—and making simple asks—"I need feedback by Thursday." Nothing dramatic.

Within weeks, support tickets were routed to owners, 1:1s got real, and her marriage softened. She didn't become cold; she became trustworthy. People finally had space to step in because she stopped filling every gap.

Restless. The Restless keeps life vivid. You're curious, fast, hungry for the new—the spark that finds fresh angles and opens doors. Overused, it skims. You sprint from idea to idea and room to room, never staying long enough to dig one well deep enough to hit water. People feel you're half a step ahead, which means you're not fully with them now.

Shella, a product lead in Amsterdam, lived in perpetual motion: ten tabs open, two half-written briefs, Slack humming. Her team admired her creativity and quietly dreaded handoffs— "She'll have a new idea tomorrow." At home, bedtime was a multitask blur: She'd scroll while her son told a story and later wonder why he seemed clingy.

She ran a small experiment. At work, she chose one "finish line" a day and closed everything else until it shipped. In meetings she put her phone face-down, laptop shut, and asked one deeper follow-up before moving on. At night she gave her son five minutes of undivided attention—phone in the kitchen, eyes up, "Tell me the best thing today."

Two weeks in, projects were actually launching, her team relaxed into ownership, and her son started asking for their "five minutes" by name. Restlessness is a gift when it fuels discovery. It hurts when it steals presence because presence is the only place where life happens.

Stickler. The Stickler is the craftsperson. You bring order to chaos, discipline to dreams, beauty to the details. People trust you because what you touch works and looks right. When fear tightens the lens, though, perfectionism takes over. You polish a leaf and miss the forest. Deadlines slip, teammates wait, and the work that needed to ship yesterday is still open in twelve tabs.

Think of Charlotte, team member of Bryan, the designer from Chicago. Her campaign brief was sharp on day three—and untouched by day ten because the spacing on slide four still "wasn't singing." Her team went quiet around her; nobody wanted to present half-finished work to the Stickler.

We made two shifts. First, "vital few" before "trivial many": Agree upfront what actually moves the outcome (the story, the offer, the call to action), and ship those at 90 percent before you tune kerning. Second, celebrate substance before surface. I'd seen a version of this with a teenager practicing a talk: She finished glowing, and the first comment was about the font. Her shoulders fell. When we named the courage and clarity first and only then tweaked slides, the human returned—and the slides got better, fast.

The Stickler at its best is excellence: perfecting the handful of things that truly matter. The Stickler overused is avoidance. A simple question brings it back on track: "What, if improved by 1 percent, would change the outcome—and what can be 'good enough' so this ships?" Define "done" before you start, time-box polish at the end, and send the draft even if your jaw is still tight. Craft remains craft when it serves the mission, not when it stalls it.

Victim. The Victim carries depth. In love, it shows up as the part of you that feels everything and names what hurts. At its best you're a witness and a truth-teller—you can say, "That crossed a line," or "I felt unseen," and the relationship has a chance to heal. Overused, the story hardens around hurt: life happens to you, not through you. Sympathy becomes a poor substitute for love. Friends tiptoe. You replay texts and let one person's choices become the headline.

After a painful breakup, Clara told the tragedy version on loop. "He wasted my time." "Everyone leaves." Nights blurred into scrolling his socials, collecting new evidence that confirmed the worst story about herself. None of it was exactly false— only incomplete.

When we treated her pain as real and her agency as real too, the story shifted. She put facts on one page (We argued about X, he moved out, no new messages) and on the next wrote three things she could influence in ten minutes. She blocked his feeds for thirty days. She texted, "No-contact for a month so I can heal; drop the keys in the mailbox." She told two friends, "Please don't give me updates; take me for a walk instead." She boxed the souvenirs and moved them to a high shelf. Then she added small, body-first anchors: a morning loop around the park, dinner at the table without her phone, a weekly class where her hands had something to make.

The facts didn't change. Her place inside them did. Shoulders dropped. Space returned for people who could meet her where she was now. The Victim isn't "weak"; it's a protective stance that asks to be met. The pivot is simple and powerful: from "Why did he do this to me?" to "What do I need, and what is one step I can take today?" Pain is real; choice is, too. When you let the pain be honest and your agency be loud, you stop auditioning for rescue and start building a love life that holds you.

None of these saboteurs are evil. They were built by a younger you who did the best they could with limited tools. The problem is that they still run the show long after their job is done. Gut leadership doesn't erase them. It recognizes their costumes, thanks them for their past service, and invites a different part of you to drive—the power brain that's calm, clear, and guided by what you know is true.

In part 2, you'll learn how to retrain your system so these voices lose their grip and your days start to reflect who you truly are.

You've seen it now: Your brilliant brain is also a bodyguard. It chases comfort, whispers "I'm fine" when you're not, and—when tired or stressed—lets the Judge and its saboteur friends run the show. We mapped the three systems sharing the wheel (survival, emotional–social, planning), showed how chemistry and habit carve highways, and why rest, food, light, breath, and tiny "Pepper Reps" matter. You learned that negative emotions are alerts, not homes; that overthinking is a safety play; and that praise/criticism can hijack your day if you hand them the keys. Next, we add the missing co-pilot: your gut—the bottom-up compass that helps you tell safety from growth and turns insight into action.

Chapter 4:

Listening To Your Gut

We've spent three chapters getting friendly with your brain. Now it's time to invite the second guide to the table: your gut.

For years I lived by spreadsheets and strategy decks. Then, during my first pregnancy, something quieter kept tapping. I started studying and paying attention. The results were too consistent to ignore. When I included my gut in the conversation, insight began turning into action. The brain doesn't drive alone. If you want real change, your gut is the copilot. When you listen to it, decisions get cleaner, boundaries get simpler, and courage stops being a pep talk and becomes a felt state. Ignore it, and you can understand everything and still feel stuck.

Your gut speaks first—not in sentences, in signals: a lift behind the navel before a pitch, a quiet drop when you agree to something you don't want, a tight, churning "no" that shows up before your mouth says "yes." This isn't superstition; it's biology. Woven through your digestive tract is a vast web of nerves (often called the "second brain"), connected to your heart and lungs by the vagus nerve. All day it listens to your world and "votes": safe or not, move closer or move away, speed up or slow down. Learning to hear it is recovering a sense you were born with—the ability to steer from the inside.

Your Inner Compass

Think of what the gut is doing every minute. It digests your life—food, yes, but also experience. As it breaks down a meal it sends constant updates to the brain: energy incoming, trouble brewing, repair required. It helps regulate immunity and inflammation, manufactures chemical messengers that shape mood and motivation, and hosts a bustling community of microbes that turn food into signals—compounds that soothe and stabilize, or sparks that make everything feel harder.

When the gut is calm and fed well, the brain plans better, sleep deepens, and patience widens. When it's inflamed, empty, or jittery from caffeine and sugar, the inner world tilts; you get short and foggy and reach for quick hits. We often blame character for what is mostly chemistry. And the street runs both ways: One sharp email can knot your stomach before you've read the second line—your survival system throwing a flag—while a morning of light, protein, and movement can turn an anxious meeting into a solvable puzzle; now the gut votes "yes," and your planner can hear it.

This is why a whole-body approach wins. Talk, understanding, and technology can help. But to truly reclaim the wheel after stress or old hurt, the body needs experiences that contradict the old story. A long exhale proves the tiger is gone. A steady meal keeps blood sugar even so the brain stops chasing. A brisk walk turns adrenaline into fuel.

You don't think your way out of a body alarm; you regulate your way out, then you think clearly again. If you've lived through too much, your survival brain keeps scanning for the next hit. Emotions surge; the body clenches; behavior follows. Those imprints are not destiny. We change them from the top down—naming what's real and telling the truth in good company; from the outside in—medicines and tools that quiet the alarm; and from the bottom up—physical experiences that teach, again and again, "I am safe, I have choices, I can move." The gut sits at the center of that bottom-up lane. Meanwhile the brain builds loops—neural highways that save energy. Check phone, tiny dopamine, repeat. Say yes to avoid awkwardness, feel relief, repeat. Stress snack, crash later, repeat.

Gut leadership is the moment you feel the tug of an old road and choose a new turn. It's your inner compass whispering, "Not this" or lighting up: "This way." One rep changes little; sets, done daily, build muscle. Pepper Reps are the gut-brain handshake in action; each one interrupts an old loop, settles the body, and installs a better default.

A core skill here is telling intuition from alarm. Alarm is hot, fast, and catastrophizing. Intuition is cooler and consistent— a gentle yes or no that remains after you breathe. Try a sixty-second check with a decision you're circling: sit, place a hand low on your belly, and take three slow breaths with longer exhales. Ask yourself what yes feels like in the body, then what no feels like. Don't hunt for words; notice whether things settle or tighten. The cortex will try to argue either way; the gut votes through sensation. With practice you'll recognize its signature.

Courage a metabolic state. Expecting boldness from a brain running on little sleep and junk food is like expecting a car to cross a country on fumes. Real food matters: protein to build the neurotransmitters that drive motivation, fiber and fermented foods to feed the gut ecosystem that steadies mood. Hydration, movement, and morning light complete the circuit. "Trust your gut" stops being a poster and becomes a skill.

What changes when you live this way is simple and profound. You make faster, kinder decisions, set cleaner boundaries, and overthink less because your body is part of the vote. The pages ahead will show you how to practice Gut leadership day to day—how to hear the signal, regulate the state, and choose the next clean action—so your life is steered by a calm, truthful compass rather than by sirens.

Children and animals have this built in—they don't overthink. A child doesn't debate for an hour before running across the grass barefoot. They feel, they move, they trust. Somewhere along the way, most of us lost that instinct. We trained ourselves to ignore the body's quiet signals in favor of logic, fear, or other people's expectations. This Pepper Time is your way back to listening to your gut in practice.

PEPPER TIME 4: GUT CHECK-IN

Timing: 3–5 minutes.

What you'll need: Just a quiet space.

What it's about: Training your body to recognize the subtle "yes" and "no" signals it's already giving you. This builds trust in your gut's language before you apply it to bigger choices.

How to do it:

1. **Settle In. Sit comfortably.** Take 2–3 slow breaths, hand on your belly.
2. **Ask a True Question.** Ask yourself a yes/no question you already know the answer to, like: "Is my name [your name]?" Notice your body's response: expansion, warmth, lightness, openness = yes.
3. **Ask a False Question.** Now ask a false statement, like: "Is my name [not your name]?" Notice the shift: contraction, heaviness, tightness, darkness = no.
4. **Repeat & Observe.** Repeat once or twice with other obvious truths and falsehoods (e.g., "Am I sitting?" vs. "Am I standing?").

What to expect: You'll start mapping your body's baseline signals for yes vs. no. With practice, these cues get clearer. Over time, you can use them when facing real choices—projects, conversations, commitments—so your gut always has a seat at the table.

Reflection

____

____

____

____

____

____

____

*   *   *

For a one-minute rescue for hard moments, use the gut reset we teach teams before high-stakes conversations. Stand up. Let your exhale be a little longer than your inhale while your palm rests on your belly. Feel your feet spread inside your shoes. Let your eyes find the farthest visible point. Whisper, "Safe, here and now." Then choose a single next action: Ask one clean question, tell one clean truth, or take one clean step. It's astonishing how often this tiny ritual turns a spiral into a decision.

As you practice, remember why this matters. The life you want doesn't live on autopilot. Your scaling brain—paired with a steady gut—lets you tell the truth faster, say no sooner, say yes with your whole body, and build the kind of day you don't need a vacation from. You are not the passenger of your history; you are the coder and the gardener. Every small check-in with your gut is a line of new code and a seed in fresh soil.

On the days you sleep badly or live on espresso, expect more static. Be kind and fix the fuel before you judge the signal. On the days you move, eat, breathe, and see the morning sun, expect the compass to click. Listen. Act. Repeat. The loop will become a way of life, and that quiet voice in your belly—the one that has been trying to guide you since you were small—will finally have a clear line to the wheel.

Female Cycles

Let's start with something people still call "controversial": female cycles. Guys, stay with me—this will help you understand the women you love and work with. You've probably heard the line, "We're about 60 percent water; the moon moves the tides, so it must move us." Whether or not you buy the moon bit, here's the part that matters: human bodies run in rhythms. Many men ride a twenty-four-hour hormonal arc; many women move through a roughly monthly arc. Those rhythms change energy, focus, mood, cravings, sleep, and even digestion—because hormones are in constant conversation with the gut and the brain.

Our culture rewards an "always on" pattern—decide in the morning, sell at noon, network at night, repeat tomorrow. That's great for a daily cycle. But cyclical bodies get told to flatten out and perform the same every day. When you try to override your rhythm, you end up fighting yourself. When you work with it, you get more done with less push. So yes, we're going to talk about cycles as a practical map. Once you see the pattern, you can plan with it: lean into phases that boost focus and visibility, protect the windows that want recovery and depth, and let your gut be part of the steering, not background noise.

Many women move through four distinct phases over about twenty-eight days, and each phase offers a different kind of power if you pay attention. I had no idea how much wisdom lived in my own body until I started tracking it; maybe you haven't either. No matter your parenthood status, what organs you still have, or how they're functioning, you still carry this energetic blueprint. Even if you're past menopause, pregnant, nursing, on contraceptives, or not menstruating for any reason, you'll notice tides in mood, sleep, hunger, focus, and gut comfort.

And here's the relief: You don't have to rewire your whole job or life overnight. Even syncing 10 percent of your projects with your rhythm makes a difference. Imagine scheduling your big pitch during a week where your body feels magnetic or letting yourself off the hook for three social events during your period so you can come back recharged instead of drained. That's the power of cycles. You can use the twenty-eight-day map as a template, or simply track your own signals. Either way, the moment you stop ignoring your body, you start gaining power.

Follicular: the "green light" phase. This phase begins after bleeding ends. Estrogen rises, your body rebuilds, and suddenly the fog lifts. Energy comes back, ideas spark, and life feels possible again. It's the week where you feel like you can start something new. What this means in real life: Start projects, brainstorm, set up exploratory meetings, sketch out the first draft, experiment. At work, your creativity flows; in relationships, you're more playful and lighthearted; in well-being,

movement feels energizing instead of heavy. Your gut also tends to feel calmer here, so fuel it with protein-rich meals and lots of light in the morning. Think of it as your body's natural springtime—plant seeds, literally and metaphorically.

Ovulation: stage time. This is when estrogen peaks, an egg is released, and you feel magnetic. Verbal clarity sharpens, confidence feels natural, and your social sparkle is at its highest. Pheromones even shift, making you more attractive to others on a biological level. This is the week to show up. Pitch the client, run the workshop, film the video, host the team dinner, have the courageous conversation. In relationships, you connect effortlessly; you may feel more flirty, generous, and open. Gut-wise, many notice fewer issues during this window—your system feels light and cooperative. Support it with colorful fiber-rich foods and steady hydration so your energy doesn't crash.

Luteal: detail and completion mode. After ovulation, progesterone rises, and energy begins to turn inward. Outward sparkle dims, but your focus deepens. This is when you suddenly care about the details—editing, checking quality, tightening systems, finishing what you started. If you've ever wondered why you feel like a "starter, not a finisher," chances are you've been ignoring this phase. This is the natural time to close loops and tie things up. In real life, use this window to finalize your presentation, clean up your processes, or even declutter your home. In relationships, you may feel less social, but this can deepen intimacy in smaller, more honest conversations. Gut-wise, some notice bloating or slower digestion. Warm meals, magnesium, and gentler movement support you here. Protecting this phase can change your life—it's not about being antiso-

cial; it's about honoring the biology that wants you to complete and conserve.

 # Menstrual: the reset. Bleeding is the body's built-in reset button. Energy is lowest, but intuition and clarity are at their highest. Science shows the two hemispheres of the brain talk more to each other now—logic and intuition meet. This is not the week to power through or stack your calendar with events. This is the week to review: What worked, what didn't, what do I want to release? Rest here isn't laziness; it's maintenance. Your gut often wants simple, soothing foods—soups, stews, tea. Say "no" more often. Give yourself quiet. If you've ever felt guilty for needing downtime, know this: Rest here powers everything else. Think of it like a CEO retreat—you step back, reset the vision, and only then return to execution.

If you identify as a "starter, not a finisher," honoring the luteal phase alone can change your life. If you're a lifelong extrovert who feeds on rooms full of people (hello, me), learning to protect menstrual-phase quiet may feel awkward at first—and then strangely like power. My body didn't really get my attention until pregnancy, when it staged an intervention: time to rest, time to listen, time to see who you are when you're not constantly doing. The lesson stuck.

If you don't bleed—or your cycle is irregular—use your personal data instead of dates. Notice when you naturally want to initiate, when you crave collaboration, when you're drawn to completion, when reflection calls. Some people like to borrow the lunar calendar as a poetic structure; others mark four weekly "seasons" on their planner. The point isn't astrology, it's alignment. This is also where gut-brain work pays off.

Premenstrual days can amplify sensitivity; that's not a character flaw. It's your nervous system running hot while your gut is a little more reactive.

Bottom-up tools help: longer exhales, a slow walk after meals, warm showers, magnesium, fewer ultra-processed "quick fixes" that spike and crash. Top-down tools help too: Name the wave, simplify the to-do list, batch decisions for follicular/ovulatory days, and keep room for one thing that's just for you. When old hurt lives in the system, survival circuits don't do denial—they pull the fire alarm.

We regain mastery three ways: top-down (truth telling in good company, therapy, coaching), outside-in (medicines and technologies that calm alarms), and bottom-up (physical experiences that say, again and again, "Safe, here and now"). Most of us need a blend. The gut sits in the center of that bottom-up path.

Here's what this looks like on a Tuesday. A founder notices her calendar is loaded with external meetings during late luteal. She's been snappish, her stomach tight, sleep thin. Instead of muscling through, she swaps two coffees for deep-work blocks, eats something warm and protein-forward at lunch, and takes a ten-minute walk before the one meeting she keeps. She ends the day with three tasks finished—no fireworks, but an exhale so loud it feels like music. Another client times her launch webinar for ovulation week and reserves menstrual days for strategy review and next-quarter planning. Same number of hours, new outcomes, far less friction.

If you want to start gently, treat your next cycle as a listening project:

The morning after your period begins, write "Season 1" at the top of a page. For a week, notice your energy, focus, appetite, and gut comfort without judgment; feed the upswing with protein, light, and movement.

Week two, notice your social pull and schedule one outward-facing thing that matters.

Week three, protect two finish blocks and give your digestion some kindness.

Week four, let your calendar soften and review the month with the kind of honesty you'd reserve for a dear friend.

If you don't menstruate, begin any Monday and run the same four-week arc. The magic is in the noticing and the matching.

A word to the men reading: This isn't a secret manual you're excluded from; it's a chance to be a wiser partner and leader. Your biology also cycles—mostly on a daily rhythm. Knowing that the person across from you may be in a different "season" than you are optimizes performance. Fewer pointless conflicts. Better timing. More wins that cost less.

 **# PEPPER ASK: Three questions to keep handy, regardless of gender:**

- *Who am I when I'm not doing anything?*
- *Who am I when I'm not producing?*
- *Who am I when I'm not in action?* 

Great teachers do this with kids' art all the time: Instead of "Good job," they ask, "What colors did you pick? How did the brush feel?" That shift—from rating the result to noticing the process—is the point. The joy isn't only at the finish line; it's in the rhythm that gets you there. Cycles aren't problems to beat; they're power to steward. Your gut helps you time the work, your brain helps you plan it, and your calendar proves you respect both. When those three are in sync, you force less, flow more—and, oddly, get more done.

Most of us were raised to believe that we have to earn our right to be here by doing. Real satisfaction comes from the process of progress and growth, not just the moment you tick the box.

Feminine Vs. Masculine Qualities

First, a sanity check: This part isn't men versus women. It's two kinds of energy we all carry. Think of them as two gears on the same bike. One gear (often called "masculine") loves structure, analysis, clarity, competition, and doing. The other (often called "feminine") loves intuition, receptivity, collaboration, process, and being. Both are essential. Too much of either throws us off.

There are hundreds of qualities that makes us human, they define our attitudes and the way we behave. I will only focus on seventeen: intuition, resilience, inclusion, creativity, empathy, awareness, passion, communication, compassion, discipline, responsibility, action orientation, courage, focus, strength, linear thinking, and assertiveness.

Overused, any tool becomes a hammer in a room full of glass. Take linear thinking. It's brilliant for scoping a project or landing a plane. Overdo it and you miss weak signals—the sideways comment from a teammate or the off note in a customer interview—that would have saved you months. Or take intuition. It helps you integrate a hundred data points into one felt sense when info is sparse or overwhelming. Overdo it and you drift past hard facts that deserve their say.

Your gut is the switchboard that picks the right gear for the terrain. When a moment demands deadlines and clean execution, your gut will nudge you toward discipline, responsibility, action, courage, focus, strength, linear thinking, and assertiveness. When a moment calls for connection or creativity, that same gut draws you toward intuition, resilience, inclusion, creativity, empathy, awareness, passion, communication, and compassion. It doesn't deliver a thesis; it delivers a nudge—more structure here, more listening there.

A lot of modern life rewards the daily, "always-on" gear: Decide by nine, perform by noon, network by six, repeat tomorrow. That's one reason so many people succeed on paper and starve inside. The "feminine" set—presence, process, relationship, recovery—gets treated like a luxury, even though it's the fuel that lets the other gear run without burning out.

You're not a fixed type. Your mix shifts by season and context. Saying "I'm 62 percent feminine" makes for a cute quiz, but the truer frame is simpler and more liberating: You are your own category. Notice what the moment needs, then shift.

Gut leadership is learning to ask, "What does this moment need?" and then letting your body's signal help you blend the gears. When you do, you force less, flow more, and your results start to feel like you. Labels can be helpful, but when they harden, they mislead. Your gut isn't asking you to be someone else; it's asking you to use all of you. The more you practice this toggling—being and doing, flow and structure, we and me—the more natural it becomes. And like everything else in this book, it's trained in reps: small, repeatable choices that, over time, turn balance into your default.

Here's the catch though: Most of us don't know which qualities we're overusing and which ones we've left dormant. We think, "I'm disciplined," or "I'm creative," but rarely pause to map the full picture. Without noticing, you may be leaning too heavily on one gear—pushing so hard with focus and structure that empathy gets lost, or floating so much in intuition and passion that action keeps stalling.

That's why I love this next Pepper Time: It gives you a mirror, a way to spot which qualities are loud, which ones are whispering, and how to rebalance so you're leading from your whole self.

PEPPER TIME 5: DISCOVER YOUR QUALITIES

Timing: 15 minutes (do it once now, then 5-minute weekly refresh).

What you'll need: A timer, a pen, and your journal.

What it's about: Spotting your natural "default drivers" so you can lead with more balance—drawing on both feminine (receptive, relational) and masculine (directive, structuring) qualities—instead of running on autopilot.

How to do it:

1. **Ground yourself.** Sit tall with one hand on your belly. Breathe in for 4 counts and out for 6 counts, five times. Let the noise settle and give your gut a say.
2. **Score each quality.** For every quality below, rate how strongly it shows up in your current behavior (not how you wish it did) on a scale of 0–100.

Feminine Qualities	Masculine Qualities
Intuition	Discipline
Resilience	Responsibility
Inclusion	Action Orientation
Creativity	Courage
Empathy	Focus
Awareness	Strength
Passion	Linear Thinking
Communication	Assertiveness
Compassion	

3. **Sort into three buckets:**
. Core Drivers (70-90): Your go-to strengths.

- Overused (90–100): Core drivers turned up so high they create friction (e.g., Focus → tunnel vision; Assertiveness → steamrolling). Mark these with a star.
- Dormant / Untapped (0–35): Capacities you're underusing but could develop.

What to expect: You'll see which qualities drive your behavior, where you lean too heavily, and which untapped traits could bring more balance to your leadership.

Reflection

____

____

____

____

____

____

____

*   *   *

The last exercise wasn't about labels; it was about learning your gears. Nothing in you is "good" or "bad." You're learning to notice, without judgment, which gear a moment needs—and to let your gut help you shift.

Attention Trains Reality

You've had those days when life clicks into place. You wake before the alarm feeling strangely rested, the commute flows, the barista gifts you a free pastry, and an email lands with the exact opportunity you've been circling. We call it "good luck," but most of what we label luck is alignment: your attention, your actions, and your energy quietly pointing in the same direction long enough for momentum to build.

Your brain's attention system is a filter. What you aim it at you start to notice; what you notice you start to choose; what you choose you start to become. That's the "law of attraction" stripped of mystique and given a steering wheel. Here's the simple, body-first way to hold this chapter: Attention is training. What you point your mind and body at starts showing up more in your day.

 # MINDSETS: how you see. Start with how you feel a mindset in your body. Abundance is the stance that there is room: room for your voice or a bigger pie. Scarcity makes the gut clench and the mind grab; abundance softens the belly and widens your field. Patience is abundance across time. It lets seeds be seeds without demanding fruit by Friday. Harmony is the head-heart-gut handshake: Your plan makes sense, your values are honored, and your body says yes. And clarity is choosing a real target. Vague asks get vague results; a precise request gives your brain and gut something to hunt. Hold these four—abundance, patience, harmony, clarity—and your nervous system stops flagging every shadow as "danger" and begins scanning for fit.

 # PRACTICES: what you do. Then put those mindsets in motion with small, physical practices. Journaling makes desire visible. When you put a murky want into words each morning, you're training your filter to find its shape in the wild. Visualization is rehearsal: A few quiet minutes running the future scene—voice steady, room warm, questions answered—lays down a pathway your body can follow under pressure. Meditation lowers static so you can hear the signal; ten unglamorous minutes of breath is often the difference between reacting and choosing. Gratitude isn't a greeting-card trick; it retrains the bias toward threat by forcing your attention to collect evidence of "already good," which calms the survival layer and returns choice to the system. And none of it matters without aligned action—small, honest steps that prove to your nervous system this isn't just a mood. Send the email. Make the call. Draft one slide. When practice and physiology agree, the world starts answering in kind.

 # ENERGETIC DRIVERS: what fuels you. Manifesting is simply sustained coherence between what you want, what you feel, and what you do. Magnetic desire is the felt spark in your belly that makes the next step obvious and the hard part worth it; it's not drama, it's current. Universal connection is the reminder that we regulate in relationship. You move faster when you let yourself be supported—by teammates who co-regulate your nerves, by places that steady your breath, by routines that signal safety. And trust is the permission slip to release the timeline and keep showing up. It isn't passivity; it's active faith: I will do my reps, and I will let timing have a say.

Seen through this lens, those "lucky" stretches aren't cosmic accidents. A promotion "out of the blue" is more often the cumulative effect of months of consistent delivery plus a reputation for being easy to work with. A chance meeting "meant to be" looks a lot like you choosing to attend, to be open, to ask one more question. Life isn't just happening to you; you're coauthoring it with what you attend to, how you care for your body, and which tiny risks you take when the gut gives you a nudge.

When I first met Lotte, her marriage was dissolving. Two kids, a partner lost to work, weekends that felt like single parent-hood. She had rehearsed leaving a hundred times and then rehearsed the fear—housing costs, disruption, the unknown—until her body shut down. We started not with spreadsheets but with attention. I asked her to build a Pepper Board, not aspirational fluff but a visual contract with herself: images that felt like oxygen. At the center she placed a woman with her back to the camera at the foot of a mountain, shoes laced, ready to climb. Around her she placed photos of her kids laugh-ing, a map with three cities circled, a kitchen table big enough for Sunday meals, a legal pad that read "Work I'm proud of."

Naming the picture sharpened her clarity; seeing it daily stabi-lized her energy. From there we layered practices: two difficult conversations scheduled with a friend on call, one meeting with a financial planner. It wasn't magic. It was a nervous system moving from alarm to agency. Within months she had renegotiated home logistics, found part-time counsel to shore up finances, and—most importantly—stopped treating herself like a passenger of her own life. The Pepper Board didn't save her; her attention did.

PEPPER ASK:

- *Here's how you make this chapter yours. Begin with a gut intention—a sentence you can feel under your hand when it rests on your belly. Sit up in bed tomorrow and breathe in for four, out for six, five cycles. Ask: What would make this season feel true?*

If you want a playful but surprisingly powerful way to discover your "why" and get clarity on which path you belong to, try the Gingerbread experiment. You're letting head, heart, and gut speak in the same place. Tuck the page where you'll see it. Let it become a compass more than a command. This 5-minute sketch bypasses overthinking and gives you raw, gut-led insights into what really matters for your future.

PEPPER TIME 6: GINGERBREAD

Timing: 8 minutes.

What you'll need: A timer, a pen/markers, and your journal.

What it's about: A fast, gut-led snapshot of your life that bypasses overthinking. By "asking" different parts of your body for signals and translating them into quick icons on a gingerbread figure, you'll distill a bold intention. This becomes the seed for your Pepper Board and future planning.

How to do it:

1. **Settle your system.** Sit tall. One hand low on your belly. Inhale for 4, exhale for 6, five cycles. Let your belly soften—this primes intuition.
2. **Draw the gingerbread figure.** Sketch a simple gingerbread outline: a head, two arms, two legs, and a belly.
3. **Draw your icons.** One symbol in each spot below—the first image that pops in is the right one. Keep it messy and fast. Set your timer 1 minute, as that's the time you have per category. Seven in total.

Head = Work/Thinking. What your mind is full of (road sign, lightning bolt, book, popcorn).

Heart = What/whom you love most (people, craft, place).

Gut = Happiness. What reliably lights you up (smiley, sun, food, nature, laughter).

Left arm = Past Gift. One thing from your past you'll carry forward (ball, cross, school, friend).

Right hand = Future Pull. One concrete future you want (keys to a home, "Teacher," globe, venture).

Left foot = Work Stance. How you're standing at work now (smiley, growth chart, question mark).

Right foot = Joy/Hobbies. What play looks like (skis, mountain, waves, canvas).

What to expect: A raw, intuitive draft of what matters most to you right now. From this snapshot, extract one bold, big-picture intention—an aspiration that reflects the area of your life you most want to shift. This vision will fuel your Pepper Board and guide your next moves.

Reflection

____

____

____

____

____

____

*   *   *

Now weave the pieces. Keep mindsets clean (abundance, patience, harmony, clarity). Keep practices light and daily (a page of journaling, a one-minute visualization, ten breaths, one real thank-you, one aligned step). Fuel it with desire you can feel, connection that steadies you, and trust that lets the calendar breathe. When old loops flare—doom-scrolls, brittle timelines, people-pleasing—use a body reset: long exhale, unclench your jaw, feel your feet, name the moment cleanly, choose one action that honors your sentence.

Run a seven-day experiment. Each morning, write your gut intention at the top of a page and the smallest step that moves the day toward it. Take the step before noon. Each evening, note one moment—however minor—when the world met you halfway: a timely reply, a needed resource, a conversation that opened a door. You're not collecting miracles; you're training your filter. By day seven, most people report the same thing: The world didn't flip, yet the day felt lighter, more directed, "luckier." That's the law of attraction as a body practice.

The head wants certainty. The heart wants safety. The gut offers direction. When all three point the same way, you'll feel it: jaw softens, belly eases, breath deepens, and the next step looks both braver and somehow easier. Follow that. Attention is training. Train it where you want your life to grow.

 # ABUNDANCE (Mindset). An abundance mindset isn't about blind optimism or pretending everything is perfect. It's about the lens you choose to look through—the belief that you have enough space, time, opportunities, and second chances. When you choose abundance, you stop bracing against life and start leaning into it.

Fear is primal. It sits in the oldest parts of your brain and whispers through your belly: What if I fail? What if there isn't enough? What if I'm not enough? Left unchecked, it narrows your world until every step feels risky. Think of the times you stayed in a job you had outgrown, tolerated a friendship that drained you, or said no to a chance you wanted because lack-thinking told you it was "too late" or "too dangerous."

When you practice abundance, you see options where fear saw dead ends. You allow yourself to test, to try, to explore. Instead of fearing failure, you reframe it as training data: Not yet. A business pitch that doesn't land teaches you clarity. A relationship that ends shows you what you deeply need. A door closing directs you to another path. Abundance is fuel. It makes you generous with others, because you're no longer afraid that giving will leave you with less. It builds resilience, because bumps in the road don't mean the journey is over. It frees your energy, because you're not stuck in the tunnel vision of "not enough."

Here's the gut piece: Your body knows the difference. In lack mode, your gut tightens, your breath gets shallow, your world shrinks. In abundance mode, your belly softens, your breath deepens, your chest opens. That physical shift is your compass. When you notice your Judge sneering "You'll fail," that's your cue: Pause, exhale, and choose again.

PEPPER ASK: Ask yourself:

- *Where do I live in lack—work, love, friendship, money, trying new things?*
- *How does that scarcity thinking shape my choices, relationships, and dreams?*
- *Where could I lean into abundance—one honest ask, one bold email, one playful experiment?* 

Scarcity lives in the body first. Jaw tightens, stomach knots, breath shortens. Your brain then spins the story: I don't have enough time or courage. I don't have what it takes. When you live here, you shrink. You say no to opportunities, stay in jobs that drain you, and hold on to friendships that don't fit anymore.

Abundance flips the script. You train your system to see more options than your fear allows. When your belly softens and your breath deepens, your nervous system registers "safe." More doors appear. A "no" at work becomes space for the right project. A breakup becomes clarity about the partner you want. Failure becomes training data instead of a dead end.

 # PATIENCE (Mindset). Patience isn't about sitting still or doing nothing. It's about trusting the right pace. When I live with patience, I remind myself: I'm not late: I'm in process. There is space for me and time for what I'm building. My body knows the difference. Scarcity makes my jaw clench, my belly knot, and my mind spiral into "I should have been there already." Patience softens me. My breath drops lower, my shoulders ease, and suddenly I can see the bigger field. From that place, I stop grabbing at quick fixes or making fear-shaped choices. Instead, I can pick one clean next step and trust it's enough.

Think seasons, not sprints. Brains rewire through repetition, not one-offs. Relationships deepen through consistency, not intensity. The gut speaks clearly when it isn't whipped by panic. Patience honors this natural timing—it keeps your body in abundance and stops your mind from confusing urgency with importance. Sometimes we give up too quickly or get anxious and desperate for results to show up overnight. But growth doesn't bend to our panic. It unfolds in its own good time. Patience is the discipline of staying open long enough for the work you've planted to take root.

Rather than obsessing about when it will happen, shift your focus to practices that strengthen the soil: daily visualization, Pepper Boards, and small consistent reps. Every time you repeat, you're laying down stronger pathways in your brain. At first it may feel like nothing is changing. But trust the process: Small shifts in confidence, attitude, and courage stack quietly. Then one day, what felt impossible suddenly feels effortless. Patience is the active choice to enjoy, trust, and keep showing up—steady, honest, and on time.

HARMONY (Mindset). Harmony isn't about being nice or keeping everyone happy. It's about integration—your head, heart, and gut playing the same song instead of fighting for the mic.

Your **head** plans, organizes, and finds words.
Your **heart** gives meaning, care, and connection.
Your **gut** keeps you safe, grounded, and points the way forward.

You can feel when they're out of tune: a clenched jaw (head pushing too hard), a heavy chest (heart drowning in emotion), a tight belly (gut on alarm). You can also feel when they're aligned: Your breath drops low, your shoulders go back, and the next step feels clean and obvious. Harmony doesn't mean a perfect 50/50 split between logic and emotion—it means the right blend for this moment. Sometimes you need structure and focus, sometimes connection and empathy, and sometimes a gut-led no before your head even finishes the sentence.

Bodies are often treated like taxis—just carrying us from one meeting to another, from one relationship to the next. But they're constant messengers signaling your real-time compass. Ignoring them creates burnout and disconnection. Listening creates power. When your logical brain, emotional brain, and gut speak the same language, you stop wasting energy in inner conflict. Instead, you're integrated. You say yes only when it's a full-body yes. You rest without shame and move when your body wants motion.

In performance, harmony looks like clarity + warmth + pace: grounding your body before a pitch, naming what matters, speaking simply. Not bulldozing (head only). Not hedging (heart only). Not hiding (gut on fear). Integrated words land. Saying no when your belly tightens. Resting without guilt. Choosing food, movement, and light that keep your system steady so your brain and gut can stay clear.

In relationships, harmony looks like presence. You stop rehearsing the next argument in your head and hear what's in front of you. Your inner Judge quiets, patience returns, and abundance feels possible. Courage is no longer a dramatic leap—it's simply the next clean step. Harmony is the foundation for thriving in a changing world. Your body already knows the tune. The work is to listen.

CLARITY (Mindset). Clarity is power. Without it, we spin, procrastinate, and waste energy on things that don't move us forward. With it, we suddenly feel lighter, sharper, and more in control. Clarity isn't about being cold or harsh—it's about being kind enough to yourself and others to stop hiding behind vagueness. Vague goals, asks, and boundaries drain you. They leave your gut restless, your mind cluttered, and your relationships confused.

When you strip away the noise and name what's real, your gut relaxes, your jaw softens, and the next step becomes obvious. Think of clarity like switching on a spotlight in a dark room. Suddenly, you see what's in front of you. One problem you can name in one sentence. One clear metric that shows progress. One clean yes or no instead of fishing for approval. You've felt the difference:

- Saying, *"I want to grow my business"* is vague. Saying, *"I will land three new clients this quarter"* is clear.

- Saying, *"I should spend more time with family"* is vague. Saying, *"Every Sunday night is no-phone dinner with my kids"* is clear.

Your body knows the difference, too. If the plan looks good on paper but your belly still tightens, something's off—you're missing a value or pretending. When you're clear, your breath drops, your chest opens, and momentum flows. Clarity only works when paired with the other mindsets. Abundance opens the field, patience sets the pace, harmony aligns your head with your heart and gut, and clarity sharpens the beam. Together, they give you a compass you can trust.

Clarity is about freeing your brain and body from the fog. That's how you stop wasting energy and start moving with purpose toward the life and business you truly desire.

 # JOURNALING (Practice). Your head spins stories all day. Journaling is where you cut through the noise. Not pages of overthinking. Just a short, honest check-in between your head, heart, and gut. On paper, fog turns into facts. You begin to see the loops that keep you stuck—the Judge whispering "not enough," the fears that shrink your choices. But you also start to see the small wins you normally skip over—a morning that felt calm, the brave email you sent, the tiny moment your belly said yes. That's data. That's gold.

And two minutes is enough:

- One line for Body (what you felt physically).
- One for Emotion (one word).
- One for Story (what your mind told you).
- One for Choice (the next step you took or will take).
- One for Win (something that went right).

That's it. Consistency beats length. At first, it might feel awkward—like you're writing to no one. But give it two weeks. The page doesn't judge; it reflects. Patterns will pop. Insights will land. And the more you do it, the more your brain learns: I can trust my signals. I can choose cleanly.

This whole journey is basically a guided journal. Every Pepper Ask, every Pepper Time, every mindset shift—those are invitations to write. To pause, put it down on paper, and track what your gut and brain are telling you. This isn't busywork. It's how you build your own playbook. So don't just read. Write. Capture the raw stuff—what's working, where your belly tightens, where you showed up braver than last week. Over time, you'll have a private dataset of your growth. That's how clarity deepens, courage builds, and your autopilot starts rewiring in the direction you want.

 # VISUALIZATION (Practice). Elite athletes do this all the time. Before they step on the track, into the pool, or out of the gate, they've already "run" the race in their minds a dozen times. Eyes closed, muscles twitching, body carving an invisible path. They're not daydreaming—they're training. Why? Because to the brain, there's surprisingly little difference between experiencing something in real life and imagining it vividly.

Research shows this is more than woo. People who only visualize flexing a muscle can gain measurable strength. Without moving a finger, their brains light up the same pathways as if they were lifting weights. The body begins to respond to the mind's rehearsal. That's the power of visualization: it tells your nervous system, This is familiar, safe, doable.

New = uncertain. And uncertain often feels like danger. Visualization shrinks "new." By imagining the moment with all your senses on you trick your system into believing it's already been there. That way, when the real moment comes, your gut doesn't throw up alarms. It nods: I know this. I'm ready.

I use this with clients before interviews, pitches, keynotes, or tough conversations. We walk through the scene in full detail:

- **What you're wearing:** Picture yourself looking down at your shoes, feeling the fabric on your shoulders.
- **Where you are:** See the room. If you've been there, replay it. If not, Google images or do a walk-through.
- **Who's there**: Imagine the faces—the nod of a colleague, the raised eyebrow of an investor, the smile of a friend.
- **What you hear:** The hum before you begin, your own voice steadying, the pause before the good question lands.
- **How it ends:** The handshake, the email, the "yes," the quiet relief in your chest.

The more sensory detail you add, the stronger the imprint. You're not just visualizing the outcome—you're rehearsing how it feels: the confidence in your shoulders, the taste of success, the warmth of belonging, the relief of having said what matters. The brain and gut learn best through repetition, and visualization gives them a safe training ground. Over time, it strengthens your abstract thinking—the what if muscle. You see more patterns, imagine different outcomes, and build flexible ways forward.

Visualization surfaces the unconscious patterns you've been running on autopilot. It shows you what you're really expecting—and gives you the chance to write a new script. When you pair this with gut signals, you're not just hoping for courage. You're practicing it. And throughout this book, we'll use guided visualizations to help you pre-run the moments that matter so your body says "yes" when the opportunity lands. You'll map how your body, thoughts, feelings, and sense of meaning shift between stress and confidence—and then train yourself to flip the switch on purpose.

 # MEDITATION (Practice). You don't need to sit cross-legged and say "Om" to meditate. You can practice by cultivating full presence and deliberate attention every moment. When I stopped treating meditation like a posture and started treating it like deliberate attention, it finally stuck. I sprinkle tiny practices through the day that settle my body, quiet the noise, and bring my planning brain back online. To do that, I use brain games. Think of these as Pepper Games—short, light, repeatable. Pick one or two and sprinkle them through your day. Simple = doable = sticky.

PEPPER TIME 7:
TINY BRAIN GAMES

#1 WALKING

- **Timing:** 5–10 minutes (commute, lunchtime, between meetings, or whenever).
- **What you'll need:** Shoes, phone camera (optional).
- **How to do it:**
  - Walk and let your eyes widen; find the horizon, then scan near/far.
  - Hunt one beautiful thing (shadow, brick texture, tree bud). Snap a photo or name three details out loud.
- **What to expect:** A quieter head, softer jaw, and a small hit of calm/clarity you can reproduce on demand.

2 GOOD MUSIC

- Timing: 3 minutes.
- What you'll need: Pick 1 song you love.
- How to do it:
  - Sit with your phone on do not disturb.
  - Press play on a song you love.
  - Just listen to the song: Contemplate the lyrics, hear the guitar and subtle tones.
  - Repeat as often as you like.
- What to expect: More presence.

3 DOING NOTHING

- Timing: 5 minutes.
- What you'll need: Nothing! No phone, no emails, no writing.

- How to do it:
  - Just do nothing.
  - Observe the thoughts that come and go.
  - Find how you feel, acknowledging it, sit with it.
  - Don't react; just do nothing.
  - Embracing it requires deliberate intention.
- What to expect: A clearer head.

 # 4 TENSION RELEASE

- Timing: min 5 minutes.
- What you'll need: A chair.
- How to do it:
  - Scan and observe your body: jaw, eyes, tongue, throat, shoulders, belly. Find one tight spot.
  - Focus on the tense spot.
  - Practice directing your attention to those areas of your body that feel tense.
  - Stretch or massage that part gently
  - Try to listen to what your body is telling you instead of ignoring it or swallowing medicine to silence it.
  - Focus not on stopping the thought, but on releasing the tension.
- What to expect: Less bracing, easier breath; over time your body flags tension earlier.

 # 5 HUMAN CONNECTION

- Timing: 90 seconds before or at the start of a conversation.
- What you'll need: Your attention and another person.
- How to do it:

- Make kind eye contact; notice two neutral details (eye color, cadence).
- Ask one open question; don't interrupt. Reflect back one exact word they used.

- What to expect: People feel seen; you hear what's actually being said, not just your projection.

Reflection

____

____

____

____

____

____

____

*   *   *

Mediation is a skill you learn by doing: Take it one thing at a time. Likewise, to fully experience life, do your best to do one thing at a time. If you talk to a friend, fully enjoy the conversation. If you play music, fully tune in and dance; even when filing your taxes, fully tune in and give it your undivided attention. Always do it like it's the first time. Be curious, focus on every step, and do what you do as well as you can. Your first email of the day should have the same attention as the last.

Meditation is simply presence on purpose. Treat these experiments like micro-workouts for your attention, and watch your baseline of calm, clarity, and courage rise.

 # GRATITUDE (Practice). By now you know that your survival brain is built to scan for what's wrong and is holding us back from our default happiness state. Gratitude is the counter-training: a daily practice of loving what's already here. When I practice gratitude, I'm reminding my nervous system that, in this moment, much is working: breath is happening, people I love exist, small joys keep arriving. This shifts attention away from the "nothing is good enough" loop and back toward the default of steadiness and connection.

We must remember more of what we are grateful for and recognize the truth that every one of us has more reasons to be happy than to be sad. Gratitude reminds us that many events in our life are not only meeting our expectations but exceeding them by so much that we should feel grateful.

Here's a simple Pepper Time to make gratitude both a habit and a lever for your gut-brain alignment.

PEPPER TIME 8:
NIGHTLY GRATITUDE

Timing: 3 minutes each night, right before sleep.

What you'll need: A journal or notes app; optionally, a partner to share with.

What this is about: Each time you recall a specific good moment, you teach your brain's value-tagging system to prioritize more of it tomorrow. This shifts you from survival bias (spotting threats) to aliveness bias (spotting what fuels you).

How to do it:

1. Name 3 specifics from your day—make them concrete and sensory:

   "Sun on my face walking to the train."

   "My kid's laugh when the pasta slipped."

   "Colleague's text: You nailed that slide."

2. Skip the generic. "Family/health" is too vague. Specifics wire faster.
3. Say them out loud—to yourself, or to someone you love.
4. See them in your heart. Close your eyes, replay them like a movie, and feel your chest expand.

What to expect: A small mood lift at night, easier sleep onset, quicker recovery from negativity spirals, and more generosity with others over time.

Reflection

____

____

____

____

____

____

*   *   *

As you know by now, I have been through very hard times. Saying goodbye to many close ones, many miscarriages, sexual abuse. But still daily my partner and I find the joy that life is beautiful and focus the good things. Don't give up too easily if you don't find your three things. See if the Happy List experiment from Chapter 1 can help. Start small. Make it a habit.

ALINGED ACTION (Practice). Aligned action is the quiet bridge between what you mean and what you make. You choose a direction that matters, then move the world a notch in that direction—today. Not a dozen tasks, not a heroic sprint. Just one step that is specific enough to exist in the real world and true enough to your values and current energy that your body can say "yes."

Anxious action tries to silence a feeling and leaves you emptier. Aligned action is smaller and calmer. It names something concrete—an email sent, a call placed, a page written, a meeting put on the calendar—and when it's done, there's a residue of relief, a little click behind the navel that says, "That was the right move." This practice builds self-trust. Each time intention and deed line up, your nervous system learns you can rely on yourself. Momentum follows. Miss a move? No drama. You notice it, tell the truth about capacity, and return to the next honest move. Over time the pattern shifts: Head, heart, and gut point the same way, friction drops, and the life you intend becomes the life you're living—one honest step at a time.

MANIFESTING (Energic). The idea of manifesting is often dismissed, but we aren't doing rain dances or anything. Look at the people around you when something great happened to them. Don't just focus on the obvious success stories but also

look at those who might have made huge health changes or found the perfect house for their needs by talking to someone they met randomly. To commit to actively trying to "manifest our dream life" may seem crazy, but manifesting isn't magic; it's alignment.

When my gut intention is clear and I let myself feel it, my attention starts tagging the world for matches. I say it, see it, hear it, and my nervous system treats the vision as familiar instead of threatening, and I take cleaner actions. Your brain runs selective attention and value tagging. What you mark as important (consciously or not) becomes easier to notice. Name a yellow Mini and suddenly you see one on every corner. Name the life you're building and you start catching the micro-openings you used to miss. This isn't superstition; it's perception-steering behavior. The shift is from "what to avoid" → "what to advance."

Once you have set your intention, close your eyes, and imagine it becoming real. See the picture in your mind and feel it in your gut. It should make your heart swell with desire: "Develop the confidence to build a flourishing business and find a great life partner," "Turn around a difficult relationship and master emotional regulation," "Find happiness in life through great health and life purpose." Aim high. You can achieve anything you might want.

If our desires and intention/gut are aligned, we can begin to manifest the life we want by saying it, hearing it, visualizing what it looks, feels, smells, and tastes like. This makes our dreams feel tangible to our brain. A great deal of brain energy is focused on working out who is friend or foe as this was critical in tribal times. In the. Today, we need to actively direct our brain away from prioritizing these unconscious biases to being more open toward our goals and choices that feel new and dangerous. We need to raise our aspirations and future from unconscious and vague to fully conscious.

As part of selective attention, value tagging is the importance your brain assigns to every piece of information it is exposed to. One person will note an old yellow Mini parked on their street and recall fond memories of their first car and smile at the thought. Their subconscious clue-tagging system is tapping into an old memory that may have been long forgotten, and they might start a conversation with the car's driver. Someone else who doesn't have that label in their brain may not notice that car at all. It's easy to assign a disproportionate value to things we care about or a negative value to things we fear or feel uncertain of.

After a painful breakup, your brain's value-tagging often shifts to protection. The inner voice says, "Stick to work. Don't risk more hurt." Your attention stops noticing the warm conversation at the café or the friend's intro text; instead, you spot every promotion posting. That's your filter steering you away from what you want and toward what feels safer. When you name a different aim—"I'm ready for a healthy partnership"—and let your gut vote for it, the filter retunes. You notice the spark in a chat, you accept the dinner invite, you choose rooms where your people gather. Our selective attention naturally prioritizes avoiding shame or rejection; bringing your true goal into consciousness flips it toward approach. It's your nervous system finally letting you see the chances that were there all along.

That's the point of the next Pepper Time. It's time to stop holding vague hopes in your head and start putting what really matters to you on paper—so your brain, your gut, and your daily actions finally line up.

PEPPER TIME 9:
DISCOVER WHAT MATTERS TO YOU

Timing: 10 minutes today + 5 minutes each evening for 4 days.

What you'll need: Your journal, a pen, and magazines or saved images.

What it's about: Your calendar tells the truth. Most people say family, health, or purpose matter—but their days tell a different story. This is about closing the gap and surfacing what lights you up. Make it visible so you can lead with meaning instead of autopilot.

How to do it:

1. Name it. In your journal, jot down what you want to achieve or experience. Don't overthink—buzzwords, fragments, anything that lights you up.
2. Picture it. Flip through magazines, Pinterest boards, or saved images. Pull out pictures that match your dream life—the ones that give you a spark in your chest. Keep them. You'll use them later in this book.

3. Repeat daily. Each evening for four days, add one or two images or words that still feel true. This repetition builds awareness like a muscle.

4. Reality check. If you want to go deeper: Look back at your calendar for the past 3 months. Compare it to your list. How much of your time served what you say matters? How much went to things that don't even make the list?

What to expect: A raw mirror of your life. The split between what you say matters and what you live becomes impossible to ignore. That clarity stings—but it's also fuel. Every word, every image sharpens your compass until your days start matching your truth.

Reflection

____

____

____

____

____

____

____

*   *   *

MAGNETIC DESIRE (Energetic). Life will always hand you the expected and the wildly unexpected. What changes your life isn't the event; it's your response. Magnetic desire is that clean, body-felt wanting that gives you energy to act. It isn't

daydreaming. It's the quiet yes in your belly that pulls you out of hoping and into doing.

My turn came in 2018. I had a safe, growing corporate job in Chicago. On paper, I was set. Inside, a sentence kept repeating: I want to build something of my own. I felt it as a lift behind the navel every time I thought about leaving—and a drop in my stomach every time I imagined staying. People thought I was crazy. I quit anyway. I didn't even have the right visa yet. I applied for the E-2, lived on an ESTA's 90-day clock, and learned taxes in two countries the hard way—reading forms at midnight, calling offices at 6 a.m., figuring out what each choice meant.

I read books, went to meetups, asked questions, and found mentors who told me the truth. Each small "yes" to that desire made me braver. I landed my first big client while still piecing the legal puzzle together. I held my breath at O'Hare's passport booth more than once. I even flew to Japan and Canada not knowing for sure I'd be let back in. Fear was loud; the pull was louder.

In 2020 I couldn't re-enter the US, so I went back to Belgium. I worked US hours from my dad's house, laughed with friends, traveled when I could, and I kept building, one steady day at a time. In October I started dating the man who's now my German husband. We based near Düsseldorf; I added European clients while keeping American ones. Money was great. Life had joy in it again. In 2021 my E-2 visa was approved. I remember the exact exhale—jaw soft, shoulders down. Around the same time, we started a side hustle in Florida real estate because the opportunity felt alive and aligned.

The more I honored that inner pull, the more doors appeared because desire focused my attention. I saw the email to send, the room to walk into, the person to ask. I stayed flexible—plans changed, borders closed, paperwork multiplied—and the current kept carrying me.

Once you feel magnetic desire and answer it with action, it compounds. Each iteration builds proof: I can do hard things. I can build what I see. Suddenly what felt out of reach starts to live within reach. If you're standing where I stood—safe on paper, restless inside—listen for the clean signal. Let it light one next step. Then another. That's how daydreams turn into a life.

UNIVERSAL CONNECTION (Energetic). You're not built to go it alone. As humans, belonging is a biological need. Your nervous system is social: Hearts sync, breath syncs, and stress settles faster in good company. Love, trust, and honest teamwork release chemistry (oxytocin, dopamine) that calms the gut, steadies the mind, and helps you see solutions more clearly. Isolation does the opposite—your belly tightens, your brain scans for threat, and small problems feel impossible.

The people you spend the most time with become your weather. Their energy, words, and habits set the climate you live in. If you choose a storm, you carry it. If you choose sunlight, you grow differently. This is why connection is so powerful—and why it belongs in the three buckets we keep coming back to: relationships, performance, and well-being. Here, the relationship piece is critical.

In part 2, we'll dig deeper into which relationships you want at your table, why they shift over time, and why we can't always hold on forever. For now, it's about awareness. Who's around you most? Who energizes you? Who drains you? Who's steady? Who keeps you small? These answers shape your growth. People will come and go—that's life. But you have to notice first, otherwise you're running on someone else's climate.

PEPPER TIME 10: THE PEOPLE TREE

Timing: 10–15 minutes this week.

What you'll need: Your journal and a pen.

What its' about: Your inner circle isn't neutral. The five people you spend the most time with quietly shape your energy, mindset, and the size of your dreams. Time to make the invisible visible—and choose your tribe with intention.

How to do it:

1. **Draw your tree.** Sketch a tree with five big branches. On each branch, write the name of one person you spend the most time with (family, friends, coworkers— it all counts).
2. **Add their imprint.** Along each branch, write five words that describe that person. Be honest: kind, restless, generous, sharp, negative, curious, rushed—whatever is true.
3. **Mark the mirror.** Re-read all 25 words. Put a star next to traits you recognize in yourself. Put a cross next to traits you don't want to amplify.

4. **Reflect.** For each person, answer these two questions:
    - **Impact on me:** Fuels or drains?
    - **Effect on mindset:** Helps me think bigger, or nudges me to play small?

5. **Make three micro-moves:**
    - Lean in: Choose one person to spend more time with or learn from. Name the next coffee, call, or walk.
    - Upgrade: Choose one relationship to gently recalibrate—set a boundary, ask for what you need, or shift the setting/topic.
    - Prune: Choose one small step to create distance from a draining tie—fewer unplanned chats, less screen time, or a kind but firm "no."

What to expect: The tribe effect gets real. The more you lean into energizing ties, the more doors open—opportunities, ideas, support. Your attention and energy follow what fuels you.

Reflection

____

____

____

____

____

____

____

*   *   *

#TRUST (Energetic). Trust is the fuel that lets alignment move. It isn't blind optimism; it's the steady sense that you can handle what comes. When trust rises, the body shows it—jaw softens, breath drops, belly unknots—and your attention returns to the work instead of circling the what-ifs. Self-trust is built in Pepper Reps, small promises kept until your body believes you. Send the note you said you'd send. Stop when you said you'd stop. Give the clean "no" you rehearsed. If you miss one, repair it: name what happened, shrink the promise, try again today. Over time your nervous system learns: I can rely on me.

Trust with others is also built through clarity. Make crisp requests, name boundaries, and then believe people when they show you who they are. Sometimes that means deepening the bond. Sometimes it means stepping back. Trust in timing is the hardest one, because we want to force results. But it means doing your Pepper Reps and giving the calendar oxygen—moving when your gut says move, and letting things ripen when your gut says wait. When trust thins, you feel it: racing thoughts, shallow breath, compulsive refreshing, over-managing. But when trust strengthens, you unlock quiet momentum. You stop strangling outcomes and start compounding actions. Life begins to meet you halfway.

Here's the deeper why: Trust is the bridge between alignment and joy. When we trust ourselves, we act instead of looping in hesitation. When we trust others, we allow connection instead of building walls. When we trust timing, we stop fighting life and start dancing with it. That shift doesn't just change our inner state—it ripples back into the three buckets we care about most: relationships, well-being, and performance. Trust makes you more open in love, more grounded in health, and more consistent in your work. Without it, fear runs the show. Trust isn't a luxury—it's the foundation. Without it, success feels shaky. With it, uncertainty feels alive with possibility.

Abundance is a stance your whole body can feel. Scarcity tightens—jaw clamps, breath stays high, gut goes on guard—and your world narrows to what might go wrong. Abundance softens—exhale lengthens, belly loosens, gaze widens—and suddenly your world opens to what might work. From that wider field, you notice more: cleaner options, truer yeses, kinder noes. You're not pretending everything is perfect—you're choosing to start from the idea that there is room, and there is time. And from that place, your gut can guide you toward what really matters.

Abundance doesn't stand alone. It partners with the other mindsets you've been practicing. Patience sets the pace so you don't force it. Harmony keeps your head, heart, and gut playing one song. Clarity sharpens your focus so action has direction. Together, these mindsets transform possibility into movement.

And this is where the deeper principle—what some call the "law of attraction"—comes alive. Not as wishful thinking, but as embodied practice. What you focus on, you begin to filter for. What you feel in your gut, you begin to trust. What you rehearse with your senses, you begin to act on. That's why visualization, journaling, meditation, and all the other reps matter: They aren't just mental games; they are rewiring your filter to see opportunities where your old self only saw threats.

 **# PEPPER ASK: Carry this line with you into to-morrow morning:**

- *There is room for me and what I care about today—especially ____.* 

Fill in the blank. Feel the click behind your navel. Take one aligned step. That's abundance made real.

Remember: You don't need to master everything at once. Each breath, each journal line, each tiny step—adds up. You've already seen how your brain and body can shift. Now, with these mindsets alive in you, you're ready for the next phase: listening even deeper to your gut and letting it steer—not just your thoughts, but your relationships, your work, and your well-being. This is where awareness turns into leadership. The law of attraction isn't about waiting for life to hand you gifts— it's about becoming the kind of person who notices the gifts already here, trusts herself to act, and keeps stepping toward the life and business she wants.

Your gut is speaking. Are you ready to listen?

Chapter 5:

The Six Pathways

People often ask me, "How long does it take to build a new habit?"

But it depends. Not just on the habit itself, but on which pathway you're training. Picking up a dumbbell at the gym is one kind of pathway. Staying calm after rejection is another. Both are trainable, but they run on different circuits. Your brain and body are constantly wiring and rewiring. Every thought, choice, and feeling is like walking a trail. The more you walk it, the easier it becomes. That's neuroplasticity—the everyday truth of how you become who you are.

You have six pathways: Physicality, Emotions, Intuition, Motivation, Logic, and Creativity. Some are strong. Some you may have ignored, avoided, or even shut down. And when one is blocked, the others try to compensate—often leaving you overthinking, pushing, or stuck in loops that don't serve you. But the rule stays the same: Repetition lays the track.

Try a tiny proof right now. Close your eyes. Think back to last Friday. Where were you? Who did you see? What happened first, then next, then last? How did your body feel—light, heavy, tight, glowing? Just by recalling it, you strengthened the network that stores it. And if that moment carried strong emotion—joy, embarrassment, anger, love—the signal doubled in power. That's neuroplasticity in everyday clothes.

We've already met your brilliant (and sometimes overprotective) brain. We've listened to your gut as a quiet, reliable guide. Now it's time to bring them to the same table. When they work together, your whole system unlocks.

Clearing The Blockages

None of these pathways is fixed at birth. They are trainable circuits. Overuse one and underuse another, and the system compensates—usually with more stress and poorer results. But when you balance them, effort compounds. And the best part? Integration doesn't take hours of work. It happens in seconds.

Picture this: You're walking down the street and spot a close friend coming toward you. The afternoon sun catches the sparkle of an engagement ring. Within seconds, your entire system lights up: Your body shifts: a skip in your step, your chest warming, your shoulders pulling back as you lean toward her. Your body prepares to embrace her, to share in her joy. Your emotions spark. A flood of happiness rises for her, mingled with a sharp pinch in your stomach—jealousy you weren't expecting.

Maybe you've been waiting for your own big commitment, and the contrast stings. Both emotions surge at once, and you feel the tug-of-war inside. Your intuition tunes in. Even before she says a word, you sense the deeper story behind the glow. Is she radiating joy—or also nervousness? You know her well enough to catch the micro-signals: the slight hesitation in her smile, the way she adjusts the ring as if reassuring herself it's really there. Your logic steps in. You recall that she'd mentioned a big promotion at work and make a mental note to ask about it, to show you remember the things that matter to her beyond this engagement.

Your motivation surges. This friendship has carried you through heartbreaks, late-night calls, and years of laughter. You feel pulled to invest in her again, to show up for her in this new chapter as fully as she's shown up for you. Your creativity leaps ahead. Instantly, your mind sketches the future: her as your bridesmaid, you as the godmother to her children, the two of you still walking side by side decades from now.

All of that unfolds in less than a heartbeat. One moment on a busy street, one flash of light off a diamond, and your entire system—body, emotions, gut, brain—ignites.

Here's the catch: If we ignore one pathway, the whole system tips out of balance. When one pathway shuts down, the others twist themselves into shapes they were never meant for. Logic tries to do intuition's job. Motivation tries to drown out emotion. Creativity hides because the body isn't being heard. The brain ends up working harder, but with worse results—like a car driving on five cylinders instead of six.

The six pathways don't just make you effective; they keep you balanced. Every pathway can grow or become blocked. When you practice certain behaviors—suppressing emotions, ignoring your gut, overthinking every choice—your brain wires that in as "normal." Even if it costs you energy, clarity, or joy. But no block is permanent. What was wired in can be rewired out.

Here are the six pathways we'll train—and some of the most common ways they get blocked:

#1 Physicality & Interoception. Your body is your first messenger—breath, posture, hunger, pain, energy shifts. But many of us stop listening early. Maybe you were teased for your weight, skin, or height. You learned to shrink your posture, avoid eye contact, or push through exhaustion. You stopped trusting your body's signals, and now low physical presence or poor self-care holds you back.

#2 Emotional Intelligence. This is your ability to notice, name, and regulate emotions instead of being hijacked by them. But if you grew up in a "don't cry, toughen up" household—or the opposite, where everything was high drama—you may have learned to suppress or drown in emotions. Either way, it makes it hard to stay balanced today.

#3 Intuition & Gut Instinct. This is your quiet inner compass, the whisper that notices patterns before logic can explain them. But maybe as a teen or young adult your instincts were mocked or punished. Over time you stopped listening, second-guessed yourself, and outsourced your choices to others.

#4 Motivation. This is your drive, your inner engine. But without a strong sense of meaning or purpose, it's easy to settle for the stable job or safe paycheck. You keep pushing through, but the fire is missing. Life feels like duty instead of desire.

#5 Logic & Thought. Clear thinking means framing problems, weighing options, spotting mental stories. But if someone once told you, "You're not smart enough," you may have avoided challenges that required memory or exams. Logic became a weak muscle, so you leaned harder on other pathways—while secretly fearing you're not clever enough.

#6 Creativity. This is your ability to imagine new options and connect unlikely dots. But maybe a teacher once told you you weren't artistic or your parents steered you toward the "safe" path. You shut down that playful spark, convinced creativity was for other people.

This chapter is about unlocking all six pathways so you're not driving on half an engine. When you learn to bring them to the same table, your whole system works with you instead of against you.

Take Nina. She worked in a well-known bank. Colleagues admired her discipline. She had a system for everything, especially decisions. Whether it was a huge business deal or whether to move apartments, Nina would open a spreadsheet. Columns of pros and cons. Weighted scores. Financial projections. It looked rational. But deep down, she knew something was off. The deals she approved sometimes turned sour, not because the numbers were wrong but because the people behind them were. The apartment she chose ticked all the boxes, but she never felt at home there. Even her dating life was shaped by the same algorithm. If a partner's CV was impressive, she convinced herself it would work, ignoring the quiet whisper in her gut.

Nina was strong in logic and motivation, but she had learned to distrust her own intuition. Growing up, whenever she voiced a gut feeling, she was told she was being "irrational." At work, emotion was seen as weakness. When we walked through the six pathways together, she had an "aha" moment. She realized her decision-making was lopsided. By ignoring her gut, she was leaving half her intelligence unused. By dismissing creativity, she was closing doors before she even saw them.

Her work wasn't to abandon logic—it was to rebalance. To invite intuition and creativity back to the table. She started small: listening to her body in meetings, noticing when her stomach tightened even if the numbers looked perfect. Pausing to ask: *"What future can I imagine here, beyond the spreadsheet?"* The result? She began making decisions that felt aligned in her gut. And for the first time in years, she wasn't just surviving her career—she was shaping it.

Awareness was the turning point. Most of us run on autopilot, leaning on the same channels over and over without realizing which ones are silent. That's why the first step is mapping your own system. Before we decode each pathway in detail, try it yourself. This Pepper Time will help you see which parts of your intelligence you naturally use—and which ones might be underplayed or blocked.

PEPPER TIME 11:
MAP YOUR PATHWAYS

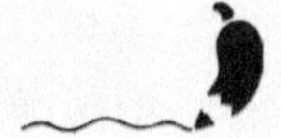

Timing: 15–20 minutes, once this week (and revisit monthly).

What you'll need: Two blank journal pages and a pen.

What it's about: Your brain runs on six pathways: Physicality, Emotions, Intuition, Logic, Motivation, and Creativity. Some are strong, others underused. Seeing the balance makes the invisible visible—and reveals where growth is waiting.

How to do it:

1. **Set up one page.** Draw a circle in the center and write "Brain." From the circle, draw six spokes like a wheel and label them: Physicality, Emotions, Intuition, Logic, Motivation, Creativity.
2. **Recall key moments.** Think of three recent situations where you had to use your full brain power *(For example: a high-stakes work meeting, a family crisis, or a big life decision).*
3. **Allocate percentages.** For each situation, assign a % to each pathway showing how much you relied on it. Be brutally honest—not how you wish you acted, but how you actually operated.
4. **Spot your patterns.** Look at the six spokes: Which pathways are barely activated? Do certain ones always dominate? Are you leaning mostly on one side— e.g., Logic + Motivation, while ignoring Intuition or Creativity?

5. **Reflect and note.** On the second page, write a few lines on what you notice: the balance (or imbalance), surprises, or any recurring themes.

What to expect: Patterns jump out fast. Some pathways carry the load, others barely show up. This isn't about fixing overnight—it's about awareness. Awareness is growth's ignition. Over time, balance shifts: emotions support instead of overwhelm, gut instincts get trusted, logic clarifies without dominating, and creativity sparks again.

Reflection

____

____

____

____

____

____

____

*   *   *

PEPPER ASK:

- *Which of your pathways might be blocked or inaccessible right now?*
- *What do you want from life that this block has kept you from?* 

Start noting it down. Go further: Collect images, words, scraps of inspiration that speak to your inner desires. These will later fuel your Pepper Board. Remember: Blocks are not life sentences. They are signals. With practice, you can overwrite old wiring and bring each pathway back online.

Now, let's walk through each of the six pathways in depth—and explore how the gut-brain connection helps you strengthen them.

Physicality & Interoception

Your body tells the truth long before your mind does. It carries the story of your health, habits, emotions, and past. Sometimes it whispers through a restless night of sleep, a tense shoulder, or the heaviness in your gut after a conversation. Other times it shouts—through illness, burnout, or a complete crash. Are you listening? Building a connection between your mind and body is the foundation of self-care.

A body that feels strong and comfortable in its own skin is a sign that you're looking after it well. When you're disconnected, you push past signals until they become symptoms. When you're connected, your body becomes a guide—pointing you toward balance, energy, and truth. Start small. Try smiling more. Not a forced grin, but a gentle lift. The moment your face shifts, your body responds. Your mood lifts with it. And when you're around others who smile, their energy changes yours too. This is how emotions and body mirror each other. Your physicality is always speaking.

You hear it all the time: pregnant women craving pickles, ice cream, salty crisps at odd hours. But often, cravings are the body's way of signaling a deeper need: sodium when blood volume is expanding, sugar when energy dips, calcium when bones are building. The mind might split the experience into "bad snacks" and "healthy foods," but the body knows what it needs.

When I was pregnant with Gisele, I craved yogurt drinks constantly. I would go through bottles of them. It wasn't about indulgence—it was my body demanding something it needed. Later, with George, it was different. My body only wanted plain milk. If I had listened to my brain, I might have judged myself. But when I tuned in, I realized my body wasn't betraying me—it was guiding me. This is interoception in action.

We all know the five outer senses: sight, sound, smell, taste, touch. Interoception is your ability to sense what's happening inside your body: hunger, thirst, heart rate, fatigue, digestion, temperature. It's knowing you need water before your lips feel dry, that you need to step away from a heated conversation before saying something you regret, that your energy is flagging long before you collapse. The problem? Many of us were taught to ignore these signals. Parents said, "You're fine" when we cried. Workplaces rewarded pushing through exhaustion instead of resting. Strength meant hiding weakness. Over time, we've overridden our interoception until we no longer hear the whispers and only respond when the body is screaming.

The good news is you can relearn this skill. You can notice the whispers before they become symptoms. You can pause when your chest tightens, hydrate when your energy dips, say no before your body collapses. And every time you do, you strengthen the connection between body and mind. Your body is your first messenger, pointing you back to balance—if you choose to listen. To train yourself back into awareness, strengthen the muscle of listening. You don't need big life changes to start—just small daily practices.

The Body Scan teaches you to slow down and hear the story your body tells in real time. It's about sharpening your ability to tune in, to catch the whispers before they turn into shouts. And it will help you build the foundation for every other pathway that follows.

PEPPER TIME 12: BODY SCAN

Timing: 5–10 minutes, once a day for a week.

What you'll need: A chair or a quiet place to sit, bare feet on the floor if possible, and your journal. Phone off, arms and legs uncrossed.

What it's about: Rebuilding the connection between mind and body. Learning to listen to subtle signals before they scream as symptoms.

How to do it:

1. **Get settled.** Sit upright, arms and legs uncrossed, hands resting in your lap, feet flat on the floor. Close your eyes.

2. **Breathe.** Take five slow breaths: inhale through your nose for 4 counts, exhale through your mouth for 6 counts. Feel oxygen enliven your body as you inhale and tension leave as you exhale.

3. **Feel your base.** Notice the weight of your body in the chair—the contact points of legs, bottom, and back. Sense gravity holding you.

4. **Scan from feet to head.** Move your attention slowly upward, pausing at each area:
   - Feet & legs: Notice pressure, warmth, tingling, heaviness or lightness.
     Ask: *Tension, discomfort, or ease?*
   - Stomach & torso: If tight, let it soften; feel your breath expand and release.
   - Hands & arms: Notice if your hands are clenched; soften each finger.
   - Shoulders & back: Let them drop naturally; feel where tension sits.
   - Neck, jaw & face: Loosen your jaw, let your tongue rest, soften your eyes.
   - Crown of the head: Imagine a line from the top of your head down through your spine, connecting your whole body.

5. **Integrate.** When you've scanned each area, expand your awareness to sense your whole body as one unified, breathing system. Take three deep, slow breaths, then open your eyes when ready.

6. **Reflect.** Jot down any sensations or patterns you noticed.

What to expect: At first, you'll catch only the loud signals—tight shoulders, heavy fatigue, gravity pulling you down. With practice, subtler cues emerge: a stomach that clenches in stress, a jaw that tenses in certain conversations, a chest that feels lighter with certain people. Over time, your body becomes an early warning system, guiding daily choices and major decisions. Listen early, conserve energy, and prevent burnout—the body whispers before it shouts.

Reflection

____

____

____

____

____

____

____

*   *   *

If you're ready to get hands-on with the physicality & interoception pathway—really tuning into the signals your body sends from the inside out—try a Food, Mood & Bowels Diary. This one-week practice is simple but eye-opening: Each day, jot down what you eat and drink, rate your mood from 1–5, and note how your digestion feels—comfortable, bloated, energized, sluggish. By week's end the patterns speak for themselves: Maybe coffee after 2 p.m. spikes your anxiety, pizza leaves you drained, or shrimp makes your lips tingle. These aren't random quirks; they're your body's own data points.

Your body is your ally. Tuning in, both outwardly through movement and inwardly through interoception, lays the foundation for every other pathway. If you can't hear your body, your emotions will distort, your intuition will quiet, and your logic will run on incomplete data. When you listen to your body, the other pathways finally have room to speak clearly.

And that brings us to the next guide on this journey: your emotions.

Emotions As Intelligence

This is our second pathway, to master your feelings, and there's a reason it comes after the body. Physicality and interoception give you signals: your heartbeat, breath, posture, tension, energy. Emotions are the next layer. They're how the body translates signals into meaning. You can't master your feelings without first noticing the body that carries them. We feel emotions every minute of every day: anger, happiness, excitement, anxiety, lust—the list goes on. And when emotions are absent, we notice it too. Boredom is simply the absence of emotional stimulation.

You can feel fear before you ever experience the event you're afraid of. You can feel excitement imagining a holiday that hasn't happened yet. These sensations are powerful. But what are they really? How do they arise? What is their purpose? And most importantly: How do we engage with them to steer our lives toward happiness and success?

Your likely felt the racing heart of fear before a big presentation, the lump in your throat when you miss someone, the spark of joy that floods your chest when you laugh with a friend. Emotions are short, embodied waves. They surge in the brain, flood the body, and ignite sensations and thoughts.

Most emotions, if left alone, rise and fall in about a minute and a half. You can't stop them from arriving. But you can choose how you meet them, how you ride them, and what you do after they pass. That choice is your true power.

The Eight Primary Emotions

To work with emotions, we need to know the basic terrain. Psychologists group them into eight primary emotions.

The first five are survival emotions: fear, anger, disgust, shame, and sadness. These are fast, primal, and designed to protect you.

- **Fear** kept our ancestors from walking into danger; today, it might stop you from stepping onto a stage.
- **Anger** once fueled fighting off threats; now it flares when your partner leaves dirty dishes in the sink.
- **Shame** was a signal to protect your place in the tribe; today it silences you in meetings.
- **Sadness** slowed people down to grieve; today it leaves you curled up after rejection.
- **Disgust** kept early humans from eating rotten food; today it makes your stomach turn when you see injustice.

Then there are the two emotions of attachment and reward: love/trust and joy/excitement. These activate your brain's reward circuits. They explain why you crave a hug, why you run for the high that follows, why you light up when someone affirms your work. Your brain wants to repeat what gives you these feelings.

But rewards cut both ways. Alcohol, toxic relationships, and even overwork can feel rewarding in the moment, tricking you into spirals of addiction. Even something "positive" like working out can become unhealthy if you chase it compulsively to fill an emotional void.

The eighth emotion is **surprise**. It doesn't fit neatly into survival or attachment. Surprise is a potentiator, flipping you from one state to another in an instant. It's the thrill at the top of a roller-coaster, or the suspended breath in a suspense film. Surprise destabilizes, then reorganizes, priming you for whatever comes next.

These eight emotions are the palette we all paint with. If you don't recognize them, they'll hijack you. But if you can name and meet them, you can work with them. Later in this book, when we explore Pepper Reps—tiny, repeatable practices that rewire your brain—you'll see that they only work because emotions are the raw data we're sculpting. You can't retrain what you can't first identify.

Family Imprint

Of course, no one meets emotions on a blank canvas. We all grew up in emotional classrooms. Some families modeled avoidance. Others taught dismissal or that love was earned only through achievement. In some families, conflict exploded into shouting and slammed doors. Children in those environments adapted. Some learned to bury their feelings, pushing through with a smile while their bodies screamed. Others copied the drama, letting storms rule every conflict. Some shut down completely because staying silent felt safer.

Those imprints follow you into relationships, parenting, and leadership. My partner carries echoes of his parents' style, just as I do with mine. Sometimes an argument between us isn't about us at all—it's an old family script replaying. Recognizing that is the first step to rewriting it.

PEPPER ASK:
Take a moment to reflect:

- *What was the emotional style in your family growing up?*
- *How were disagreements handled?*
- *How in touch are you with your emotional responses today?*
- *How easy is it for you to regulate—can you pull yourself back from rage, fear, or sadness?*
- *How easily do you build rapport with someone new?*
- *How often do you feel emotional resonance—that sense of being met and understood in conversation?*

Start mapping your strengths and your edges. One simple practice: Swap half your "I think" statements for "I feel." One of my Scaleurs tried this in her journal. At first it felt strange, even artificial. But over time she shifted from *"I think I'd like to..."* to *"I feel I want to..."* and eventually to *"I've decided."* The vocabulary of feeling gave her clarity that pure thinking never did.

It's important to catch emotions in the moment. Emotions like anger rise fast, hijack the body, and push us into reactions we later regret. This next Pepper Time gives you a safe way to practice noticing anger's early signals before it runs the show. Think of it as building a "pause button" into your nervous system, so you can choose your response instead of being dragged by it.

PEPPER TIME 13: THE STOP SIGN

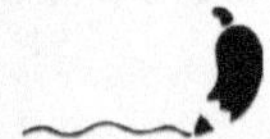

Timing: 3–5 minutes. Practice in calm moments first; then use it in real time when anger rises.

What you'll need: A quiet space and a vivid memory of something that made you angry.

What it's about: Anger builds fast and hot. This practice trains your nervous system to interrupt that curve, cool the fire, and create space for choice before you react.

How to do it:

1. **Recall the trigger.** Sit comfortably, close your eyes, and bring to mind a moment when you felt strong anger.
2. **Let the feeling build.** Notice how anger shows up in your body—heat on the skin, tightness in the chest, pressure in the jaw, racing thoughts.
3. **Call up the sign.** When the feeling is vivid, picture a giant red STOP sign in your mind. See every detail.
4. **Say it out loud (or whisper).** Whisper "Stop." At the same time, exhale slowly and let your muscles soften.

5. **Stay with the shift.** Notice the wave of anger begin to fade. Feel your body relax as the tension releases.

What to expect: With repetition, your brain starts linking the STOP image to calm. Over time, you'll be able to summon it in real moments—during an argument, a heated meeting, or while parenting—and cut the escalation before it hijacks you.

Reflection

____

____

____

____

____

____

____

*   *   *

The 90-Second Rule

Research shows that most emotions crest and fall within about 90 seconds—if you don't feed them with new thoughts. If you let the wave pass, the chemicals disperse. If you start attaching thoughts—*"I'll never be good enough," "She always does this," "I'm such an idiot"*—you pour fuel on the fire and the wave becomes a storm. You have the power to let emotions move through without turning into loops.

The emotions themselves are not the enemy. The real trouble comes from what we do with them:

- Suppress them, and they don't disappear—they pile up until they leak or explode.
- Avoid them, and they sneak back in disguised as stress, illness, or conflict.
- Overidentify with them, and they drag you around like a storm cloud, dictating how you speak, act, and even think.

The idea is to feel emotions fully without letting them run the show. To treat them tenderly, the way you'd hold a crying child—acknowledging, soothing, and allowing them to rise, crest, and fall while you choose your response. Most emotions really do rise and fade within about ninety seconds if you don't add fuel. It's your thoughts that keep them looping. A single spark—"She hasn't texted me back"—can trigger anxiety. That anxiety then breeds more thoughts: *Am I too clingy? Did I do something wrong? Maybe I'm not attractive enough."* Each thought births a new emotion, which births another thought, and the storm swirls on.

Once you see this pattern, you realize emotions are not as unpredictable as they feel in the moment. They follow a rhythm. You know the triggers. You can anticipate the wave. And that predictability gives you a chance to pause, breathe, and steer. Based on this, what can you conclude? Because emotions are predictable, you are not at their mercy. You can anticipate the wave, and when you know it will only last ninety seconds unless you feed it, you can choose differently. That is where your freedom begins.

Why The World Feels Low-Emotion

I believe there are four reasons we've created a world stripped of authentic emotion. The first is cultural: We're taught to have a stiff upper lip. But three more forces live inside us: emotional storms, emotional camouflage, and emotional discomfort. Understanding all four is how you take your power back.

#1 EMOTIONAL STORMS. No one feels one clean emotion at a time. Life is storms. You can love your child and worry about her health in the same breath. You can feel pride in your work and envy a colleague. You can be optimistic about the future and grieve your past. Our inner world is a swirl of contradictions. In a single moment you might feel joy at your progress on a project, pride that you're nearly there, tenderness for your daughter, worry because she's unwell, deep love for her presence in your life, sadness because you miss her, humility at the gift of it all—and simple hunger because you haven't eaten. That's a weather system.

I am very happy with the progress I'm making on this book. I feel optimistic I'll be ready soon. Then Gisele, my daughter, tells me she isn't feeling well. Instantly, I feel intense love for her, concern for her body, and sadness because I can't fix it right away. At the same time, I feel humbled at the gift of being her mother—and, honestly, hungry because I haven't eaten lunch. Joy, love, pride, sadness, humility, hunger—all present in the same hour.

The point is to ride the storm by deconstructing your inner weather into components—love, fear, hunger, pride—so you can see clearly. Then you stop letting other people's emotional immaturity hijack you. Their guilt trips, tantrums, or explosions are not your responsibility. You can't control how anyone else feels or responds. You can control your next right move—even if it upsets others. That's emotional adulthood.

#2 EMOTIONAL CAMOUFLAGE. Emotions rarely announce themselves with words. They arrive in the body first:

- Anger shows up as flushed skin, a clenched jaw, a racing pulse.
- Fear as a pounding chest, shallow breath, the urge to run.
- Disgust as a stomach twist, nausea, recoiling.
- Sadness as heaviness, fatigue, withdrawal.
- Excitement as bright eyes, open chest, quickened breath.

Beneath these general patterns, each of us has personal signatures. For me, missing my mom is not just "sadness." It's a sharp hollow ache in the bottom-right of my chest, as if that piece of me is missing. And it feels just as intense today as the day she left. That is my body's language for loss. You have your language too. When you start noticing the camouflage—how feelings wear themselves—you begin to see your map. That personal map is the key to navigation.

#3 EMOTIONAL DISCOMFORT. Even painful emotions remind us we're alive. The problem isn't the feeling—it's refusing to feel. And life gives us plenty of reasons to want to numb out.

It isn't fair that some carry student debt while others inherit wealth.
It isn't fair your sister looks like a supermodel and you buy your own drinks.
It isn't fair your boss keeps giving you the late shift.

It isn't fair your country is torn by war.
It isn't fair you were born diabetic and will manage insulin for life.

Life is unfair. Those feelings are real. But you can either accept emotions as they are, or convert them into fuel. Accept sadness as sadness—and let it cue rest. Accept anger as anger—and let it power a boundary, a conversation, a change. Pretending the emotion isn't there guarantees suffering. Buried feelings don't vanish; they ferment into resentment, anxiety, depression, illness.

We need to master these emotions by learning when to accept and when to convert. Acceptance might sound like: *"I feel vulnerable, and that's okay."* Conversion might sound like: *"I don't like how I look today, so I'll go for a run to feel stronger."* Both are valid. It's ignoring the emotion altogether that destroys you.

#4 CONTAGION, COMPARISON, AND THE MASKS WE WEAR.
Emotions are contagious. You'll never control the weather around you or stop your automatic waves from rising. But what you can always choose is how you respond. And often, the right choice will be the hardest to make. Comparison is one of the most common escapes from discomfort. Looking upward—at those who seem "ahead"—can torture you with the feeling that you're not enough. But it can also teach you, if you treat it as a mirror: *If they can do it, so can I. What's their formula?* Looking downward—at those who seem "behind"—can either inflate arrogance or cultivate gratitude. The problem isn't comparison itself. It's how you use it.

Ask yourself: *Is this comparison torturing me, or teaching me?* Sometimes comparison is the mirror that calls you out. Sometimes it's the spark of anger that finally gets you moving. Let it fuel you, not destroy you.

But comparison is only half the story. The culture we grow up in hands us masks and scripts. Emotions become something to hide. Vulnerability gets labeled as weakness. "Fake it till you make it" becomes the rule. But emotions don't disappear just because we bury them. They turn into resentment, sarcasm, shutdowns, explosive outbursts, even illness. An emotion that isn't allowed to be felt, expressed, and shared takes root inside of us. It's an explosion waiting to happen. And when we don't open up to others, we also shut down toward ourselves.

That's why masks are so costly. They may protect us from judgment or rejection in the short term, but they cut us off from our truth. And you only feel truly alive when you allow yourself to feel. Vulnerability isn't weakness—it's the birthplace of intimacy, connection, and authentic power. Our emotions are fragile, delicate, worthy of care. They need to be met with tenderness, the way you'd comfort a hurt child. When you stop fighting your emotions and allow them to be felt instead of hidden—you get your life back.

When You Feel, You Begin To Be

Feeling is the only way to fully *be*. It is the first step on the path to happiness. At first, this feels hard—sometimes impossible. Sitting with rawness can feel like sitting in fire. But like every other pathway, neuroplasticity works in your favor. The brain reshapes itself around whatever you practice. If you practice avoidance, you wire avoidance. If you practice presence, you wire resilience.

Predictability is the key to freedom. Because if emotions are predictable, so is change. And neuroplasticity proves beyond doubt that people *do* change. I'm living proof. I used to run endlessly, working 24/7 with my laptop glued to me, chasing achievement while my body screamed for rest. Today, I am calmer, present, and unchained from my device because repetition rewired me. Step by step, practice by practice, I built new patterns.

The emotions you practice naming and feeling become easier to ride. The storms you learn to sit with become easier to navigate. Emotional mastery is about awareness and practice. The skill is to notice the shift instantly—to catch the mood as it rises, bring it into awareness right away, and in doing so, reclaim your choice. That is the moment emotions stop owning you and start serving you.

Here's the hidden reward: When the masks drop and emotions finally flow, you touch real joy—the kind that only comes when humans truly connect. True intimacy is born in those moments. And if I may be blunt—it's a joy as intense as the best sex you've ever had, only without the physical touch. It's the spark of being seen, felt, and connected to someone's essence. There is no better place to start than becoming fully convinced of how emotions work. When you trust their rhythm, you stop fearing them. When you notice their patterns, you stop being hijacked.

The biggest skill you can learn is to bring any shift in your mood instantly into your awareness. That single move puts the steering wheel back in your hands. But awareness must be practiced. As we grow older, most of us learn to suppress our emotions. The real work is the opposite: to approach your emotions. To let them surface in the same way we allow a child to cry, laugh, or shout when something feels too big to hold alone.

The invitation here is simple yet profound: Learn to hold yourself with the same tenderness you'd offer that child. Sitting with your emotions slowly tames the Judge inside you. Observe the dialogue. Notice the thought, then let it go. Remind yourself: *This thought is not me.* Because most of the thoughts that cause unhappiness stem from illusions and false beliefs.

No emotion can hurt you unless you hand it the power to do so. What you feel is always real, always valid, and always yours. The task is not to judge or resist but to acknowledge: *"This is how I feel. And that is okay."*

Let's bring this to life with a Pepper Time. You've already seen how naming emotions gives you awareness. Now we'll go one level deeper: practicing the art of simply sitting with them. This one is uncomfortable at first—that's why it's powerful. Think of it as training your nervous system the same way you'd train a muscle: by staying present under tension.

PEPPER TIME 14:
SIT WITH IT

Timing: 30 minutes. Once or twice a week.

What you'll need: A quiet space and a timer (set on your phone, then put it away).

What it's about: Training yourself to sit with boredom and raw emotions without escaping. This is emotional strength training—grit practice for the bigger waves of life.

How to do it:

1. **Find a quiet place.** Somewhere you won't be interrupted.
2. **Set a timer for 30 minutes.** Then put your phone out of reach.
3. **Do nothing.** No internet, scrolling, TV, music, books, fridge trips, or texting. No meditation or "techniques." Just sit.
4. **Notice what rises.** Boredom, restlessness, frustration, anger, grief, tears, joy. Let it all come. Don't push it away or act on it.
5. **If your nose itches, don't scratch.** Simply observe the sensation until it fades.
6. **Resist the urge to escape.** Stay with whatever comes up until it crests and falls.

What to expect: At first, restlessness screams loud: *"I'm bored!"* That's good—it means you're finally facing what you usually avoid. Stay, and deeper emotions surface—the ones buried under busyness and distraction. Boredom is loaded with hidden insights. Emotions only become toxic when buried or acted out blindly. With practice, you build resilience: the grit to hold discomfort, the strength to resist urges, and the power to act from intention, not impulse.

If you want to go deeper into emotions—why so many of us feel "low" or stuck in them—I recommend this simple, powerful practice: Hold Your Inner Child. It's one of the easiest ways to shift from judging your feelings to caring for them.

Reflection

____

____

____

____

____

____

*   *   *

PEPPER TIME 15: HOLD YOUR INNER CHILD

Timing: 5–10 minutes, whenever strong emotions rise.

What you'll need: Quiet space, imagination, and the willingness to soften.

What it's about: Meeting your emotions with tenderness instead of judgment—by picturing them as the feelings of a child who simply needs care.

How to do it:

1. **Picture a child in pain.** Close your eyes and imagine a six-year-old who has fallen and scraped her knee. She is crying, maybe even screaming. Do you scold her? Tell her she's overreacting? Or do you kneel, hold her, and whisper that it's okay to cry—that she is safe and loved.
2. **Recognize the truth.** Every time you feel overwhelmed, angry, sad, or lost, that child is you. Your emotions are not weaknesses to discipline; they are signals asking for care.
3. **Hold your own emotions.** Breathe with them. Whisper comfort to yourself: "I see you. I hear you. It's okay to feel this."
4. **Extend the practice outward.** When someone shows you raw emotion, create safety for them to feel without shutting down. Don't judge—if you had walked their path, you might feel the same. Offer empathy: Respond as you would want someone to respond to you in your most vulnerable state.

What to expect: At first this may feel awkward or "soft." Stay with it. Over time you'll notice storms inside you passing more quickly when you meet them with compassion instead of resistance. And when the masks drop—yours and others'—you'll discover the joy of true connection. Not polite small talk, but real human intimacy. The kind that can feel as powerful and electric as the best physical closeness—without needing touch at all.

Reflection

____

____

____

____

____

____

*   *   *

Building Your Strength

Emotional mastery isn't built overnight. The itch you resist scratching, the hunger you wait through, the silence you hold when you want to blurt something out—these are your emotional push-ups. Every time you resist the impulse to escape, you strengthen your ability to stay present. Boredom is a perfect teacher here. That's why the *Sit with It* experiment is so vital. Include it daily in your routine for 10 to 15 minutes. Don't numb the boredom with scrolling, food, or chatter. See the raw emotions, the memories, even the sparks of creativity that usually get drowned out.

Boredom is a doorway. Sitting with it prepares you to sit with the real storms: anger, grief, shame, heartbreak. The next time you feel anger rising, tune in. Notice your heart pounding, your breath shortening, your body heating up, your voice wanting to rise. Let the fire burn without pouring more fuel on. At the right moment, whisper: *I am calm.* When you do, the storm will pass. And each time you practice this, you rewire your brain to make it easier the next time.

But here's the challenge: Emotions don't just visit once and leave. They loop. The mind loves to replay the scene from last week, the argument from last year, the failure from a decade ago. These loops are the brain's way of keeping unfinished business alive until it's resolved. The trouble is, most of us never resolve it. We just keep replaying the tape. That's why awareness is only the first step.

To break the loops, you need to have a real conversation with the part of you that fuels them—the Judge. That's where we'll go next. Because until you learn how to meet the Judge head-on, emotions will keep circling back, dragging you into storms you've already survived. Emotions are your teachers. Learn to sit with them, train with them, and eventually dance with them. And when the loops come back—as they always do—you'll be ready to face the Judge who keeps pressing repeat.

Intuition & Gut Instincts

Intuition is one of my favorite pathways. It's where logic stops and your deeper knowing begins. How good are you at acknowledging that inner voice? Do you believe in the value of gut feeling, or do you dismiss it as irrational? When I introduce intuition in a business context, people often look skeptical. It sounds too soft, too illogical, too unmeasurable. But intuition is the key to everything—from sharp decision-making to deeper self-awareness. It's the quiet compass that points you toward alignment long before your brain has gathered enough data to explain why.

Like the earlier pathways, intuition doesn't stand alone. Physicality gives you the raw signals—tight chest, lightness in your step, fatigue that doesn't make sense. Emotions translate those signals into meaning. Intuition is the next layer: It connects the dots before your rational brain has time to catch up. Together, they form a ladder—body, emotions, intuition—that helps you climb toward clarity and aligned action.

The Gut-Brain Connection

Your gut isn't just a digestive machine; it's a messenger system. The enteric nervous system is a vast network of neurons embedded in your gut wall that communicates constantly with the brain. Some call it the "second brain," but that's misleading. The gut isn't a duplicate—it's a connected partner, one that influences your mood, habits, and relationships. The gut links back to the limbic brain, the seat of emotion and memory. It's here that habits form, patterns take root, and instincts sharpen. When your gut says "yes" or "no," it's drawing on a complex web of physical signals, stored experiences, and emotional truths.

And it isn't just emotional. Neurochemistry lives here, too. About 90 percent of your body's serotonin—the "happy hormone"—is produced in your gut. Serotonin regulates mood in the brain, but in the gut, it acts as a signaling molecule, influencing digestion, appetite, even weight. The state of your gut affects the state of your mind, and vice versa. During stress, for example, the brain goes into alert and the gut slows down digestion, reduces blood supply, and prepares for "threat." Think of the stomach ache before a presentation, the cramps in a conflict.

Self Care & The Inner Voice

Your intuition works like a compass, but only if the signal is clear. That signal is carried through your body—and your gut in particular. When you nourish your body with proper sleep, food, movement, and stress management, the signal strengthens. Neglect these, and the inner voice becomes distorted, harder to hear through the noise of exhaustion, imbalance, or constant stress. This is why self-care is not indulgence—it's the foundation of clarity. A well-cared-for gut does more than aid digestion; it produces and regulates neurotransmitters, including serotonin, which shapes mood, focus, and even resilience. When your system is balanced, your intuition speaks with a sharper edge. When it's neglected, doubt and second-guessing take over.

And self-care goes beyond the physical. It's also the discipline of slowing down enough to notice the signals you're receiving—

whether it's fatigue telling you to pause, a knot in your stomach warning you about a project, or a surge of energy affirming a decision. Listening requires presence. Acting requires courage. Your inner voice is already there, quietly guiding you toward alignment. Are you creating the conditions to hear it? Every act of care—choosing real food, going for a walk, saying no to an extra meeting, or simply breathing deeply—sharpens that connection. When you take care of your body, you're not just fueling performance. You're strengthening your access to wisdom.

Intuition is like a muscle—you strengthen it through practice. If you've lost touch with it, it's still there, waiting to be trained back online. Go back to the Body Scan practice from Chapter 5 (Pepper Time 12). This Pepper Time is designed to help you notice what your body is already telling you—signals you may have ignored or overridden for years. Every rep builds clarity. When you strengthen your gut intuition, you stop second-guessing yourself.

Intuition isn't mystical—it's practical. It's a massive time and energy saver. Most importantly, it's the foundation of gut leadership. When your body, brain, and gut speak the same language, you don't just make decisions—you *own them*. You lead with presence instead of performance. You move faster, cleaner, truer. And people can feel it. So, start small. Ask your body about lunch, about a workout, about a meeting. Because the more you practice, the louder your compass becomes. And when you can trust your gut fully, you're not just navigating life—you're shaping it with clarity and power.

Motivation & Drive

Motivation is the fire that keeps us moving when it would be easier to give up. At its core, it starts with the most basic human drives: sleep and wake, hunger and thirst, reproduction and safety. But beyond survival, we all have personal drivers—helping others, solving intellectual challenges, achieving financial success, innovating, or building something meaningful. Motivation is what allows us to push through obstacles, but it also shapes the quality of the life we build.

Yet motivation is not a straight road. There are positive motivators—purpose, passion, contribution. And there are negative motivators—fear, revenge, anger, even addiction. Both can fuel action, but they shape very different outcomes. The challenge is to anchor yourself in a "why" strong enough to carry you when distractions, doubts, or difficulties arise.

Finding Your Why

When we visited Japan, I learned the word *Ikigai*—literally, "the reason I get up in the morning." It's a sense of purpose so deeply embedded in culture that it guides both personal happiness and collective longevity. Having a strong sense of purpose correlates directly with well-being. It gives you the tenacity to keep going when the path is steep.

The same is true here: The work we're doing isn't about short-term hacks. It's about building long-lasting habits that increase your well-being, deepen your relationships, and sustain your performance. Purpose acts like a compass. Anything can derail us. But when your purpose is clear, the reward of moving toward that outcome outweighs the lure of distraction.

The more meaningful your "why," the less attractive the detours.

People with a strong sense of purpose are more likely to feel passion. And passion matters, because when aspiring students or young entrepreneurs ask me what to study or what career to choose, I always give the same advice: Follow the path that sparks your passion. Because when things get hard—and they will—it's passion that will keep you moving.

Some of the most motivated and resilient people I've met have lived through childhood trauma. That connection is no coincidence. Learning early on how to survive life's existential challenges—bereavement, divorce, moving away from family and friends—can lead to a deep, internal determination to thrive despite the circumstances. Pain, when integrated, becomes fuel.

The Science Of Motivation

If you want to harness motivation as a consistent force, you need to understand the wiring of the human brain. Motivation isn't magic, discipline, or pressure. Motivation is chemistry and emotion, desire and meaning. If you can learn how it operates, you can stop waiting for it and start building it.

 # Adults only change when they feel like it. We like to think that if you give people enough facts, they'll change. But adults don't do what they "should." They do what they *want*. Motivation isn't about pushing—it's about desire. If motivation worked on command, we'd all have six-packs, million-dollar businesses, balanced calendars, and meditation habits. But pressure creates resistance. Push me, and I push back. Tell me to do it, and suddenly I don't want to.

Movement happens when the desire inside outweighs the discomfort outside. That's why people often change only when the pain of staying the same becomes unbearable. It's why someone finally leaves the toxic job only after their body breaks down or gets sober only after they hit bottom. Desire fuels change—not force.

Recall the man on the sofa watching TV, eating his pepperoni pizza. He knows he should work out. The treadmill is five steps away. But the couch is warm, the game is on, the chips are salty and perfect. He "knows" logically that exercise is better for him, but logic doesn't move him. Desire does. If his desire to feel strong, confident, and alive right now is greater than his desire for comfort, he'll get up. If not, the chips win. Every time. The takeaway? Stop trying to push yourself (or others) into change. Build desire instead.

We are wired to move toward what feels good right now.
The present always feels louder than the future. The Netflix binge is soothing now. The treadmill? That's sweat and soreness. The future payoff—better health, more energy, confidence—is invisible in the moment. That's why diets fail, gym memberships gather dust, and entrepreneurs never launch the business they keep daydreaming about. Unless you hack the system, your brain will default to the immediate reward—even when it sabotages the long game.

Imagine two people standing at a crossroads. One path is paved, shaded, and lined with ice cream stands. The other is uphill, rocky, with no guarantees of a view. Where does the average brain go? To the ice cream. The solution? Bring the future into the present. Make the payoff visible and emotional *now*. Don't focus on "losing twenty pounds in six months." Focus on how you'll feel stronger, lighter, prouder after today's workout. Don't frame the business as a five-year gamble. Frame it as the first taste of freedom you'll feel *today* when you take one step forward.

 # Everyone thinks they are the exception. This is the "Not me" illusion. Smokers believe they won't get cancer. Overworkers think burnout is for "other people." Procrastinators think they'll magically pull it off at the last minute. It's the mental get-out-of-jail-free card: *"The warning applies to everyone else, but I'll be fine."* That's why threats, ultimatums, and lectures rarely work. If someone deep down believes they're untouchable, your warnings bounce off like rubber bullets. They'll say, "Yeah, I know" while thinking *"but not me."* The reality? No one is the exception. Biology doesn't negotiate. Stress, poor habits, and neglected dreams always cash their checks. The only difference is whether you wake up early—or when it's too late.

Unlock The Power Of Influence

A question I hear often is: "How do I motivate someone else to change?"
The honest answer: **You can't.**

People only change when they feel like changing. It doesn't matter how strong your reasons are, how right you think you are, or even if they fully understand the consequences. If they don't feel it inside, they won't move. And worse—when you pressure someone to change, it usually backfires. Instead of progress, you get tension, resentment, and distance.

I experienced this firsthand with Tobi. I kept pushing him to adjust small habits. The more I nudged, the more he began to resent me. Suddenly, everything I did was seen through a negative lens—even when I did something good. And if I forgot just one small thing, like leaving a cup in the sink, all the frustration came flooding back. We all have a deep, hardwired need to feel in control of our decisions. When you pressure people, they resist even if your intentions are loving. Lack of change doesn't mean someone is lazy or doesn't care. More often, it means they feel discouraged, overwhelmed, or like they *can't* change. Think of it this way: you can't demand that someone start eating healthier while raving about the croissant you just devoured. But you can influence by modeling another way—cooking colorful, delicious meals and sharing how much better you feel. That's influence in action.

The route to influencing others isn't through pressure—it's through compassion and example. You want the best for your partner, friend, or colleague. You love them, care about them, and want to see them healthier, happier, and fulfilled. That desire is good. But pressure feels like judgment, and judgment rarely inspires. Think about how it feels when someone does this to you—when they make it sound like change should be easy. You feel attacked, defensive, even offended. Change is hard for everyone, which is why the most loving thing you can do is stop pushing and start meeting people where they are.

This is where trust comes in. Without it, nothing sticks. Safety—created through unconditional love, kindness, and acceptance—relaxes the nervous system. And in that space of acceptance, *real* change becomes possible. People want to feel they're in control of their own growth.

That means you need to decide: What can I accept, and what is a deal-breaker? Maybe your partner vapes, struggles in their career, makes promises they don't keep, or lounges in sweatpants too often. Can you accept them as they are? Or is it a fundamental misalignment? Adults must be allowed to be adults—but you get to choose the relationship you want to be in. And here's where your real power lies: The only behavior you can fully control is your own. That's the lever. The first change is to stop pressuring and start accepting. Doing so transforms all three areas at once:

- **Your well-being:** Less stress from focusing on things you can't control, more clarity and alignment with your gut.
- **Your relationships:** When you stop pushing, safety and trust grow. People lean toward you instead of pulling away.
- **Your performance:** More energy goes into building the business and life you love, rather than battling resistance.

Behavior is contagious. You can't demand someone live differently while you model the opposite. But if you walk the talk, show the benefits, and make it look fun, you unlock the power of influence. Change spreads not through pressure but through inspiration. That's why finding your own motivation is crucial if you hope to influence others.

To get to the root of your motivation, you need honesty. What do you really want from life? Why do you want it? Plant these questions like seeds and let them germinate. It doesn't matter whether your goal is health, balance, a career change, or building a company. What matters is cultivating a motivation strong enough to switch you from imagination into action. Motivation is about creating conditions where the feeling grows. For your dreams to become reality, you need two things: action and resilience. The patience to keep going through distractions. The willingness to accept setbacks as part of the process. And the ability to return, again and again, to your why.

Motivation isn't willpower—it's alignment. It's about finding the spark that pulls you forward. When you clarify your why, you lead with conviction. Resilience is the decision to keep showing up when it would be easier not to. And that decision, repeated day after day, is what makes you unstoppable.

Logic & Thought

If you want to thrive, you need a tuned body, mastered emotions, and trusted intuition. Still, logic matters. It's how you test stories, weigh options, and choose actions. Most of us need a cleaner environment for logic to work: fewer emotional hijacks and unexamined biases and a tighter loop from noticing → testing → acting.

We used to believe logic lived in the left brain and creativity/ emotion in the right. Modern neuroscience shows complex decisions are *whole-brain:* Information flows left↔right, back↔front, bottom↔top. The healthier and more connected your brain, the better your judgment. Plenty of people make brilliant calls at work and disastrous ones at home. Strong reasoning does not equal emotional mastery—and without emotional mastery, logic gets dragged around by mood.

Thought first, emotions second

It feels like emotions come first, but the spark is almost always a thought. The chicken is the thought; the egg is the emotion. And those eggs hatch more thoughts, which hatch more emotions—until you're caught in a storm.

Here's how it plays out. Your partner hasn't texted back. The first thought flickers: *Maybe I'm not important.* That one seed sparks anxiety. Anxiety fuels new thoughts: *Should I call? Am I too clingy? Maybe I need to lose weight to stay attractive.* Each thought pours gasoline on the fire. Suddenly, you're not just waiting for a message—you're in a spiral of irritation, insecurity, even self-criticism.

This is why emotions feel overwhelming—they're stacked on layer after layer of thought. But this also means they're predictable, because if you know your thought triggers, you can anticipate the emotional wave before it crashes. That's the leverage logic gives you: the ability to step in, name the first spark, and stop the avalanche.

A single thought can drag you through years of suffering. We still believe them, hand them power, and let them dictate our happiness. A thought might even bring relief. But the moment that fades, negative thoughts rush back in to reestablish suffering. Just like painkillers: When one wears off, you reach for another. Eventually, regular strength no longer numbs the pain, and you start reaching for stronger doses. In life, that shows up as chasing more extreme pleasures—wilder parties, bigger risks, extreme sports, endless indulgences. All in an attempt to outrun what started as a single thought.

The Three Types Of Thought

Logic isn't about thinking harder; it's about thinking cleaner. In this pathway, we'll explore the four modes of thought that move you forward so you can separate the noise from the signal and make decisions that serve both your head and your gut.

#1 NARRATIVE. This is the running commentary in your head—the voice that replays the argument, critiques the email you just sent, or imagines what others think of you. It's the "grumpy brain" in action. Narrative thought is useful for storytelling and identity, but when left unchecked, it hijacks logic and pulls you into loops of judgment, fear, or self-doubt.

#2 EXPERIENTIAL THINKING. This mode is pure seeing/feeling/hearing the present—no commentary. It's listening attentively to a friend, noticing your partner's posture shift after your remark, smelling the bread, watching the butterfly's wings. It's also the basis of interoception: noticing the tight jaw or loose belly now. Deliberate attention is the switch that turns this thinking on.

And speaking of attention, it's worth noting that there is no such thing as true multitasking. Task-switching wastes cognitive fuel and degrades accuracy. Train single-task presence, and you instantly improve judgment—which brings us to our next Pepper Time experiment.

PEPPER TIME 16: THE MULTITASKING MYTH

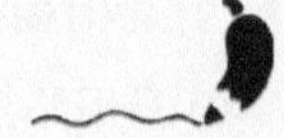

Timing: 5 minutes.

What you'll need: Your journal, a pen, and a timer.

What it's about: Multitasking feels efficient, but your brain pays a hidden tax every time you switch. This game shows you how costly it really is.

How to do it:

1. **Game 1:** Straight run. Write the alphabet A–Z in order. On the next line, write numbers 1–26. Time yourself.
2. **Game 2:** Alternating. Write A1, B2, C3 ... all the way to Z26. Time yourself again.
3. **Compare.** Notice how much slower and more draining the alternating sequence feels.

What to expect: The second round takes longer and feels surprisingly exhausting. That's the *switch cost*—the mental toll of splitting attention. It's the same tax your brain pays every time you juggle emails, calls, and tasks instead of focusing on one thing.

Reflection

____

____

____

____

____

____

____

*   *   *

#3 SOLVING. Solving is where logic rolls up its sleeves. It's the bridge between awareness and action. Without solving, awareness just keeps you circling the same storm. Solving takes the raw data of your experience and runs it through intelligence—debugging the faulty code your brain writes in survival mode.

Most thoughts that drag you down are illusions and false beliefs. Holding onto them is ostrich behavior—burying your head in the sand, thinking you're safe while leaving yourself vulnerable. It feels protective, but it deepens suffering. You already practiced this earlier in the *Sit with It* experiment—watching thoughts rise and pass, realizing *a thought is not you*. Now, Solving asks you to take the next step: Test the thought before you obey it.

So how do you actually solve? Six questions cut through the noise, expose faulty code, and move you from looping to leading.

Question #1: Am I happy right now? It sounds basic, but most of us rush through life without ever asking. If the answer is yes—pause and enjoy it. Let your system register the moment as joy. For example, you're sitting with a coffee, laughing with a friend. Instead of scrolling to the next task, you breathe it in and think: *This is happiness*. That simple act of naming reinforces a positive loop in your brain and gut. If the answer is no—don't judge it. Just move to the next question.

Question #2: What do I feel? Here's where you get specific. Don't just say "bad." Label the storm. Is it anger? Fear? Sadness? Shame? *Disappointment*? The act of naming the feeling reduces its grip. Picture this: You get feedback at work. Your chest tightens, and you mutter, "I feel anxious." But when you pause and really name it, you realize it's disappointment—you wanted praise. The moment you say, "This is disappointment," the fog lifts. Your brain stops spinning a vague panic and starts working with the truth. Notice where it shows up in your body, too. Go back to the Body Scan experiment (Pepper Time 12) if you need help here. Maybe it's a knot in your stomach, pressure in your jaw, or heat in your chest. Naming the feeling and locating it in the body gives your gut a voice in the solving process.

Question #3: What triggered it? Every emotion has a thought behind it. Trace the spark. For example: Your partner hasn't texted you back. The thought: *They don't care*. The emotion: sadness. Or maybe it's *I'll never get this promotion* → emotion: fear. Or *I'm not good enough* → emotion: shame. When you catch the thought, write it down. This one step already weakens its power. Because once the trigger is out of your head and onto paper, you can see it for what it is—a story, not the whole truth.

These three questions—Am I happy? What do I feel? What triggered it?—are the starting point of solving. They move you from vague overwhelm to specific clarity. They connect your brain and gut so you can see the storm for what it is, not just drown in it. And the more you practice, the faster the cycle runs. You feel the knot in your belly, you name it as fear, you spot the thought ("I'll fail at this"), and already the storm has lost half its force. That's the beginning of rewiring to change the game within.

Now that you've practiced the first three questions, you've seen how quickly they can bring clarity. But clarity alone isn't enough. Awareness is step one—solving means we also start testing the stories that fuel our storms. This is where part 2 comes in: rewiring. But before we move on, let's add three more questions to your gut-logic toolkit to stop the spin, cut through the noise, and help you separate fact from fiction. The first of these is a game-changer:

Question #4: Is it true? Your brain wants to protect you. It scans constantly for danger. But in doing so, it often hands you stories instead of truth. And when you believe those stories, you pay the price—in peace, energy, and trust. Think about it. Your partner doesn't text back for a few hours. Your brain leaps in: *They're upset with me. They don't care. Maybe they're losing interest.* Suddenly, you're not just waiting on a message— you're in a storm of fear and rejection.

But pause. Is it true?

Did you see or hear anything that proves it? Your brain genuinely wants to protect you, but it doesn't always give you the truth. Every second, life throws endless amounts of data at you—sights, sounds, smells, sensations, fragments of conversations, memories. Your brain cannot possibly capture all of it. So, it makes its best guess. And that guess often becomes the "story" you believe.

If I asked you to describe the room you're sitting in right now, could you list every detail—the exact number of books on the shelf, the way the light hits the floor, the faint smell of coffee, the sound of a car outside, the precise shade of paint on the wall, or the tiny scratch on the table? Of course not. What your brain does instead is fill in the blanks: "The wall is white," "There's a chair in the corner," "The room is quiet." But is it exactly white or slightly beige? Is it truly "quiet," or is there a low hum from the fridge you've tuned out? Your brain gives you approximations, not reality.

Now apply that same mechanism to emotional thoughts. Let's say your best friend doesn't reply to your message all day. Your brain jumps in to protect you with a "story": *She's mad at me. Maybe she's replacing me*. Is it true? Probably not. But because your brain wants to keep you alert, it serves you this dramatic version. And once that first thought lands, it hatches new ones: *I must not be good enough. I'll end up alone*. Before you know it, you're in a full-blown storm—all built on a foundation that may have zero evidence.

That's why you need to test your thoughts. Most of them aren't clean—they're filtered through past pain, strong emotions, and other people's opinions. Solving means stripping those layers off and asking: Is this real, or is this just a story? Here are four simple rules to help you check:

- **Rule 1:** No sensory proof = no truth. Did you *see, hear, touch, taste,* or *smell* it? If not, it's a story. You assume the chef cooked your meal from scratch. Maybe. But unless you saw it, it could just as easily be frozen food reheated. Without sensory proof, you don't know. The same goes for thoughts like *"They're talking behind my back."* Unless you were in the room and heard the words, it's just your brain filling in blanks.

- **Rule 2:** Anything stamped past or future is fiction. Your brain loves to time-travel. *"He's like this because of his childhood..."* or *"I know my team won't do anything when I'm not there."* Both are guesses, not truths. You can't know the past you didn't witness, nor the future that hasn't happened. The only thing you can verify is here and now. Ask yourself: *"Can I actually prove this in the present?"* If not, it's fiction.

- **Rule 3:** Drama ≠ truth. Events themselves are neutral. It's your mind that adds drama. A colleague doesn't say hello in the hallway. The raw fact = they walked past you silently. The drama = *"They're mad at me. They don't respect me. Maybe I'm about to be fired."* The first is an observation. The rest is your brain's script. Don't confuse drama with reality.

- **Rule 4:** Trauma isn't truth. Old wounds color new events. Maybe a parent once abandoned you, so when a friend cancels dinner, your brain screams, *"Everyone leaves me."* But that's your past pain leaking into the present—not the truth about this one event. Separate the two. Hold the event in isolation without layering past trauma on top.

The way you frame the question matters. Keep it clean. Use closed yes/no questions. If I ask, *"What color is this page?"* you could go on: *"Well, it was in the rain, so it lost some color, it's not pure white, maybe beige..."* That's your brain storytelling. If I ask, *"Is this page yellow?"* the answer is simply yes or no. That's how you cut through the noise.

For a thought to count as true, your brain must provide evidence. If it can't, assume it's false and drop it. You always have the choice to stop letting stories hurt you. The moment you call it out, you move from being run by your brain to leading with your gut. Solving is about forcing positivity. It's about looking at the raw data honestly, identifying the faulty coding, and choosing your next move with clarity. The faster you cycle through awareness → problem → solution, the less time you spend in unnecessary suffering.

Question #5 What can I do about it? Thoughts without action keep you stuck. When you take a step, you move from paralysis to momentum, from helpless to capable. That shift alone is often enough to break the cycle. The kinds of thoughts that make us suffer tend to be the incessant, looping ones. Alarms tell us something in our environment doesn't meet our expectations of safe, fair, or desirable. Then, it's time to act.

Take the example of a fight with your partner. If you sit in thoughts like *"We're breaking up. This is over. I can't handle this,"* you'll only prolong your suffering. The only way forward is action. Text them. Own your part. Suggest a conversation. If it works—great. If not—you move on. Either way, you've shifted from being stuck in the storm to steering through it.

Even micro-steps matter. Write down a plan. Make one call. Send one email. Do *something*. This is what I call adding "pepper" into your life—the bold move that kicks you out of rumination and into creation. You'll learn more about this in Chapter 7 when we dive into your Power Brain. It's about activating the right part of your brain for what's needed now and navigating one small step at a time. Action rewires your brain. The moment you shift from looping on *what's wrong* to *what's possible*, you activate your prefrontal cortex—the part of your brain responsible for clarity, focus, and forward motion. You don't even need to solve the entire problem. The simple act of identifying a possible solution and taking the first step lowers the noise.

Your thoughts are the fire alarm, blaring through the house. You can either sit there covering your ears—or you can get up, look for the smoke, and take action. The alarm will soften the moment you move. Sometimes we delay action because we're scared we're not good enough, or because the problem feels too big. But most situations are simpler than they appear when you're stuck in the storm. You just need your next right move. And once you take it, you'll feel the shift immediately.

So here's the mantra for this step: Stop looping. Start moving. Add pepper.

Question #6 Can I accept & commit? Life will test you. Sometimes brutally. Jobs disappear. Loved ones die. People betray you. Money gets stolen. I've lived through every one of those storms, and in each case, I had to fall back on my ultimate defense: committed acceptance. Some things you simply cannot change. Acceptance isn't weakness. It's clarity. When you stop fighting the unchangeable, you stop wasting your energy on resistance. And once you've accepted reality for what it is—not what you wish it were—you regain the ultimate power: **the power to choose how you respond.**

Most people I work with, when asked, "Would you erase your hardships if you could, knowing that erasing them would also erase the growth, the resilience, and everything that followed?"—answer no. Because even suffering has a gift. This is the turning point. You can remain an object—resigned, bitter, complaining, waiting for someone else to rescue you. Or you can step into being a subject—taking charge, rewriting your story, using your pain as fuel. Acceptance is the first move.

Commitment is the second. You may never get your old job back, but you can commit to finding a new path. You may never recover stolen money, but you can commit to rebuilding. You may never bring back a loved one, but you can commit to honoring their memory and living in a way they would be proud of. Acceptance opens the door. Commitment walks you through it.

You don't have to fix everything in one step. Just commit to making tomorrow a little better than today, and the day after that a little better still. That's how resilience compounds. This is where your Power Brain comes in (see Chapter 7). The Power Brain is your ability to activate the right mental gear for the moment. That might mean slowing down the fear-driven circuits and switching on your logic, calling on motivation to take one micro-step, or leaning into creativity to imagine a different future. Acceptance is the *reset*. Commitment is the *navigation*—choosing the right brain pathway to move forward, one step at a time.

This pathway of logic is about pairing clear thinking with emotional mastery. Thoughts spark emotions, emotions trigger stories, and stories shape the way you act—or don't. The power comes when you can slow down, ask the six questions, and intervene before the storm hijacks you. Logic is about seeing more clearly, deciding more wisely, and choosing to move forward even in the hardest conditions. You are not a victim of your thoughts. You are the author. And authors don't wait for a happy ending—they write one.

You are a legend. Start playing like one.

Creativity Unleashed

Creativity is the pathway that turns all the others into possibility. To create the life you want, you need to see the opportunities, signals, and openings that are always around you. Creativity is freedom to imagine, combine ideas in new ways, and shape your future instead of being dragged by the past. A creative brain doesn't just consume—it designs. It pulls from the other pathways—intuition, logic, motivation, emotions—and fuses them into something bigger.

That's why this pathway is the bridge: It's the one that turns "knowing" into "becoming." You create every day. You create your home, your friendships, your career, the meals you eat, the conversations you start, the energy you bring into a room. Imagine what would happen if you took the wheel fully.

You may not think your career is creative, but creativity isn't just for "artistic" jobs. It's what helps you find new ways to solve problems, pitch bold ideas, or break through roadblocks others see as fixed. Jessy, an entrepreneur I worked with from Zurich was stuck on product messaging. She tapped creativity: rewriting the copy in three voices—a customer's, a rival's, and her five-year-old nephew's. The child's voice cut the jargon and revealed the one line that clicked with buyers. That shift tripled conversions. Creativity reframes performance from "work harder" to "work differently."

Relationships thrive on novelty. Without creativity, love becomes routine; conflict becomes stuck. One couple I coached used to fight every Friday evening. Same argument, same exhaustion. Instead of another "serious talk," they created a ritual: Friday Connection Hour. Phones in a basket, one high and one low from the week, plus one dance song together in the living room. It was silly, even awkward at first—but the play broke their pattern.

Creativity can be about shaping your environment so it serves you. One client kept saying she lacked "discipline" to eat healthy. We didn't work on willpower—we worked on design. Fruit at eye level in the fridge. Running shoes by the front door. Snacks out of sight. Suddenly she didn't need to "try harder." Her environment was making the healthy choice the easy one. That's creativity at work: not pushing through, but designing conditions where your best self shows up automatically.

Neuroscience reveals that creativity is a whole-brain activity. It comes from the dance between mind wandering and focus, between divergent thinking (expansive, idea-generating) and convergent thinking (choosing and refining). Both can be trained. Give your brain space—time without distraction—and it will connect dots you didn't know belonged together. Then shift into focused attention, and you'll see how to turn sparks into action.

Visualization is one of the most powerful tools here. When you bring your hopes and desires to the forefront of your mind repeatedly, your brain begins filtering the world differently. The reticular activating system—the same system that makes you suddenly notice every red car after you think about buying one—starts noticing the opportunities that align with your vision.

Pepper Boards, journaling, or even daydreaming with intention all strengthen this muscle. But beware: Negative filtering kills creativity. If you train your brain to focus on scarcity, what's missing, and why something won't work, you'll find endless evidence for that story. Flip it to abundance, and your brain starts finding possibilities everywhere. It's a simple but powerful way to sketch out the life you want, underline the feelings that matter most, and start taking gut-led micro-actions today that pull that vision closer.

Make creativity the steering wheel of your life. When you practice it across performance, relationships, and well-being, you'll stop replaying old tapes and start composing new music. You begin to design, not drift. And that's the essence of gut leadership—your brain observes, your gut feels, your emotions move you, your motivation drives you, your logic tests you—but creativity is the spark that combines them all into a future worth living.

And here's the truth: Each thought you think doesn't just stay in your head. It changes your chemistry, your emotions, your body, and your habits. What you think repeatedly shapes who you become. That's why awareness matters. And that's why creativity—intentional, conscious creation—is the final pathway in part 1. Because when you master creativity, you're no longer just surviving. You're designing.

Remember: You are already creative. The question is whether you're creating unconsciously, on autopilot—or intentionally, as the author of your life.

This first part has been about waking up. About pulling back the curtain on what's really running your life. Because without awareness, you stay trapped in autopilot, recycling yesterday's patterns. With it, you take back authorship. That is the first pepper: the sting of realizing you have always had more power than you thought. Carry that with you as you move forward: Awareness isn't something to earn; it's already yours. Will you use it?

"You can't create a new future by holding on to the emotions of the past. The moment you decide to change, everything changes. "

— Dr. Joe Dispenza

Rewiring Your Brain & Gut

We've looked at neuroplasticity as a practice where every repetition wires you closer to who you want to become. You've learned the transformative power of shifting from scarcity to abundance, of holding an expanded vision, and of imagining a future that feels true to you. We've explored the science of visualization and how the brain filters the world differently based on what you repeatedly bring to mind.

Now comes the turning point. This part of the book is about integration and rewiring—taking the insights you've gained and making them real. This is the pathway to a new you. It's about training your brain and aligning with your gut so you can build a life on *your* terms—across the three domains that matter most:

1. **Relationships:** Building deeper, more authentic connections without masks or loops.
2. **Well-being:** Strengthening your body, energy, and resilience so you can thrive.
3. **Performance:** Aligning your drive, intuition, and creativity to achieve both authenticity and success.

Resist the urge to rush. Each practice is designed to rewire you step by step. Move forward only when you've received real insights and tangible benefits from the current one. That's how transformation compounds.

Chapter 6:

Training Mental Fitness

Happiness depends less on controlling every thought and more on training your brain the way you'd train a muscle. This is what mental fitness is all about. In part 1, we explored how your brain and gut shape reality. In part 2, we move from noticing to actively training. Remember: What you use grows; what you neglect shrinks. Neuroplasticity doesn't ask whether you're rehearsing something good for you or something toxic. It simply strengthens whatever circuit you repeat.

Think of your muscles. You don't strengthen them by going to the gym once—you go back again and again. The fibers tear, repair, and grow. Your brain works the same way. Every loop you repeat—worry, gratitude, presence, self-criticism—lays down stronger circuits. Your brain doesn't care *what* you practice. It just gets better at whatever you repeat. That's why tracking matters.

In business, we measure numbers to improve performance. In life, you need to track your mental reps. See where your attention goes. Notice how quickly you bounce back from stress. What gets measured gets trained. Without tracking, old patterns creep back in. With tracking, you can deliberately build resilience, clarity, and focus. Mental fitness is made up of daily reps that rewire your defaults, interrupt autopilot, and put you back in a choice mindset. These reps make your wiser brain and your gut the leaders of your life. And it starts here with Pepper Reps: ten seconds of attention, repeated often, that compound into lasting change.

Pepper Time

A Pepper Rep is at least ten seconds of laser-focused attention on one physical sensation—your breath, your fingertips, your feet on the floor, a sound in the distance, the warmth of a sip of tea. Thoughts will come and go; you don't chase them. You simply return to sensation.

Why call them Pepper Reps? Because they add spice, energy, and sharpness to your system. They wake you up, interrupt the autopilot spiral, and bring you back to presence. When you're caught in negative emotions, your brain narrows into tunnel vision. Pepper Reps are the interruption. By anchoring on a sensation, you light up the parts of your brain that go quiet under stress. You shift from survival mode into the higher networks that can think clearly, regulate emotions, and find solutions.

The beauty is in their double effect. In the moment, a Pepper Rep creates a state shift: You feel calmer, clearer, and more grounded. Over time, repetition creates a trait shift: Your brain learns to return to calm more quickly, rewiring itself for resilience. One rep won't change your life. But dozens, scattered throughout your day, absolutely will.

From Triggers To Choice

The easiest way to start is to use your triggers. Every time you feel stress rising, a negative thought looping, or a conversation beginning to spiral—drop into a Pepper Rep. Ten seconds of breathing, touch, or sound is enough to create a pause. And from that pause, you choose your next move. But you don't have to wait until you're upset. Pepper Reps also work as a daily routine to keep you steady, help you begin a project without procrastination, or prepare yourself for a difficult conversation or tough negotiation. They are as much a warm-up as they are a reset.

Well-being: Your inner voice says, *I'm not good enough*. Instead of spiraling, you close your eyes and feel your heartbeat in your chest. You're alive, right here, right now. The critic loses its grip.

Relationships: Your partner snaps at you after a long day. Your instinct is to snap back. Instead, you catch the trigger. You close your eyes, feel your chest rise with one breath, unclench your jaw. The urge to escalate softens, and you respond with curiosity instead of anger. That single shift changes the tone of the interaction.

Performance: Imagine you're about to walk into a high-stakes meeting. Normally, stress would tighten your chest, scatter your thoughts, and leave you fumbling for words.

Instead, stop for ten seconds, plant your feet on the ground, breathe into your belly, and feel the air move in and out. The tension drops, and you walk in sharp and steady.

Stress from a hundred small things can be stopped with ten seconds of listening to the farthest sound you can hear — the hum of a fridge, birds outside, the murmur of traffic. Your nervous system resets before the spiral snowballs.

Every Pepper Rep is a micro-investment in your power brain— the part of you that is calm, creative, and clear. No more rehearsing the critic until it becomes your strongest muscle. Instead, every rep trains you to come back to presence, again and again. And over time, the compound effect transforms you in thousands of tiny, peppered steps.

Before we jump into the heavy lifting of rewiring, let's begin with something simple but powerful: noticing. You can't change what you can't see. Most of us walk through our days pulled around by emotions without realizing when they rise, how long they linger, or what sparks them in the first place. That's why the first experiment is your training ground for awareness. Think of it as putting on night-vision goggles to spot the signals that were invisible before. This isn't about "fixing" yet. It's about building the muscle of noticing. Once you can see clearly, you can choose differently.

PEPPER TIME 17:
MONITOR YOUR EMOTIONS

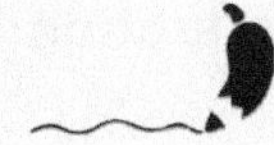

Timing: Daily for 1–2 weeks (5 minutes each evening to record).

What you'll need: Your journal or notes app.

What it's about: Emotions don't just appear—they signal, peak, and fade. Training yourself to track them builds awareness so you can spot shifts instantly, before they run the show.

How to do it:

1. **Pick one emotion.** Choose a negative emotion you often feel—anger, shyness, boredom, frustration.
2. **Track it.** For 7–14 days, stay alert and note the exact moments it surfaces.
3. **Record each instance.** Use a short note (situation + feeling).
4. **Compare with calm.** Contrast your baseline (relaxed body, ease) with the physical signals of the emotion (tight chest, tension, racing thoughts).
5. **Observe only.** Don't fix or fight it—just learn how your body signals the emotion.

What to expect: Patterns emerge fast: triggers, times of day, specific situations that pull the emotion forward. Simply monitoring sharpens awareness. Awareness is the first step to shifting your emotional state with intention.

Reflection

____

____

____

____

____

____

*   *   *

The Power Of Pause

Picture a parent with three kids: One needs a diaper change, another is crying, and the third is demanding a cookie. The parent copes by handling each need in turn. First the diaper, then the tears, then the cookie. It may look chaotic from the outside, but the parent is practicing a deep truth of the human system: We cannot attend to everything at once. We prioritize, complete, and move forward. We must pause, feel, then act. If you try to jump straight into analysis without first acknowledging your body and emotions, you get stuck in half-truths and spirals.

Your brain functions are not confined to your skull. A huge part of the nervous system stretches throughout your body, carrying intelligence in every fiber. Signals are constantly collected through your senses—sight, sound, smell, touch, taste—and relayed upward so the brain can become aware of its environment. Gut leadership is about respecting this wider field of intelligence: not just the mind in your head, but the wisdom spread throughout your body's entire network.

Your emotions are the first messengers. They show up in your face, posture, breath, and tension long before you consciously know what's happening. Smiling is a trigger that shifts your inner state. Your body softens, your nervous system calms, and your mood lifts. Even better, smiles are contagious. Being around others who smile changes your own biochemistry, nudging you toward ease and connection. Time to try it out!

Pepper Challenge: Each day, make it a point to smile on purpose at least three times. Notice what happens inside your own body when you do—the slight lift in mood, the softening of your energy. Watch how the people around you react, and how their returning smiles shift your own state again. This simple act isn't about faking happiness; it's a gentle way to spark a lighter atmosphere and create a ripple of connection that can brighten an entire day.

Be Here Now

Presence is the next layer of mental fitness. It's about bringing attention to the experience you're in right now. Presence can be as simple as noticing the taste of your coffee, the rhythm of your footsteps during a walk, or the expression on your partner's face while you're talking. Formal practices like yoga or meditation help, but everyday presence is where the real rewiring happens. Mindful eating, mindful walking, truly listening when someone speaks—these small habits, repeated daily, build a calmer, clearer, more resilient brain.

Even a few minutes a day can shift the chemistry of your nervous system. Neuroscience shows that within 2 to 3 months of regular practice, your brain physically changes—networks of calm, empathy, and focus strengthen while stress circuits quiet. As little as twelve minutes a day of deliberate presence makes a measurable difference.

For me, presence became nonnegotiable during pregnancy. Before, I lived in constant distraction—jumping from one shiny thing to another. But while carrying my daughter, my body screamed for rest. Although I had practiced yoga for years, I wasn't listening deeply enough. I started using meditation apps like Headspace, then layered in my own Pepper Reps to strengthen my inner calm. Later, when exposed to harsh words and external pressure, I trained my brain to move out of that negativity.

Presence became my shield and my source of strength. I began to treat meditation not as another thing on the to-do list but as future-proofing my brain, especially when life felt overwhelming. A monk once told an executive who claimed he had no time to meditate: *"Then you must meditate for two hours a day."* The point wasn't the number but the paradox: When you feel you don't have time, presence is what you need most.

Recall the Body Scan exercise in Chapter 5, where you learned how to notice subtle signals in your body. That scan is a doorway into presence. It teaches you to sense the small shifts between stress and calm so you can reset quickly in the middle of the storm.

This is also where your Power Brain (discussed in detail in Chapter 7) comes in. Your power brain is the state where all three of your centers—head, heart, and gut—work together instead of pulling in different directions. Being present is the fastest way to activate it. When you're present, you quiet the noise, notice what really matters, and can respond from clarity instead of autopilot. That's how you improve not only your relationships (because you actually hear and see the other person) but also your well-being (your body softens, stress lowers) and your performance (you focus only on the moves that count).

This is exactly where Pepper Reps help. A single rep—pausing to breathe, anchoring into your senses, or shifting focus—pulls you back into presence in seconds. Presence isn't about hours of meditation. It's about building the ability to return, again and again, in small, doable ways. That's how you strengthen your power brain and make presence your everyday advantage.

Pepper Reps In Daily Life 

We sabotage ourselves every single day. Every time you spend more than a second in stress, anger, or shame, you're practicing self-sabotage. That's where Pepper Reps come in. They're your reset button. Ten seconds of feeling your breath, rubbing your fingertips together, or listening for the farthest sound you can hear. Each rep interrupts autopilot, energizes your brain, and strengthens your self-command muscle. Over time, you build a brain that is wired not for sabotage but for resilience, presence, and possibility.

Start simple: Anchor your Pepper Reps to your morning routine. Notice the pillow under your head before you get up. Feel your feet on the floor. Savor the taste of your first sip of coffee or tea. Do two reps each morning and let them snowball. The point isn't perfection—it's momentum. Just like riding a bike, the first pedal takes effort, but once you're moving, the ride becomes smoother.

This chapter is about rewriting you by building habits that make you unshakable. Each Pepper Rep, moment of presence, and act of feeling before analyzing compounds into a brain and body aligned with your deepest values. The payoff shows up everywhere: sharper performance, stronger relationships, and steadier well-being. This is how you stop letting your saboteurs run the show and start living as the author of your own mind.

Let's start with your very first Pepper Rep, the easiest one: the Breath Rep. Close your eyes if you want, place a hand low on your belly, and take three slow but deep breaths. Ten seconds. That's all it takes to shift from autopilot into presence. Your survival brain may be spinning, but your body now has proof: You're safe, you're steady, you're here. And this is only the beginning.

There are many more Pepper Reps, each designed to pull you back into alignment. You'll find a full collection in the appendices at the back of the book, but the goal isn't to try them all at once. The goal is to integrate them into your mornings, because the way you start your day sets the tone for everything that follows. If your first move is reaching for your phone, you hand your nervous system over to stress. But if your first move is a Pepper Rep, you hand the wheel back to yourself. Let's look at the Sensory Pepper Reps:

- **First sensation of the day:** You wake up and notice the pillow or blanket around you. For 10 seconds, let yourself really feel it—the weight against your body, the warmth it gives, the texture of the fabric against your skin, the contours pressing into you. Instead of rushing up, let your body register: "I am held. I am here."

- **Feet on the floor:** As you swing your legs down, pause. For 10 seconds, notice the exact sensation where your feet meet the ground—the coolness or warmth of the floor, the firmness or softness, the subtle texture of wood, tile, or carpet. Feel how gravity grounds you, how the earth carries your weight.
- **Water on your skin:** When you wash your face, slow down. For 10 seconds, feel the temperature of the water, the way it runs across your skin, the pressure of your hands, the freshness. Let the water reset you, as if it's rinsing off yesterday's noise.
- **First sip of the day:** With your coffee or tea, pause for 10 seconds before swallowing. Notice the rising steam, the aroma, the warmth against your lips, the taste spreading across your tongue, the way it moves down your throat. Let it be more than fuel—let it be presence.
- **First sound you hear:** When the radio comes on or the room stirs awake, give the first 10 seconds fully to your ears. Notice melody, tone, rhythm, or the subtle layers of sound around you. Pick one detail—the hum under the music, the cadence of a voice—and stay with it.

None of this adds time to your morning. Your simply turning what's already there into training reps. A sip, a sound, a touch—tiny anchors that pull you back into alignment. Do two or three each morning and let them snowball. The point isn't perfection; it's momentum. Every rep is a vote for your Power Brain. Over weeks and months, those votes stack into a new default: mornings that begin with clarity instead of chaos, days led by presence instead of reactivity, and a life steered by you—not your saboteurs.

And this is just the start. Pepper Reps work because they're simple, repeatable, and sneak into daily life until they become second nature. One rep won't change your life—just like one push-up won't build a body. But hundreds and then thousands over time rewire your brain. Pepper Reps are the quickest entry points to snap you out of autopilot and back into presence.

You can do them with your kids, too. Children naturally live in their senses. They notice the crunch of toast, the shape of a cloud, the hum of the fridge. When you join them, you're not only training your Power Brain; you're modeling presence for them. It becomes a shared reset, a small moment of connection that teaches them how to regulate, while keeping you grounded, too.

A Pepper Rep is the ten-second clutch pedal that lets you take back control. Each one energizes your brain and strengthens your power to choose. Instead of running on half-power, you run with your whole brain switched on.

Could something so simple matter? Yes—but only if you practice. With time and consistency, soon you'll see the difference: fewer spirals, faster resets, clearer thinking. It's about rewriting who you're becoming. Each rep is a vote for your future self— the one who stays calm under pressure, present in relationships, and powerful in the moments that matter.

Start small. Anchor a rep to your mornings. Add one before a meeting, one in a hard conversation, one as you close the day. Stack them. Compound them. And watch what happens. Your autopilot won't run the show anymore—you will.

Chapter 7:

Activating Your Power Brain

Have you ever walked out of a meeting or a conversation and thought: *"Why did I say yes when I meant no?"* Or sent an email, then instantly replayed it in your head, worrying how it would land? Or maybe you've sat down to work on something important and, two hours later, found yourself deep in emails, snacks, or scrolling instead. That's your Judge running the show.

The good news? You already have a different operating system inside you—your Power Brain. And the reset button you practiced in the last chapter—those ten-second Pepper Reps—are your way in. Your Power Brain is the version of you that shows up steady, clear, and resourceful even when stress is loud. Think of it like five core muscles, each carrying a superpower:

- **Empathize:** The warmth that lets you connect and love without judgment.
- **Explore:** The curiosity that sees more angles and asks better questions.
- **Innovate:** The creativity that plays with fresh ideas instead of looping the same old ones.
- **Navigate:** The discernment that knows your values and can choose with clarity.
- **Activate:** The bold energy that stops overthinking and gets you moving.

These five muscles don't replace your rational mind—they expand it. Together, they give you access to your whole brain, not just the Judge's narrow voice. This how you reclaim choice, ease, and flow. But you cannot fully step into your Power Brain without self-love. Each of these muscles rests on the belief that you are already worthy—not because of what you achieve or how others see you, but simply because you exist. Without that foundation, every tool collapses back into the Judge's grip.

You were born whole. Over time, saboteurs layered fear, shame, and judgment on top of that wholeness—like plaster covering gold. Eventually, you forgot what was underneath. But your Pepper Self—your true essence—never broke. It was only hidden.

Your job is not to change your essence but to rediscover it— and love it. Over time, the saboteurs whispered lies: that you are *not enough, not yet, not until.* And so, you worked harder for a love that never lasted, because the Judge always moved the finish line.

It's exhausting. Endless. Unless you remember: **Your Pepper Self is already worthy. You don't need to earn love—you need to return to it.**

Meet Your Pepper Self

Let me tell you two stories, the first from 1700s Thailand. When invaders threatened a village, monks covered their massive golden Buddha in layers of plaster to disguise it, and the invaders left it behind. But over centuries, everyone forgot what was hidden beneath. Until one day, a crack revealed the truth: Inside that plaster statue was a solid Buddha of pure gold. Covered, disguised, and forgotten for 200 years—yet untouched at its core.

You were born golden. Over time, you covered yourself with plaster to survive—fear, shame, judgment, "not enough." Eventually you forgot what was underneath. But your essence remains—unchanged, unbroken, waiting.

The second story is from Italy. When Michelangelo was asked how he carved his statue of David, he said: *"I saw the angel in the marble and carved until I set him free."* David was always inside the block of stone. Michelangelo didn't invent him—he simply chipped away everything that wasn't David.

The plaster of the Buddha, the marble around David—those are your saboteurs. They are not you. Your Pepper Self has always been there. Your job is not to become something new, but to **chip away everything you are not.**

When you begin returning to love—when you chip away the plaster—everything shifts. Compassion toward yourself softens how you see others. The colleague who snaps may look arrogant, but under their mask is a brutal Judge. The partner who criticizes may look harsh, but underneath is fear. For ten seconds, if you picture them as a five-year-old—cheeks flushed, eyes wide, desperate to be accepted—something in you melts. Judgment turns to compassion. You bypass the armor and meet the essence.

And it doesn't stop there. The warmth of a cup of tea, the sound of birds at dawn, the miracle of your own breath. These aren't small things. They're proof that life isn't just survivable—it's beautiful. This is also where the law of attraction (as discussed in Chapter 4) comes alive. When you shift from fear to gratitude, your nervous system opens instead of contracts. What you radiate, you attract. The more you practice seeing beauty, the more beauty appears. Even your body—so often attacked by the Judge—becomes different. Instead of criticizing wrinkles, weight, or imperfections, you see it as miraculous: the vehicle that carried you through every single day of your life. It deserves care, not punishment. And when you love it, you naturally treat it better.

This is where the Power Brain begins, not with strategy or effort but with **remembering your worth.** And from that place of unconditional love, you're ready to step into practice. Each Pepper Rep is a mental push-up—small in effort, huge in return. Every Rep loosens the Judge's grip, strengthens your Power Brain, and invests in your true self. And from here, we begin.

PEPPER REP:
SELF-LOVE

Self-love is a practice. Most of us learned to tie love to conditions, but true self-love begins when you remember who you already are—your Pepper Self, your essence. That part of you never changed. It's as unique as your fingerprint, as steady as your heartbeat, and as worthy of love now as the day you were born. This Pepper Rep helps you activate the part of your brain that can feel unconditional love: your Power Brain.

How to do it:

- Find a quiet spot. Optional: hold a childhood photo.
- Close your eyes and take a few deeper-than-usual breaths. Feel your chest rise and fall, then let your breath settle.
- Imagine yourself as a child. If you don't recall a happy moment, create one—running outside, laughing, or being held by someone who loved you. Let the details fill in: colors, sounds, smells, the look in your eyes.
- Step into that scene as your adult self. Approach your child-self with care. Notice what they might long to hear. Say it. Offer love without conditions.
- When you're ready, embrace that child. Feel them merge into you, reminding you of who you've always been.
- Open your eyes. If you have the photo, look at it—not with judgment, but with truth: *This being is precious. This being is worthy. This being is me.*

- Whisper: *"This is the plaster. Underneath, I am my Pepper Self. I am worthy. I am love."*

Your Judge may interrupt: *"This is silly."* Ignore it. With practice, you'll feel a softness grow. Stress lightens; compassion spreads. You'll notice that you begin treating your body, choices, and relationships with more care—not because you *should*, but because love makes care natural. Keep a childhood photo where you'll see it often—on your desk, your mirror, or your phone background. Each time self-criticism shows up, pause and whisper: *"This is just the plaster. Underneath, I am my Pepper Self."*

At night, wrap your arms around yourself in a gentle hug and thank your body for carrying you through another day. But don't stop there. Pepper Reps aren't only about loving yourself. They extend outward—toward others, your body, and your life itself. Each of these reps helps you shift from judgment to compassion, from criticism to care, from scarcity to abundance.

- **Love Others:** When irritation or judgment rises, this rep helps you see past someone's plaster to the Pepper Self beneath. It softens conflict into compassion.
- **Love Your Body:** Instead of attacking your body with criticism, thank it for walking you through life, for breathing, for protecting you. This shifts pressure into gratitude.
- **Love Your Life:** This rep reopens your eyes to joy and possibility, reminding you that even small moments are enough to savor.

Together, these reps form a circle: inward (self-love), outward (others), and upward (life itself). Practiced consistently, they loosen judgment, strengthen compassion, and let you keep returning to your Pepper Self. You'll find the detailed versions of Love Others, Love Your Body, and Love Your Life in Appendix B. For now, know this: When you train yourself to practice love in all directions, you build the strongest foundation for the Power Brain—the place where empathy, curiosity, creativity, clarity, and courage take root.

*   *   *

Empathize With Love

Empathize is about warmth, love, and connection. It's what happens when you pause long enough to tune in and ask: **"What's the human need here?"** Your rational mind is like a hammer: perfect when the job is to hit a nail. But when the need is for care, reassurance, or trust, the hammer only makes dents. Empathy is the brush that lets you paint with softness, step into someone else's world, and see through their eyes. You may solve problems without it, but you won't sustain relationships, navigate conflict well, or engage your whole brain.

Empathy is one of the fastest routes to influence and collaboration. Influence is built on making others feel seen. Collaboration grows in the safety of connection. Empathy activates the relational and creative circuits of your brain, balancing logic with heart. Autopilot wants you to defend, explain, or bulldoze through. Empathy whispers: *Slow down, feel, connect.*

Picture Bryan, leading his ad team in Chicago. The deadline is crushing, and Charlotte delivers late—again. The Judge in Bryan's head hisses: *She's unreliable. She's dragging us down.* His first impulse is to snap. But he remembers that Charlotte's Judge is already brutal on her. Adding more fuel won't help. He tries empathy: *"I can see this was tough. I'll handle slide 6. Could you finalize slide 7?"* Criticism gives way to collaboration. Charlotte doesn't leave smaller—she leaves stronger.

Beneath every mask—arrogance, coldness, defensiveness—lies the same basic need: safety, belonging, love. When you see the child inside, you bypass the armor and meet the essence. And empathy isn't only for others—it's also for yourself. Autopilot either believes negative self-talk or fights it. Empathy responds differently: *"Yes, this is pressure. It's okay. What do I need right now?"* Sometimes it's a glass of water, a two-minute walk, or a phone call to a friend. Sometimes it's naming the truth: "I'm tired. I need rest."

Self-compassion doesn't mean complacency or excusing harmful patterns. It means creating the inner safety that allows growth. When you're no longer at war with yourself, you have the strength to keep going. When you soften your gaze, relax your jaw, and lower your shoulders 2%, your nervous system shifts into safety. Your body tells your brain: *"It's safe to connect."* From there, you can meet others without defensiveness.

But beware of false empathy: confusing empathy with fixing, rescuing, or pleasing. True empathy listens to understand instead of rushing to solve. It doesn't erase boundaries—it respects them. Empathize is the antidote to disconnection, building trust through presence. That is the foundation of real influence.

Exploring With Curiosity

Explore is curiosity with teeth. It's the Power Brain move that widens the frame when life collapses into "This is bad." The Judge loves narrow certainty: *You failed. There's no way out.* Explore interrupts that spiral and asks, **"What's the fuller truth here?"**

Start small. You're stuck in traffic or waiting in a checkout line. Judge: *Wasted time.* Explore reframes: *Training time. Drop your shoulders 2%, soften your jaw, do sixty seconds of Pepper Reps.* By the time the light turns green, your body is steadier, your focus sharper. Waiting became practice.

You ship a deck with the wrong date on the title slide. Judge: *Careless. Amateur.* Explore notices the tight belly, takes one breath, and asks, "What's the smallest useful lesson?" You implement a two-line pre-send checklist. A $100 embarrassment prevents a $1,000 failure later. Conflicts shift, too, when you move from reacting in anger to looking for the opportunity to collaborate.

Hardship needs nuance. You feel pain. Explore asks, "What might this be training me for?" Resilience? Boundaries? A clearer picture of who you want to be? You wouldn't wish it on anyone, and yet there's a seed to water. Explore steps back until the whole picture appears. Learn to Explore in the moment:

- **Zoom out:** Ask, "How will this matter in a month?" or "How might other stakeholders be seeing this?".
- **Zoom in:** Ask what exactly happened vs. what you're assuming.
- **Flip the angle:** Ask, "What would prove my take wrong?"
- **Five Whys:** Keep asking "Why?" until you hit the root.
- **One breath in the body:** Tension = tunnel vision; one slow exhale = a wider lens.

Explore doesn't sugarcoat—it reclaims perspective so you can move from *Why me?* to *What now?*

Innovating With Play

Innovate is the Power Brain's spark. It's the mode that turns raw material—setbacks, routines, even pain—into fresh possibilities. Where the Judge insists there are no good options, Innovate answers: "Let's play." It's about loosening the Judge's grip and generating options without pressure. It's creativity with a purpose.

Take a lost pitch. The Judge says you blew it. Innovate runs a 7-minute blitz: no criticism, no editing, just flow. Write every idea down—no matter how silly. And here's the key: **Every idea carries at least 10% that's worth keeping.**

- Publish what we learned.
- Ask the client for a two-minute debrief.
- Cut the deck into modules so the next version is 50% faster.

When the storm clears, you circle the 10% in each idea—transparency, feedback, speed—and stack them into a concrete plan. Suddenly what looked like failure becomes leverage. Or picture a fight with your partner. The Judge wants the same tired script: rehearse, accuse, defend. Innovate shifts the stage: go for a walk instead of sitting across the kitchen table. Pretend you're teammates solving a puzzle, not opponents in court. Add humor to crack the tension. Play doesn't erase the issue—it creates new ground for connection.

Innovate thrives on the 10% rule. You just need a starting idea, a fragment you can build on. Ten scraps of "10%" combine into something solid. Sometimes the gift is small: a checklist to avoid a repeat mistake. Sometimes it's life-shaping: a layoff that frees you to chase work that truly fits. Either way, Innovate interrupts *Why me?* and shifts you toward acceptance: *What now?*

PEPPER TIME 18: UPSET & ACCEPT

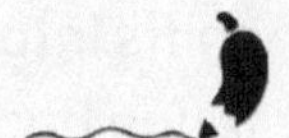

Timing: 1–3 minutes, anytime you feel upset, tense, or stuck in negative emotions.

What you'll need: Just yourself (optional: private space for full-body release)

What it's about: Pairing a clear mental choice—*I choose to accept*—with a physical release so your nervous system feels the shift.

How to do it:

1. **Bring up the trigger.** Call to mind something that genuinely upsets you or stirs tension.
2. **Tense your body.** Tighten everything—jaw, fists, shoulders, toes—for 10 seconds. Really feel the strain.
3. **Release and accept.** Exhale fully, let tension melt away, whisper, *"I choose to accept"*—add a small, gentle smile.
4. **Use discreet versions when needed:**

- Jaw reset: Clench your jaw for 10 seconds, relax, think, *I choose to accept*, and smile.
- Hidden hand version: Squeeze fists under the table for 10 seconds, open your hands, think, *I choose to accept*, and smile.
- Toe press: Press your toes into the floor for 10 seconds, release, think, *I choose to accept*, and smile.

What to expect: The bigger the contrast between tension and release, the deeper the relief. With practice, stress shifts into calm faster, and the Judge's grip loosens. Acceptance becomes a real, felt choice.

Reflection

____

____

____

____

____

____

____

*   *   *

Here are three important things to understand about acceptance:

1. **Acceptance isn't passive.** It's an active, conscious decision to release tension and create space, even if the situation hasn't changed.
2. **Acceptance must be repeated.** The Judge will rarely give up after just one round. Each repetition is like a bicep curl for your Power Brain.
3. **Acceptance doesn't have to be forever.** Acceptance brings relief now; conversion creates growth when you're ready.

 # Start with yourself. When we judge ourselves, so much of our suffering comes from repetitive self-attacks. The suffering repeats not because of the slip, but because of the Judge's replay. That's where you practice the switch. Notice it. Accept the sting in both your body and your words—tense, release, whisper: "I choose to accept." And then, when you're ready, convert it into repair, a Pepper Gift: Apologize, create a checklist, set a boundary.

I used to beat myself up for having a bad memory. At some point, I started practicing acceptance. I did a Pepper Rep, let go of the tension, and stopped spiraling. Later, I converted it by putting in systems that supported me—writing things down, delegating details. That turned what felt like a flaw into fuel for becoming a better leader. Instead of trying to micro-manage, I focused on the big picture and built teams around me who were great with details.

Ask yourself: What is one situation you haven't made peace with yet? One recurring problem that keeps bringing you suffering? Now choose—accept or convert.

 # Apply it to others. About 69% of problems in long-term relationships are unsolvable differences in personality, values, or preferences. The same pattern shows up at work with colleagues or family members. The Judge says fight, resist, complain. Power Brain says accept or convert. Accept might look like doing a quick Pepper Rep when the irritation rises, tensing and releasing your body while whispering, "I accept." The thought may return, but every time you release it, your sage muscle grows stronger. Convert is when you convert it to a Pepper Gift like setting a boundary, writing a script for responding, or creating a workflow that reduces friction. Either way, you reclaim peace instead of fueling the cycle.

 # Apply it to circumstances. Health conditions, financial stress, caretaking responsibilities, chronic challenges in work or family life. Acceptance here means actively releasing the tension that keeps you locked in unhappiness. Tense your fists, jaw, or toes for ten seconds, release, and whisper: "I choose to accept." Do this every time the Judge returns, even if it's twenty times a day. Over time, the Judge will visit less often, and when it does, it won't hit as hard. Conversion can come later. You also don't have to convert everything—some situations aren't worth the energy. Prioritize the ones where a gift or opportunity is possible, and accept the rest.

If you don't accept, you stay stuck. Acceptance doesn't make the problem disappear, but it gives you peace now. Conversion to a Pepper Gift, when you're ready, gives you growth later. Together, they keep you from wasting energy on battles you cannot win. And when you're ready to move, Innovate will always give you the next step.

Navigating With Clarity

Navigate is the compass of your Power Brain. The Judge wants to pull you into panic. Navigate slows the spin and asks the deeper question: What really matters here? Without Navigate, you can hustle, generate ideas, even act boldly—and still end up climbing the wrong ladder faster. With Navigate, every step lines up with your values, your vision, and the life you want to build.

You feel the difference in your body. Out of alignment, your chest is tight, breath shallow, shoulders tense, mind buzzing with "shoulds." Back in alignment, you exhale longer, plant your feet, let your shoulders drop, and ask: *"What's truly important right now?"* That small pause is how Navigate opens the door to wiser choices.

Think of an argument with someone you love. Your partner says, "Yesterday I felt like I didn't matter." The Judge shouts: "Defend yourself. Prove your point." Autopilot jumps to explain your busy schedule. Navigate asks instead: *"What matters most—being right, or protecting love and trust?"* You Accept the sting with a breath ("I choose to accept"), Explore the fuller truth (they felt unseen), then Activate a small, aligned step: "Friday, let's put phones away and just eat together." What could have become distance becomes closeness again.

Or picture your workday. Your list has 14 tasks the Judge deems urgent. Navigate steps in: *"Which three tasks actually move the needle? Which protect my health and relationships?"* Suddenly, you see clearly: one revenue driver, one health boundary (log off at 7 p.m.), one relationship deposit (call a key client). The rest gets parked without guilt. You traded busyness for meaning.

The Judge wants you to fight conflicts, temptations, and decisions forever. Navigate teaches another path: **Accept** what won't change, **Convert** what you can into a Pepper Gift (learning or boundaries), and then steer by values. Navigate in action means:

- Asking: *"What value is at stake here—trust, health, integrity, freedom, love?"*
- Pausing before yes or no, and weighing short-term relief against long-term alignment.
- Choosing the small step that reflects who you want to be, not who the Judge says you are.

Navigate doesn't erase hard trade-offs, but it removes regret. Even in loss, you know you acted in line with what matters. That lets you move forward with peace instead of spinning in "What if."

Activating With Courage

If Navigate is your compass, Activate is your engine. It's the muscle that takes clarity and turns it into motion. The Judge screams: *"It's too much. You'll never manage this. You'll fail."* Autopilot responds with avoidance—emails, scrolling, cleaning. Activate cuts through the noise with one simple question:

What's the next step? Big projects and scary moments don't need big hero moves. They need one clear action. That's how you break paralysis.

Picture yourself at your desk. The deadline is looming, but you're stuck in a loop of distractions. The Judge calls you lazy. Autopilot keeps you busy without progress. Activate interrupts: *"One minute."* Open the document. Write the first sentence. Momentum begins. Even if you stop after that, the engine has turned over.

Now raise the stakes. You're about to walk into the board-room. The Judge whispers: *"Don't mess this up. Don't forget slide three."* Autopilot panics, speeds up, and spirals. Activate reminds you to ground your feet, breathe deep into your belly, soften your jaw. You walk in steady. When the tough question lands, you pause, breathe, and ask for clarification. What could have been collapse turns into presence.

And it's not just for big moments. Everyday resistance is Activate's playground. The phone call you dread. The workout that feels heavy. The Judge says: *"Too hard."* Activate says: *"Shrink it. Just the first step."* Your body is the switch. Straighten your spine. Open your chest. Plant your feet. Breathe low and slow. Suddenly, the task feels doable. The Judge's *"You'll never manage this"* weakens. In its place grows a new reflex: *"I can take the next step."*

That's how paralysis turns into progress. Activate isn't about frantic doing. It's about wise, courageous movement—one clear step at a time. And when paired with Navigate's compass, every step you take isn't just forward—it's forward in the right direction.

Orchestrating The Five Power Brains

Stress, conflict, and opportunity usually arrive messy, making it easy for the Judge to scatter your thoughts. The Power Brain is strongest when you let the five muscles work together, like beams of light focused into a laser. Scattered light is weak. Focused light cuts through steel.

Think of public speaking. Just before you walk on stage, the Judge whispers: *"You'll forget. They'll laugh. You're not ready."* Autopilot panics, throat locks, chest tightens. Then the five powers join forces:

- **Activate** breaks it down: *Step one—walk to the stage. Step two—say the first line.*
- **Empathize** says: *"Anyone would feel nervous—it means I care."*
- **Explore** widens the truth: Most people aren't judging— they're hoping you'll do well.
- **Innovate** reshapes the picture: The crowd becomes one friendly face, not a sea of eyes.
- **Navigate** reminds: *What matters isn't perfect delivery—it's connection.*

The same energy that froze you becomes fuel. You walk out steady, heart pounding—but it powers you instead of paralyzing you.

And here's the hidden gift of orchestration: when you live this way, you don't just change yourself—you influence everyone around you. Remember, people change only when they feel ready—not when you push. Pressure always backfires. I learned this the hard way with Tobias, my partner. Open communication wasn't modeled for him growing up the way it was for me. So when I tried to talk things through, what he heard wasn't "I want connection." It was "You're failing. You're not enough." His Judge piled on, louder and louder. That's when I finally saw it: No matter how valid my reasons, pressure only deepened the gap.

So, I stopped pushing. I stopped trying to explain us back into safety. Instead, I began to model what I wanted to feel. Tobias had walked away from something he'd always loved: golf. It had been his spark for years, but stress had dimmed it. Instead of asking him to return, I signed up myself. I practiced. I got certified. I went out on the course alone. At first, he stayed home. Then one day, he came to watch. He cheered me on. Slowly, he picked up his clubs again. And soon, he found his spark. I hadn't demanded change. I had lived change. That's the essence of influence.

Humans are contagious. We pick up energy, habits, and attitudes from each other. If you want your family to be healthier, don't lecture them—live it. Put your running shoes by the door the night before. Stock the fridge with food that matches the life you want to live. If you want more openness in your team, share vulnerably and then listen. If you want love to return in your marriage, lead with empathy. Model the care you wish to receive. Influence is about presence—the way you live, model, and embody the five powers. When you hold steady, others feel safe enough to access them, too. This is the true loop of success.

- **Empathize builds warmth and trust.** Connection is the seedbed of influence.

- **Explore widens the frame and reveals the fuller truth.** The fuller truth softens judgment and opens doors where walls had stood.
- **Innovate reframes setbacks into soil and play.** Playfulness loosens the Judge's grip and allows fresh possibilities to grow where only stress existed before.
- **Navigate anchors you to what truly matters.** It filters out noise so your choices reflect your values.
- **Activate shrinks the step into bold movement.** Movement breaks inertia. Small acts stack into progress. And progress compounds into real change.

Together, these powers are the architecture of a new way of being. Life won't stop throwing challenges. But when you orchestrate the five powers—and live them out loud—you stop being ruled by hardness. You model ease and presence, and presence ripples. Your willingness to listen shifts the tone of your team. Your small acts of courage give others permission to try. Influence spreads quietly, reshaping families, friendships, and workplaces.

PEPPER TIME 19:
The I.N.F.L.U.E.N.C.E. METHOD

Timing: 5–15 minutes per conversation or reflection. Best when you feel the urge to push someone to change.

What you'll need: Yourself, curiosity, and patience. Optional: Your journal to track patterns.

What it's about: Influence is presence—combining empathy, curiosity, creativity, action, and clarity—creating space where others *want* to change while you keep your peace.

How to do it: follow I.N.F.L.U.E.N.C.E.

I – Inquire (Empathize & Explore). Ask. Open-ended questions are about uncovering the fuller truth and meeting the other person's need:

- "How do you feel about this?"
- "What's working for you right now?"
- "Have you thought about what you'd want to do about it?"

N – Notice (Activate presence). Ground yourself before reacting. Breathe, soften shoulders, check: *Am I in Judge or Power Brain?* One calm presence can shift the whole exchange.

F – Frame (Navigate). Set the bigger picture. Why does this matter—for you, for them, for the relationship? Name it in one sentence.

L – Let go. People only change when they want to. Release pressure. Think seed-planting: water, don't force.

U – Uplift small steps. Acknowledge even tiny progress. Encouragement fuels momentum.

E – Evaluate deal-breakers. If nothing shifts after months, ask: *Could I accept this forever?* If not, the choice is yours.

N – Neutralize loops. Stop rehashing the same complaints. If you choose to stay, accept them fully. Resentment kills connection faster than flaws.

C – Check compatibility. Sometimes it's not habits but values. If you can't imagine peace long-term, it may be a life decision, not an influence problem.

E – Embody change (Innovate). Model it. Eat the healthy meal, put down the phone, live the presence. Behavior is contagious.

What to expect: At first, your Judge screams: *"It's unfair—they should change!"* With practice, you'll feel lighter, free of the impossible job of controlling someone else. Over time, people often shift—not because you pushed, but because you lived it.

Bottom line: The only behavior you can fully control is your own. But with the I.N.F.L.U.E.N.C.E. method, you stop pressuring and start inspiring. That's how real change begins.

Reflection

____

____

____

____

____

____

*   *   *

PEPPER ASK:
THE 5 POWER BRAIN QUESTIONS

Each Power Brain muscle has one simple entry point: a question. When the Judge hijacks you, ask the right question, take the small step, and you flip back into your Pepper Self.

- **Empathize:** *"What's the human need here?" Slow down, feel, soften. See the five-year-old inside yourself or the other person. Add warmth.*
- **Explore:** *"What's the fuller truth?" Zoom out. Name the bigger picture. Look for the missing angles instead of clinging to the fragment.*
- **Innovate:** *"What's another way?" Generate options playfully. Don't critique. Stack the 10% you like from each idea.*
- **Navigate:** *"What really matters most here?" Anchor back to values and priorities. Choose alignment over winning.*
- **Activate:** *"What's the one next step?" Breathe, focus, move. Shrink the task to the smallest action, and do it now.*

Supercharging Your State

Most days, the small tools are enough. A Pepper Rep. A 10-second release. A whispered "I choose to accept." And just like that, you're back in flow. But some days, the Judge comes swinging. or life stacks several problems all at once.

Suddenly, the little reps don't hold. It's not enough to breathe for ten seconds. You need something bigger. That's when you **Supercharge.**

Supercharge is your reset button. Supercharge is all-in: body, breath, and joy. It overwhelms the Judge by flooding your system with energy and celebration. The Judge only ever offers *conditional joy* with things you must do to achieve it. The Power Brain flips the script: Joy isn't earned. It's created—here, now, no matter what just happened.

How? Move, laugh, shake out your arms. Jump around, dance to the song that lights you up, playfully bounce in your chair. The form doesn't matter. What matters is that it cracks the Judge's grip and lets joy flood back in. Yes, the Judge will sneer. Ignore it. That voice is plaster. Supercharge is you breaking through to the gold.

PEPPER TIME 20:
SUPERCHARGE

Timing: 2–5 minutes, anytime a normal rep isn't enough to shift your state.

What you'll need: Music, space to move, and a willingness to feel silly.

What it's about: Break the Judge's spiral by flooding your system with energy, movement, and unconditional joy.

How to do it:

1. **Check your mood.** Rate how you feel right now on a scale of 1–10
2. **Move to music.** Put on a song you love and let yourself go: dance, jump, laugh, shake, get playful—whatever feels freeing.
3. **Stay with it.** Keep moving until you sense a real shift in your body—sometimes one minute, sometimes five.
4. **Re-check your mood.** Rate yourself again. Notice the change.

What to expect: At first, resistance. The Judge whispers: *"Don't. This won't work."* Push through. Soon your body takes over. Energy rises. Stress melts. Joy comes back online.

Once you've charged, ask your Power Brain: *What's needed now?* If the answer is clear—make the call, open the file, send the message—do it. If the answer is unclear, let the five powers guide you: Empathize to connect, Explore to widen perspective, Innovate to spark options, Navigate to remember what matters, Activate to take the next step. Supercharge isn't about pretending everything is fine. It's about giving yourself enough fuel to choose powerfully again.

Reflection

____

____

____

____

____

____

____

*   *   *

Celebrating The Wins

Every time you celebrate—even the smallest win—you're Supercharging.

- Catch the Judge? Celebrate.
- Do one Pepper Rep? Celebrate.
- Say no when you used to say yes? Celebrate.
- Take a breath before reacting? Celebrate.

Because celebration is the spark that ties everything together. And celebration rewires your brain. The Judge will resist, but big wins only happen because of countless small ones. Every micro-celebration triggers dopamine—your brain's reward chemical. What's rewarded gets repeated. That's how you lock in the Power Brain.

And you can dial celebration up or down: A subtle nod, a hand on your heart, a fist pump, a loud "YES!" or a full-blown kitchen dance. The stronger the celebration, the more it drowns out the Judge. But even the smallest smile matters. Especially when you don't feel like it. So celebrate every time you choose your Power Brain over your Judge. That's how you build momentum.

You've now met the five powers of the Power Brain—Empathize, Explore, Innovate, Navigate, Activate—and the fuel that binds them together: Supercharge. Each time you catch the Judge, pause, or take even the smallest step back into your Power Brain, celebrate. That celebration is the accelerator. So pause now. Hand on your heart. Whisper: *I caught it. I shifted. I'm building my Power Brain*. Smile, even 2%. That's a win.

Next, we'll go deeper. You'll learn how to rewrite the noise of the Judge itself, so its voice no longer drives your choices.

Chapter 8:

Rewriting The Noise

The loudest critic in your life is the voice in your own head. The one that whispers, *"You're not ready. You're not enough. Don't mess this up."* That voice isn't you. That voice is the Judge— your master saboteur. And if you don't learn to spot it, it will run your life.

You've trained your brain with Pepper Reps, felt how ten seconds of presence can interrupt autopilot and bring you back to center, and met your five Power Brain muscles: Empathize, Explore, Innovate, Navigate, and Activate. Together, they give you clarity, warmth, courage, and direction when life gets loud. But there's still one force inside all of us that doesn't give up easily: the Judge.

The Judge is the voice that insists you're not ready, not enough, not lovable, not worthy. It loops like a broken record. Sometimes the Judge borrows the tone of a parent, teacher, or boss. Other times it dresses up as "reasonable." Either way, it doesn't keep you safe—it keeps you small. As a child, that voice may have helped you avoid pain. But as an adult, it becomes a cage.

You are not the Judge. The critical voice lives in you, but it is not you. The moment you notice it and say, *"I'm hearing my Judge right now,"* you create distance. That's power. The Judge feels so convincing, but there's a difference between the Judge's pronouncements and realistic thinking.

The Judge	Realistic Thinking
"This presentation will be a disaster."	"What would make this presentation land better?"
"I always mess this up."	"Last time went fine after two rehearsals—let's repeat that."
"If it isn't perfect, it's worthless."	"Good enough here—I'll polish the key slide only."
"Am I qualified—yes or no?"	"Which parts am I ready for, and who can help with the rest?"
"We don't have resources."	"What can we ship with what we have now?"
"What's wrong with me?"	"What's needed now?"

One loops in fear. The other moves forward with clarity. Fortunately, understanding the Judge will take you a long way toward silencing it.

The Three Faces Of The Judge

The Judge doesn't always attack from the same angle. It wears three masks. Once you learn to spot them, you'll notice how often they hijack your thoughts.

 # The Judge of Self. This is the harshest voice—the one that turns inward. It says: *"I'm not good enough. I'll fail. I don't belong here."* The Judge convinces you your successes don't count—that they were luck, that you'll be found out. Over time, you stop stepping forward—not because you can't, but because you believe the noise.

 # The Judge of Others. This mask flips outward. Instead of cutting you down, it cuts down the people around you. *"She's incompetent. He's lazy. They'll never get it right."* The Judge of Others doesn't just damage them—it shrinks you too, because it keeps you locked in blame instead of influence.

 # The Judge of Circumstances. This one is sneakier. It blames the situation itself: *"This is unfair. The timing is terrible. Nothing ever works out for me."* But circumstances aren't good or bad until you decide the story. The Judge declares, "This is terrible." But often, what looks like loss today becomes training or opportunity tomorrow.

The Judge is wired into you, but it doesn't have to drive your choices. When you name it—when you say, *"This is my Judge talking"*—you break its trance. You remember: **I am not the critic. I am the one who notices the critic.** If the Judge runs your relationships, you end up defensive, withdrawn, circling the same fights. If it runs your performance, you overwork, over-prepare, and still feel like a fraud. If it runs your well-being, stress hormones spike until joy evaporates.

But once you see its masks, you can choose differently. You can catch it, name it, and shift back into your Power Brain—where empathy, curiosity, creativity, discernment, and courage wait for you. And that's exactly where we go next: not just noticing the Judge, but **rewiring its noise at the root—so it no longer runs your relationships, your work, or your joy.**

Now it's time to put this into practice with one of the simplest yet most powerful Pepper Times in the book. It's easy, it's direct, and it works—if you do it. Some days you may need it once. Other days, ten times. Occasionally, a hundred.. Each time you practice, you're reclaiming choice from your Judge. This experiment trains you to catch the Judge in the act, quiet its grip, and redirect your energy into the Power Brain—where clarity, courage, and momentum live.

PEPPER TIME 21:
TAMING THE JUDGE

Timing: 3–5 minutes, whenever the Judge's voice shows up (or once daily as practice).

What you'll need: Just you, a quiet moment, and optionally, your journal.

What it's about: This practice creates distance so you stop obeying your Judge and start choosing for yourself. The more you rehearse, the faster you'll spot it and the weaker its grip becomes.

How to do it: Follow the steps below without overthinking.

1. **Notice & Label.** The instant you hear that inner critic, pause and call it by name: *"Oh, I'm hearing my Judge right now."* That one line is the foundation. It reminds you: This isn't me.
2. **Separate "I" from the Judge.** Language is powerful here. Instead of saying, *"I'm freaking out,"* switch to, *"My Judge is having a freak-out."* Instead of, *"I'm not good enough,"* try, *"My Judge is telling me I'm not good enough."* This small shift trains your brain to see the Judge as just one of many voices.
3. **Give It a Character.** Name it. Visualize it. Personify it so it feels less like you and more like a noisy sidekick. Maybe yours looks like a cranky boss tapping a pen, a gremlin whispering in your ear, or a lawyer in a ridiculous wig objecting to everything. Humor cuts its authority. Gave it a name: Judging Jane or Becky Brain.
4. **Ask Its Motive.** This step matters because every Judge line is rooted in fear. Gently ask, *"What are you trying to protect me from?"* Often the answer is rejection, humiliation, failure, disapproval. Instead of fighting, thank it: *"Thanks for trying to keep me safe, but I've got this covered."* This flips the Judge from enemy to misguided ally.
5. **Play With the Volume.** Imagine a dial in your mind, and turn it down to a whisper. Or imagine the Judge's voice fading into the distance, like a radio losing signal.

6. **Move It Out.** Physically pantomime placing Judge-thoughts into a cup, box, or jar and setting it aside. Or visualize walking your Judge character to the door and sending it on vacation. The body loves rituals—they make the shift feel real.

7. **Find the Humor.** When your Judge says, *"You'll ruin your reputation forever,"* exaggerate it until it sounds absurd: *"You'll fail and the entire galaxy will collapse."* Laughing at its drama breaks the spell.

What to expect: More distance from self-criticism, quicker recovery from doubt, and less energy wasted arguing with yourself. With practice, the Judge shows up—but you no longer take it seriously. Attention returns to what matters.

Reflection

____

____

____

____

____

____

*   *   *

Don't wait for the "perfect moment" to start—your Judge feeds on hesitation. It will never fully disappear, but you don't need it to. The practice is to notice it, name it, and keep moving. Over time, you'll catch it faster, take it less seriously, and waste far less energy wrestling with it. You'll recover from self-doubt more quickly, reclaim focus, and free up space for what matters.

You're calmly acknowledging the Judge, then choosing not to obey. That's the muscle you're building. And the Judge doesn't just live in your head—it tightens your chest, clenches your jaw, and shortens your breath. To loosen its grip, recall a recent Judge moment. Step into it fully: Exaggerate the posture, repeat its words, notice the weight in your body. Stay long enough to recognize, *"This is what it feels like when the Judge runs me."* Then release. Straighten your spine, drop your shoulders, open your chest. Imagine warm rain washing the tension through you. Exhale deeply and whisper: *"This is not me. This is my Judge."*

This is the same muscle you train with the Stop Sign Rep (Pepper Time 13), catching the Judge mid-sentence and halting its spiral, and Upset & Accept (Pepper Time 18), feeling anger in your body, then letting it move through instead of getting stuck. Each rep builds your ability to notice, feel, and release. Anchor the shift with a Pepper Rep: rub your fingertips, follow your breath, or tune into one sound. The contrast is the proof—heavy and tight versus light and present.

Over time, this becomes one of the simplest yet most enduring habits you'll build. It lays the foundation for peace, clarity, and resilience. The Judge will always return—especially when you stretch into something new. Your job is to notice it, thank it, and lead anyway. Once you can feel the Judge in your posture and breath, it stops being "you" and becomes just a pattern. And patterns can be changed.

PEPPER ASK:

Spot Your Judge in Action. Your Judge will always show up—but you can get faster at catching it. Use these prompts to build your own action plan for dealing with your Judge: 

- What pops up when you speak in a risky meeting?
- What does it say about an exciting career move or your big idea?
- What does it whisper if you start a creative project or post online?
- What do you hear, walking into a room where you know no one?
- How does it sound when you're challenged as a parent, partner, or friend?
- What about reclaiming a hobby or sharing work publicly?
- What comes up in the mirror each morning?

Notice not just the words, but the type of Judge at work:

- **Self-Judge:** "I messed up," "I'm not enough."
- **Judge of Others:** irritation, disappointment, frustration.
- **Judge of Circumstances:** complaints, rumination, resentment.

Look ahead at your week. What situations are likely to trigger each Judge? Anticipation makes it far more likely you'll catch them in real time. And when you do—celebrate. A smile, a stretch, a checkmark in your journal. Every small celebration rewires the habit and strengthens your Power Brain.

Writing Your Contract

Being stuck in a thought that makes you unhappy works against you in two ways:

1. It makes you feel awful—and who wants that?
2. It adds no value whatsoever.

The only way to change your life is to be in charge, so I signed a contract with my brain. When my mom died, the thought was deeply painful. It triggered a physical ache in my chest. Every time Brainy said, "Your mom died," I answered: "Yes, I know, Brainy. But she also lived." I chose to hold the joyful side: remembering the laughter we shared, looking at pictures and videos, hearing her voice in memory. I refused to let the Judge keep me only in grief.

I signed a contract with myself: I will return to useful thoughts. Yes, my brain kept throwing "what ifs" at me. Each time, I came back to the same response: Give me a useful thought. With persistence, the spiral loosened its grip. Everything else? Noise. My Judge wanted me locked in pain. My contract said: Return to useful thoughts. This is what I invite you to do now.

PEPPER TIME 22:
WRITE YOUR CONTRACT

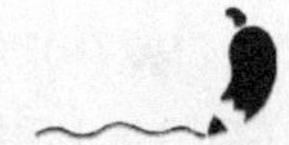

Timing: 10–20 minutes once, then revisit monthly or when the Judge gets loud.

What you'll need: Your journal, a pen, and a quiet moment.

What it's about: Your Judge thrives on vagueness. A written contract flips the script. By putting your commitment into words, you tell your brain: I choose clarity and courage over fear and paralysis.

How to do it:

1. **Create space.** Find a quiet spot where you won't be interrupted.
2. **Write your contract.** Copy the sample contract into your journal or craft your own version. Print it or write it by hand, then sign it.
3. **Read it aloud.** Speak the words slowly, and let them land in your body.
4. **Keep it visible.** Place it somewhere you'll see often—on your desk, mirror, or phone background—to remind yourself daily that you're in charge.

Dear Brainy,
I know you mean well. You try to keep me safe from pain, rejection, and failure.
But I'm no longer letting the Judge drive my life.
From today, I choose to hear you—without obeying you.

I, ___________________________, commit to noticing when my Judge hijacks my thoughts and to responding with clarity, compassion, and action.

- If the Judge says: *"You're not good enough,"*
  I will answer: *"Thanks for your input, but I've got this covered."*
- If the Judge says: *"You'll embarrass yourself,"*
  I will answer: *"Embarrassment is a teacher, not a prison. I move anyway."*

- If the Judge says: *"People will laugh at you,"*
  I will answer: *"Then they're watching. Good. I'm visible."*
- If the Judge says: *"Someone else has already done it better,"*
  I will answer: *"No one can do it exactly as me. My voice matters."*
- If the Judge says: *"You'll ruin your reputation if you fail,"*
  I will answer: *"Failure is data, not destiny. My reputation is built on courage, not silence."*

I will not sign false contracts of unhappiness. I choose thoughts that are useful: to experience, to solve, to flow, and to give.

Signed: _______________________________________

Date: ____

What to expect: At first, this may feel symbolic or cheesy. But contracts carry weight: They signal to your brain that a decision is made. Over time, you'll notice quicker recovery when the Judge attacks, more confidence to act, and less energy wasted on fear. Each time you read it, you reinforce your Power Brain circuits.

Reflection

---

*   *   *

Taming The Saboteurs

The Judge always speaks first, but it rarely speaks alone. The moment a negative feeling flickers—hesitation, fear, shame, doubt—the accomplice saboteurs pile in. For one breath, their signal might even be useful, telling you something deserves attention. But if you let them take over, they hijack the show. Where do these voices come from? Childhood. We all found ways to feel safe, accepted, and loved. Some of us learned to please, some to control, some to achieve, some to avoid. But what once kept us safe now keeps us small.

We already explored these saboteurs back in Chapter 3, where we named their patterns and saw how universal they are. Now, we're going deeper. This is where awareness turns into power. You've already practiced using the five Power Brain muscles— Empathize, Explore, Innovate, Navigate, and Activate.

Now we'll apply them directly, turning each saboteur from a hijacker into a signal and an entry point back into your power. We'll look at each saboteur one by one. You'll see what its original gift was and how that gift, when overused, backfires. You'll learn the lie it whispers in your ear, the way it shows up in real time, and how to shift into your Power Brain instead. The saboteurs won't vanish. But once you see their tricks, they lose their grip. And instead of obstacles, they become stepping stones.

#1 The Controller. The Controller starts as a strength. It's the voice that moves things forward. When others hesitate, you step in, take charge, set direction, and create momentum. Without it, projects stall and decisions drag. But when the Controller seizes the wheel, the gift flips. Clarity becomes force. Confidence becomes pressure. Instead of leading, you bulldoze. People don't feel empowered—they feel managed. And when people feel pushed, they push back. You may get short-term results, but at the cost of trust, creativity, and loyalty.

Liyana, the head of sales from Dublin we met in Chapter 3, lived this pattern. She was ambitious and bold. But as her scope grew, so did her need to control. She started issuing commands and cutting off discussion. Meetings drained the team instead of energizing them. When we began working together, this was one of the first things I noticed. Her boldness was real, but the Controller had taken the driver's seat. I held up the mirror and showed her how often her need to be efficient was silencing her team. She recognized herself instantly: the tight chest, the quick voice, the way people left meetings deflated. Awareness was the first breakthrough.

The second came in practice. One day she caught herself mid-meeting, her chest tight, her jaw hot. She realized she was about to steamroll the room again. This time she paused and invited each teammate to share two minutes of input. It felt unnatural at first—inefficient, even. But what happened next surprised her. Their ideas sharpened her own thinking. Her plan became stronger. And instead of leaving frustrated, the team left engaged and motivated. That was the turning point.

Together, we worked on rewiring her instinct by leaning into her Power Brain. **She moved from push to pull.** From commanding to co-creating. The decisiveness remained, but it was now anchored in trust and collaboration. Instead of draining the team, she inspired them. And as her leadership matured, she rose even further up the corporate ladder. Her Controller became one instrument in her orchestra, powerful but no longer overwhelming.

#2 The Avoider. The Avoider is easygoing. You keep harmony, make life pleasant, and flow with people. You're the one others find safe, the one who doesn't escalate tension. But when the Avoider runs the show, the gift curdles. Hard conversations and difficult tasks get pushed aside. Harmony turns into silence, and silence into anxiety. The work piles up. The conversation that could heal festers instead. Each delay costs energy—because the task still looms.

That's what happened with Anna, our SaaS builder from Berlin we met in Chapter 3. On paper, she was bold. But she feared not being good enough. Her Avoider kept her safe by postponing key tasks, especially the ones that mattered most, and her confidence eroded quietly in the background.

When we worked together, we broke the pattern. Instead of asking her to finish the whole deck, we agreed she would commit only to the first step: Open the file and title slide one. Then pause, acknowledge it, and allow herself to stop if she wanted to. To her surprise, once the first step was done, momentum carried her further.

By committing to the first step and celebrating it, Anna rewired the Avoider from hiding to handling. Whenever she felt that urge to delay, it became her cue to shrink the task until it was so small she couldn't say no. And with each micro-step, she built momentum, confidence, and resilience.

#3 The Hyper-Achiever. The Hyper-Achiever looks ambitious, resilient, driven. You set goals and smash them. People admire your discipline and grit. But when this drive tips into overfire, it becomes a trap. Your worth becomes welded to your wins. Rest feels unsafe. Joy shows up only for a fleeting moment at the summit—then vanishes in seconds as your eyes scan for the next mountain. The scoreboard never ends, and the Judge is always there, moving the goalpost.

Maya, a COO we met in Chapter 3, lived this rhythm to the extreme. She was the one checking Slack at 2 a.m., chasing commissions at quarter's end, running on fumes. She became addicted to the next achievement—and lost balance. When I began coaching Maya, my first task was simply to hold up the mirror. I reminded her: She was already a powerful, ambitious COO, whether she won the deal or not. Her value wasn't conditional. Together, we rewired her lens on failure—not as proof she was lacking, but as raw material for growth.

I asked her to try something new. Instead of powering through another late-night grind, she blocked forty-five minutes to role-play objections with a colleague. At first, it felt inefficient. But something shifted. She laughed. She remembered she was human, not a machine. She realized leadership wasn't about wringing out another call at midnight; it was about building her team, strengthening the company, and sustaining the whole year—not just the quarter. We worked on rewiring her focus: away from the scoreboard and into the journey itself.

What's compelling along the way? The people you connect with. The impact you make. The growth you experience. The fun you allow yourself to have. When she leaned into the game itself, the pressure loosened its grip. Her results improved. Deals landed more often—not because she was grinding harder, but because she was present, creative, and free. I also asked her to write down one story about a customer she had genuinely helped. That single act transformed numbers into meaning, and meaning became her fuel. That's the Hyper-Achiever rewired: joy baked into today. Success became a resource she could use—not a cage that owned her.

#4 The Hyper-Rational. The Hyper-Rational is sharp. You analyze clearly and stay calm under pressure. Logic is your gift, bringing clarity when others spiral. But when it takes over, emotions are cut out. People don't feel understood—they feel managed. Connection dries up. Life isn't math. People rarely change because of "evidence." They shift when they feel seen.

I saw this up close with friends of Tobi and me. He had missed her birthday; she felt ignored and unloved. She spoke with passion and vulnerability, desperate to connect. He didn't see the big deal and explained what he saw as serious priorities he was busy with. She sank back, ashamed of her feelings. "I feel unheard. I just wanted to be cared for." He truly thought he was being helpful, but without empathy, even the most rational explanation lands as cold, arrogant, or superior—even if that's not your intent.

I stepped in and told him: "This is the moment to make a Power Brain move. Put yourself in her shoes. Ask how she feels. Name it with her. Acknowledge; don't fix." He resisted at first, and I asked, "How would you feel if you missed an important meeting because someone dismissed your preparation?"

Slowly, he began to get it. He tried: "I hear you felt hurt. I'm sorry about the impact that had on you." And for the first time, she softened.

Acknowledging someone's feelings doesn't mean admitting guilt or saying they're objectively right. It means you recognize their inner world as valid. You're saying: *"I see you."* That's what rewires the Hyper-Rational. Logic stays sharp, but it is led by empathy. And when empathy leads, connection builds, trust strengthens, and your logic finally has a place to land.

#5 The Hyper-Vigilant. The Hyper-Vigilant protects. You see risks others miss. You anticipate, prepare, and keep people safe. But when Vigilance overfires, the warnings never stop. And worry doesn't prevent disaster—it only drains you and erodes trust.

This reminds me of Isabella, a digital marketeer from the UK who joined my Scaleur Mastermind. I still laugh when I think back, because she found an excuse for everything. Now she laughs too—but back then her Hyper-Vigilant was in overdrive. Every time she wanted to launch a new product, she could instantly name five potential disasters. Her brain worked like a disaster generator.

I used a simple childhood story to break through: Imagine you live in a village on the edge of the woods, where dangerous tigers sometimes roam. If you stand watch all night, every rustling branch becomes a tiger. You scream so often that by morning, no one believes you anymore. And when the real tiger comes, you're too exhausted to see it.

That landed, and Isabella realized her endless vigilance was backfiring. She wasn't protecting her team; she was exhausting them. Together we mapped out all her fears in one list. Then we categorized them. Out of dozens, maybe one or two were genuine risks. Those few she planned for. The rest, she learned to park. For the first time in weeks, she slept through the night. That's the Hyper-Vigilant rewired: not endless fear, but focused care.

#6 The Pleaser. The Pleaser shines with warmth. You're generous, attuned, kind. You sense needs before others even name them, building trust and connection. But when the Pleaser takes over, you say yes too often, sugarcoat feedback, and mute your own needs. Resentment quietly builds while you're smiling.

This was Sofia's story. We met her back in Chapter 3—early forties, running a successful consulting company in Barcelona. She had a solid reputation, but every time she raised her prices, guilt crept in. Every time she asked her team for more, guilt again. And her default response to requests was always yes. She confused leadership with pleasing. When I coached Sofia, I told her what she most wanted to avoid: "If you keep pleasing, you'll tolerate mediocre performance, and you'll lose trust—not build it."

She had to see that always giving without naming her own needs didn't strengthen relationships, it weakened them. Because when you give but never say what matters to you, the other person doesn't even know what you need. They can't give back. Slowly, resentment replaces connection. I gave her this question: *"Am I choosing to give this freely, or am I giving because I'm afraid they won't like me if I say no?"*

That became her turning point. If it was a genuine yes—she could serve wholeheartedly. But if it was a reluctant yes—the Pleaser was running the show. That was her cue to pause, to do a Pepper Rep. Each time she felt guilty raising prices, or said yes while feeling a no in her gut, she asked herself: *"What would please me here?"*

She no longer gave from fear but from strength. She started giving honest feedback and raised her prices without apology. Her relationships grew stronger. Her team respected her more, her clients trusted her more, and Sofia finally trusted herself. That's the Pleaser rewired. The warmth remains—but it comes from choice, not compulsion.

#7 The Restless. The Restless carries spark. You bring energy, curiosity, ideas. You light up a room. But when Restless overdrives, you skim life instead of living it. Ten projects started, none finished. Your phone pops up in every quiet moment. You chase the next thing, but depth feels dull. Real joy rarely comes from skimming. It comes from presence.

This reminds me of Shella, a product lead from Amsterdam. Brilliant, creative, and always *on*. Shella's Slack was green at midnight, her inbox open before breakfast, her brain buzzing with the next idea before the current one had even launched. The result? Half-finished initiatives, a team stretched thin, and Shella herself exhausted yet unable to switch off.

When we worked together, I asked her to notice the pattern: The moment one project reached stability, she jumped to the next shiny thing. To break it, we built a ritual of pause. Before saying yes, Shella had to ask herself: *"Is this the right depth, or just the next distraction?"* At first, slowing down felt unbearable. But one day, instead of replying to a late-night request, she closed her laptop and sat with her discomfort. The world didn't fall apart. Her team, in fact, stepped up.

The breakthrough came when Shella learned that presence isn't laziness—it's leadership. By staying with one project long enough, she saw it through to real impact. She had dinner with friends without checking her phone. That's the Restless rewired: from chasing novelty to choosing depth. The spark remains, but now it fuels instead of burning.

#8 The Stickler. The Stickler values standards. You care about craft, order, precision. You see what others miss and increase quality. But when the Stickler dominates, perfectionism creeps in. You zoom in on the 1 percent wrong and miss the 99 percent right. Time evaporates into fixing small details. Perfectionism is fear disguised as excellence.

Nadya, a marketing manager preparing for a major pitch, lived this pattern. She was brilliant, disciplined, and committed. But when it came time to deliver, her Stickler hijacked the process. Instead of mapping out the big storyline, she spent hours nudging font sizes and aligning icons on slides no client would notice. The more she fixed, the less progress she made. Her stress mounted, her energy drained, and her confidence wavered.

I challenged her to reframe: *"What 20% truly needs perfection?"* After reflection, she tagged safety copy and pricing as critical and left the fonts as "good enough." For the first time, she experienced the relief of letting go without losing professionalism. And once she focused on clarity instead of cosmetics, the pitch came alive. She practiced storytelling, refined her key messages, and connected with the client in the room. Nadya landed the deal not by chasing flawless slides but by showing up present, confident, and human.

That's the Stickler rewired: high standards, but with perspective. Excellence without exhaustion. The Stickler doesn't disappear, but once you spot it, you can thank it for caring about quality and then invite your Power Brain to lead with balance.

#9 The Victim. The Victim feels deeply. You bring authenticity, honesty, soul. You know life's weight, and that depth is a gift. But when the Victim overfires, pain becomes identity. Self-pity substitutes for connection. People step back. Suffering alone doesn't bring love—it repels it.

I once worked with a colleague who lived this pattern. Every situation became another chapter in his story of being wronged. One evening he was stuck in Brussels traffic, his son crying in the back seat. Instead of seeing a tired child in need of comfort, my colleague saw himself as the victim: of the traffic, of ungratefulness, of bad music on the radio, of the grim news he was forced to hear. And yet the truth wasn't that the world was attacking him—it was that he felt powerless. The suffering gave him an identity, but it didn't give him relief.

I helped him reframe. What if, instead of clinging to pain, he voiced his needs? What if, instead of collapsing into self-pity, he acknowledged the frustration and then chose one small action? He began experimenting with shifting from *"I'm trapped"* to *"I can choose."* In that car, he could have turned the music into a silly sing-along or paused the news and asked his son about his feelings. Not everything would've been solved, but he would've no longer be trapped in the passive role of suffering.

That's the Victim rewired: depth without drowning. Pain still exists, but it's met with agency. Instead of *"look how much I suffer,"* the story becomes *"look how I grow, even here."*

The reason we keep coming back to these saboteurs and voices is simple: every time you catch one and shift, you stop a leak of energy and attention. That freed-up power is exactly what fuels your Power Brain. You're not just coping—you're rewiring by building life-long habits that stick. First comes awareness; next comes practice. Because when saboteurs run on autopilot, they drain your attention, distort your choices, and keep you small.

The impact of that shift ripples outward, too. That's because when you access your Power Brain, you see not just behavior but humanity. Picture this: You're on a plane heading to an important meeting. The passenger behind you keeps sneezing. By the third time, irritation spikes. Most people stew in silence, carrying resentment through the whole flight. But with a shift, you could turn around, kindly ask if they need tissues, or check if they're okay. You could transform hours of annoyance into peace and connection. That's the Power Brain at work: reframing annoyance into curiosity and care.

It's crucial to name your saboteurs, understand them, and learn how to shift. Not just for yourself, but because you live and work with people who also have saboteurs. Recognizing them changes how you lead, love, and collaborate. Here's a simple recap:

Saboteur	Big Lie	Big Shift
Judge	"If I criticize, I'll get better / be safe."	Notice → Name → Shift to acceptance.
Controller	"Without me, nothing moves."	From push to pull → co-create.
Avoider	"If I hide, problems vanish."	From hiding → handling one small step.
Hyper-Achiever	"My worth = my wins."	From scoreboard → to journey + meaning.
Hyper-Rational	"Feelings are noise."	Lead with empathy, not just logic.
Pleaser	"If I give enough, I'll be loved."	Choose when to give, set boundaries.
Hyper-Vigilant	"If I don't worry, disaster will strike."	From endless fear → focused care.
Restless	"The next thing will fulfill me."	Depth over skimming → presence.
Stickler	"If it's not perfect, it's worthless."	High standards, yes → with perspective.
Victim	"My suffering proves I'm real."	Feel deeply → but take action + connect.

 # PEPPER ASK: Which two saboteurs show up strongest for you? Naming them is the first step toward shifting them. Then ask these questions to start catching your own patterns in real time:

- What benefits would you gain if you caught and quieted your top two saboteurs this week?
- How will you know when your top two saboteurs have taken over?
  (Example: Stickler → I feel stressed about tiny details being imperfect. Avoider → I procrastinate on anything "unpleasant." Controller → I get irritated when someone disagrees with me. Hyper-Vigilant → I spiral into "what if" scenarios.)
- Looking ahead to this week: What situations do you expect will activate your #1 and #2 saboteurs? Anticipating makes it far more likely you'll catch them before they hijack you.
- When you do catch them, how will you celebrate to reinforce the practice?

Rewiring Your Fear

Conquering your saboteurs will go a long way toward helping you tame your fears, but fear comes in many forms. For some, it's obvious, like fear of heights, spiders, or needles. Other fears are harder to spot, like fear of rejection, failure, not being enough, or not having the resources to build the life you want. But no matter how it shows up, fear is the granddaddy of illusions.

Back in Chapter 1, we explored how fear is your brain's ancient survival trick. It keeps you alive, but it also keeps you small.

Left unchecked, fear builds invisible walls around your freedom. That's why we need to tackle it head-on, rewrite it, and stop letting it run the show. The first step to freedom is simple but hard: **Admit you are afraid.** No problem can be solved until it's named. Most people never get that far. They justify, avoid, or numb instead. But once you say it out loud—"I'm afraid"—you take back power.

Ask yourself honestly:

- Can I keep the doors unlocked at night? Why not? Am I afraid someone will come in?
- Can I stop talking to that one toxic friend? Why not? Am I afraid of being alone?
- Can I drop my health insurance tomorrow? Why not? Am I afraid of sickness or ruin?
- Can I say no to that project at work? Why not? Am I afraid of disappointing others?
- Can I go live online and speak for two minutes? Why not? Am I afraid of embarrassment?
- Can I try launching that business idea I've been sitting on? Why not? Am I afraid to fail—or succeed?

The answer to "Why not?" is usually fear. Your brain whispers stories to keep you obedient and in control, piling layers of logic on top of the real source so you never face the root. But if you're brave enough to dig deeper, you'll find the truth. Beneath every fear is the same root: loss of love, safety, or belonging. That's what your child self once feared most and what still drives your survival strategies today. Kids cry on their first day of kindergarten, terrified of being left behind. But eventually, they adapt. They learn. Fear doesn't disappear because the world changes—it disappears because they do. And the same can be true for you.

So how do you face fear and rewrite it? Here's the step-by-step to this experiment.

PEPPER TIME 23: MAKE FEAR YOUR COMPASS

Timing: 15–30 minutes (repeat whenever fear shows up).

What you'll need: Your journal and honesty.

What it's about: Fear isn't a cage. It's a compass. Instead of waiting to "feel ready," you can face fear head-on, question it, and turn it into fuel for growth.

How to do it:

1. **What's the worst thing that can happen?** Get it out of your head and into the light. Visualize the worst case clearly. Once you see it, you'll realize you can only go up from there.
2. **So what?** Flip the fear into courage. So what if you lose your job? So what if your partner leaves? So what if you make a fool of yourself? You'll still be standing, breathing, alive—and able to choose your next step.
3. **How likely is it, really?** Honestly—how often have you seen someone faint on stage while giving a speech? Almost never. The probability of most fears is vanishingly small once you check the facts.
4. **Is there anything I can do now to prevent it?** This is where fear becomes action. Nervous about a presenta-

tion? Practice in the mirror. Present to your partner. Do a trial run with a small group. Action shrinks fear.

5. **Can I recover if it happens?** Suppose you lose your job. Could you cut costs, move in with parents for a season, or take a temporary gig? Recovery is usually possible—and knowing that gives you strength.

6. **What will happen if I do nothing?** This is the hidden cost of fear. If you stay in the draining job, what happens to your health, joy, or family? If you avoid love, will you live alone with regret? Doing nothing is always more expensive than facing the fear.

7. **What's the best-case scenario?** Yes, the worst could happen. But what if the best does? What if you write the next Harry Potter? What if your talk inspires someone who needed it most? What if your leap sets you free?

What to expect: At first, your brain will fight you—fear has been its favorite control trick since Chapter 1. But as you walk through these seven steps, fear loosens. Your body calms. Perspective widens. And what looked like a wall starts looking like a doorway.

Reflection

____

____

____

____

____

____

*   *   *

Fear isn't your enemy. Waiting for it to vanish is. Fear is your soul's GPS. When you know in your bones that no matter what happens, you'll figure it out, risks stop being cliffs and become doors. Once you conquer a fear, the test disappears. But if you never face it, that same fear will stalk you at every crossroads.

PEPPER ASK: So ask yourself today:

- *What fear has been running my life—and am I ready to rewrite it?*

Unhooking The Hooks

Your brain doesn't just get hijacked by fear or saboteurs—it also gets hooked on praise and criticism. Both keep you chained to other people's voices instead of your own. We've all been there. The email from your boss with one harsh line you replay for days. The compliment on your outfit you float on for hours. But praise and criticism aren't reliable mirrors of your worth. They're reflections of the person giving them. And as long as you let praise and criticism drive your choices, you'll be living in reaction instead of in creation.

This connects directly to the saboteurs. The Judge thrives on external voices. It feeds off criticism: "See, I told you you weren't good enough." It feeds off praise: "See, you only matter when people clap." Either way, you're trapped. But when you unhook, you shift back into your Power Brain. You stop outsourcing your worth and reclaim your fuel for what really matters. Here's how we rewire it:

Feedback doesn't tell you about you—it tells you about them. Once, at my corporate job, I was responsible for a big Dutch supermarket client. I prepared the full presentation and products, but last minute, they asked us to reorganize it at another location. I said, "No problem," and did the best I could. Customers were happy, but my boss wasn't. I felt crushed, even though I knew I had given it everything.

What I learned that day: My boss's reaction said more about his own stress and lack of control than it did about me. He wasn't leading from his Power Brain. He was blaming. Feedback is always filtered through someone else's state of mind.

You pitch to an investor who doesn't bite. Does that mean your idea is worthless? No. It means it didn't resonate *for them*. Or take parenting: Someone says, "You're irresponsible for working while raising kids." That doesn't define your parenting—it reveals their definition of responsibility.

So here's the rewire: Feedback is vital, but not as a mirror of your self-worth. It's tactical data telling you whether you're reaching the people you want to reach. Rewire by asking: *What does this tell me about the person giving it? What does this tell me about the people I want to reach?*

Incorporate what's useful—let the rest go. Especially as women, we often love gathering input. It makes us collaborative, humble, open. But not all feedback is equal. While pitching Jelloow to investors, I heard all kinds of advice. Some of it was gold. Some of it was absurd—like the Belgian investor who

suggested I focus less on scaling and more on "family life." Not exactly helpful. What I learned was discernment. Which voices mattered for my goal? Which were noise?

Here's the rewire: each time you get feedback, ask yourself: *Does this help me reach the people I need to reach, or is it just noise?* If it's noise, thank them politely—and let it go.

Women who play big get criticized. Period. The bigger you play, the more criticism you'll face. That's not a bug in the system—it's the cost of impact. When I was climbing, I heard it all. One of the worst: "She's probably sleeping with the boss to get promoted." Liyana, the head of sales we met earlier, was told she was "too direct." The women you admire most, the ones who led movements and changed industries, were not universally adored. They were criticized, mocked, doubted. So if you're being criticized, it just means you're in the arena. The only way to avoid it is to stay small, silent, invisible, and that's not why you're here.

The rewire is this: Stop treating criticism as a problem. Start treating it as proof you're doing something that matters. When it stings, ask your inner mentor: *How would she handle this?* Chances are, with more grace and less drama than your Judge wants you to.

Criticism only hurts when it echoes your own belief. Think back to childhood. Maybe you loved writing. You poured yourself into a story, only to hear your teacher say, "This is stiff. You're not a writer." The sting wasn't just her words. It was that part of you feared it might be true. The same happens as adults. A colleague criticizes your presentation style. If you already

doubt yourself, it cuts deep. If you don't, it bounces off. Criticism hurts most when it mirrors your own Judge.

And here's the opportunity: Each sting is not proof that you're broken—it's a clue to where the Judge still has power. It's an invitation to rewrite that inner belief.

 # Ask: What's more important to me than praise? Praise lights up dopamine. But if you live for it, you'll bend yourself to get it. That's not freedom. That's slavery with a smile. Instead, ask: *What matters more to me than being liked?* Some of my clients answer: Being useful. Inspiring others. Living fully in my own skin. Being truthful. Getting my message out. Building something real.

What about you? When you know your higher values, praise becomes nice but not necessary. Criticism becomes painful but not defining. Both lose their grip so you can start steering from your Power Brain. And that's the point: to come back to your natural state of happiness so you can build the life and business you want—not the one other people's moods dictate.

PEPPER TIME 24:
THE 5-SECOND RULE (5-4-3-2-1)

Timing: Anytime hesitation shows up.

What you'll need: Just your mind and the guts to act.

What it's about: Procrastination, fear, and overthinking feed on hesitation. The 5-4-3-2-1 rule kills it by snapping your brain out of autopilot and launching you into action before excuses take over.

How to do it:

1. **Catch the hesitation**. The moment you notice yourself stalling, count backwards: 5-4-3-2-1.
2. **Move on "1."** Stand up, press send, open the file, speak up, step on stage—whatever action you've been delaying.
3. **Skip "feeling ready."** Don't wait for motivation. Action itself creates readiness.

What to expect: Counting backwards hijacks your brain's default loop. For five seconds, fear has no grip. Once you move, momentum takes over. You'll start noticing the exact pause where your Judge sneaks in. And instead of freezing, you'll move. You'll prove to yourself: *I can act, even without permission from fear or motivation.*

Reflection

____

____

____

____

____

____

*   *   *

This isn't just about getting out of bed or sending an email. It's about rewiring trust with yourself. Every countdown becomes a micro-contract: *I move, no matter what I feel.* And those contracts compound into confidence, momentum, and freedom. **Thinking about your problems will never solve them.** Action is the answer. The 5-second rule gets you to the gym, through the pile of bills, into the hard conversation, onto the stage. It teaches you the deepest rewire of all: **Your feelings don't decide your life. Your actions do.**

Speaking With Power

Another way to rewire your brain—and put yourself firmly on the map—is through language. The words you choose shape how others perceive you, but more importantly, they shape how you perceive yourself. Each weak sentence you whisper reinforces your saboteurs. Each powerful sentence strengthens your Power Brain.

For women especially, communication can be loaded. We've been conditioned to stay "nice," to soften our edges, to shrink our presence in order not to appear "too much." As a result, our speech is littered with tiny habits that weaken our authority without us even noticing. They seem small, but they add up. When you shift the way you speak, you do more than project confidence. You also rewire your brain. Strong sentences anchor your Power Brain. They tell your nervous system: *I belong here. My voice matters.*

Here are ten of the most common speech habits that quietly sabotage your power—and how to rewrite them:

"Just." We do this when we feel apologetic or afraid of being too direct. "I just wanted to check in..." shrinks your request before you've even made it.

Rewire it: Drop the "just." Say: *"I want to check in about..."* Clear. Direct. Powerful.

"Actually." "I actually think..." makes it sound like you're surprised you have a thought worth sharing.

Rewire it: Own your thought. *"I think..., I believe..., I recommend..."*

"Kind of / Almost." "I kind of think the report should be reorganized." Weak, hesitant.

Rewire it: "The report should be reorganized." Certainty builds trust.

"Sorry, but..." We apologize for existing: "Sorry to bother you, but..." Unless you truly caused harm, stop apologizing for taking space.

Rewire it: Replace "sorry" with gratitude. "Thanks for making time. Here's what I need." (Pro tip: Start a Sorry Jar. Every time you use "sorry" without need, you pay $10. You'll break the habit fast.)

"A Little Bit." "I just need a little bit of your time." As if time isn't worth much.

Rewire it: *"I'd like 15 minutes to discuss our new product."* Be specific and confident.

 # Disclaimers. "I'm not the expert, but..." "This is just an idea, but..." These are defense shields to protect us from judgment.

Rewire it: *"Here are my thoughts."* Own your contribution.

 # "Does that make sense?" This undermines your credibility. Research shows it makes you sound less knowledgeable.

Rewire it: Try *"How did that land with you?"* or *"What are your thoughts?"* It opens dialogue without undercutting yourself.

 # Uptalk. Raising your pitch at the end of a statement makes it sound like a question: "We need to increase the budget?"

Rewire it: End firmly. Use your voice like a period, not a question mark.

 # Rushing & Piling on Words. We cram words together because we fear being interrupted or taking up too much space. But rushing weakens presence.

Rewire it: Slow down. Pause. Let silence do the heavy lifting. Power is in the pause.

 # Turning Statements into Questions. Instead of saying, "We need to increase the budget," you say, "What about increasing the budget?" Hiding your idea in a question can feel safer, but it dilutes your authority.

Rewire it: Claim it before asking the question: *"We need to increase the budget. What do you think?"*

This is more than communication coaching—it's brain rewiring. Every time you replace a weak phrase with a strong one, you build a new circuit in your Power Brain. Over time, your words reshape your identity. You stop waiting for permission and start speaking from conviction. Strong communication is about being clearer. It's about signaling—to yourself and to the world—that you are here to create impact. And when you stop hedging, apologizing, and shrinking, people don't think you're "too much." They finally see you.

Meet Your Future Self

We've spent this chapter rewiring your brain—taming the Judge, shrinking your saboteurs, building tiny habits with Pepper Reps. But there's one more powerful practice that sits right at the heart of playing bigger. If Pepper Reps are daily push-ups for your mind, **meeting your Future Self is the marathon.** I love teaching my Scaleurs this habit because it doesn't just keep you in the Power Brain today, it pulls you forward into who you are meant to become. This is where you step into your authentic vision.

Think of it like this: Your gut and brain are in constant conversation. Through Pepper Reps, you've learned you can step in and steer that dialogue. Now it's time to ask a bigger question: *Who are you steering toward*? Because if you don't decide who you want to become, your saboteurs, your Judge, or someone else's voice will decide for you. That's why Future Self work is a game-changer. It shifts you from autopilot survival into intentional creation.

This Pepper Experiment has made the single biggest difference in the lives of my clients, my Scaleurs, and myself. Here's how it works: You meet the version of yourself 10 or 20 years from now. Not the exhausted, older version your Judge might imagine, but the wiser, freer, more authentic you. You ask her questions. And here's the magic: The Future Self you meet is often not just "you, but older." She shows up more like a mentor, a guide, a voice that carries wisdom you didn't know you already had.

When I first met Lotte, our Scaleur from Chapter 3, her life was at a breaking point: a dissolving marriage, two kids to care for, a partner swallowed by work. Weekends felt like single parenthood. She had rehearsed leaving a hundred times—and then rehearsed the fears just as often: housing costs, the disruption for her children, the weight of the unknown. Each round left her body more frozen, her energy more drained. We started with her Future Self. I guided her through the visualization, and afterward she created what I call a *visual contract with herself*—a Pepper Board, which you'll learn to build in Chapter 9.

What Lotte discovered in her Future Self Pepper Experiment stunned her. She didn't meet a worn-out, depleted version of herself. She met a woman in a cozy house at the foot of a mountain. The moment she stepped inside, she felt her vitality—walking shoes by the door, raincoats for adventures with her kids, the freshness of a life that embraced movement. She saw smiling photos of her children, a big wooden table waiting for Sunday meals, and a legal pad that boldly read: *Work I'm proud of.* This Future Self radiated calm and joy. She carried a message that hit Lotte straight in the gut: Leadership doesn't mean self-sacrifice. It means modeling presence and joy.

From that day on, Lotte began making tiny, radical shifts. She ate slowly instead of rushing. She asked for help without apology. She scheduled her creative work before chores. Small choices, repeated daily. And the ripple was undeniable. Her kids relaxed. Her work sharpened, infused with new clarity. Her energy shifted from heavy to magnetic. The experiment didn't save her—her attention did. By committing to the vision of her Future Self, she stepped out of survival mode and into agency.

The first time I tried it, I was skeptical. My coach, Toby (not my partner), guided me through it. He asked me to close my eyes, breathe, and step into a scene. After some breathing exercises, he said: *"Now it's your spotlight moment. Where are you?"* Without planning, I said I saw myself on a stage. A room full of women—Scaleurs—looking at me with hopeful eyes. I was speaking about the gut, about adding pepper in their ass. I could see their faces light up as they remembered their power. I saw happy people expanding instead of shrinking.

Doing the Future Self visualization I love to practice, I found myself approaching a white house by the water. The door opened. A woman greeted me—confident, calm, radiant. She wore business casual—feminine, colorful, but with a deep sense of calm. Behind her, kids' paintings filled the kitchen wall. The house radiated warmth and balance. She smiled at me—big, open, peaceful. She took me out to the terrace with a view of a lake and mountains. I asked her what she does. She answered: *"I speak on stages. I guide female entrepreneurs. I live what I teach."*

That woman was my Future Self. She felt both unfamiliar and deeply familiar. And over the next months, I realized: I was already becoming her. Every lecture, every word I wrote, every time I helped someone bring Pepper into their life—I was stepping closer.

Maybe right your Judge is skeptical. I thought the same. But what did I have to lose? Twenty minutes of my time. That's it. I told myself: *If I do it, I'll give the full twenty minutes*. And I hope you will, too. Because your Future Self becomes an inner compass. She whispers when your Judge is shouting, offers clarity when your choices feel messy, and gives courage when your saboteurs try to shrink you. She won't replace the mentors in your life—but she'll always be available. If your mind wanders? If you fall asleep? Try again. Slow down. This isn't about *doing it right*. It's about giving your deeper voice a chance to speak.

So here's my challenge: **Give yourself those 20 minutes, and don't overthink it.**

PEPPER TIME 25: MEET YOUR FUTURE SELF

This practice—meeting your Future Self—has created some of the most dramatic shifts in the lives of my Scaleurs. When you take time to connect with your Future Self, decisions get clearer, doubts shrink, energy rises, and your vision starts becoming someone you are growing into.

Timing: Around 20 minutes.

What you'll need: Quiet space, your journal, and the courage to imagine.

What it's about: You're not just who you are today—you're also who you're becoming. This practice connects you with your wiser, freer, future self. She's the mentor inside you, waiting to be heard.

How to do it:

1. **Close your eyes.** Breathe deeply three times. Feel yourself settle.
2. **Step into the vision.** Imagine meeting your Future Self, 10 or 20 years ahead. See her space, her presence, her energy.
3. **Write the script.** Capture what you saw, heard, or felt.
4. Stay with the details. Don't overanalyze. Focus on the feeling, the symbols, the tone of her presence.
5. **Anchor it.** Give her a name. Recall her face before bed. Keep her close as your compass.

What to expect: Your Future Self may not look like an "older you." She may feel more radiant, calm, bold, or playful. Meeting her shifts leadership from sacrifice to presence and joy. Over time, her guidance becomes a source of courage in daily choices—reminding you that the path you're on is shaping who you're becoming.

Interpreting Your Vision

- **Don't overanalyze.** If you saw something surprising—like living by the ocean when you've never considered it—don't rush to literal conclusions. Stay with the feeling. That's where the wisdom lives.
- **Explore symbols.** Ask yourself: What associations do I have with this place, activity, or object? What does it connote for me?

- **Notice tone.** Was your Future Self calm, playful, powerful? That's a clue about the energy you're growing into.
- **Stay open.** Your Future Self may communicate through words, body language, or even silence. Trust the form it takes.
- **Keep it close.** Give her a name. Recall her face before bed. Keep the memory in your heart. She's not a fantasy—she's the wiser you that already exists inside.

The Journey: Step Into Your Future

Close your eyes.
Find a comfortable place to sit or lie down.
Feel your body supported by the chair, the floor, the bed beneath you.

Take three slow, grounding breaths.
Inhale deeply through your nose.
Exhale fully through your mouth.
Again: Inhale... and release.
One more time: Inhale... and let it all go.

Now soften your jaw.
Drop your shoulders.
Feel the tension melt from your arms, your chest, your belly.
Your breath deepens.
Your body loosens.
You are safe here.

In front of you, a beam of light appears—strong, steady, waiting just for you.

Step onto it. Feel it welcome you.
It lifts you gently, effortlessly, carrying you upward above the room.
You rise above rooftops, above treetops.
Clouds drift by. Sunlight shimmers at their edges.
The air is lighter here, and so are you.

The beam carries you higher and faster now.
Below, landscapes blur—mountains, rivers, oceans, cities.
Time itself begins to shift.
You are being carried forward, into your future.

The light slows.
Below you, a new landscape appears—the world of your Future Self.
You float down gently until your feet touch the ground.

Look around.
Notice the place where your Future Self lives.
Is it a warm home tucked into trees?
A sunlit apartment above a lively street?
A studio filled with art and tools?
A home with a balcony overlooking the sea?

Take in the surroundings.
Notice the air, the smells, the sounds.
How do you feel here? Lighter? Excited? Calm?

Walk toward the entrance of your Future Self's home.
See the path under your feet—stone, wood, earth.
Notice the door, the handle, the color, the little details.

Reach out and ring the bell.
Listen to the sound echo.
Take a breath.

The door opens.
Someone is there.
It's your Future Self.

Notice her attitude, the calm or spark in her eyes.
Notice her clothes and how she moves.
Notice how she welcomes you—warm, open, steady.
How does it feel to be welcomed by her?

She invites you in.
You step inside and follow her through her home.
Notice what you see: light, colors, textures, smells.

She leads you to her favorite place in the house.
It might be a big wooden table, a reading nook, a garden, a
sunlit balcony.
Observe every detail: how the light falls, what's on the
walls, the view out the window.

She asks you to sit.
Notice what she offers you: food, drink, a cup of tea, a
piece of fruit, a glass of water.
Observe how she behaves as she serves you.
How does her presence feel?

As you sit with her, take a moment to breathe.
Then ask her: "What are you doing now in your life?"
Let her show you. Listen.

Then ask: "What do I need to do to get here?"

Stay quiet.
Keep breathing.
Listen closely.
Let her answers wash through you—not just words but feelings, images, knowing.
Absorb her guidance.

After a while, it's time to go.
Your Future Self stands and walks you back to the door.
Notice how she looks at you and what she places in your hands—an object, a symbol, a reminder.
Thank her.

Step outside.
Step back onto the beam of light waiting for you.

It lifts you gently and carries you up, back across time.
The landscapes pass in reverse—cities, rivers, mountains, clouds.

You return to the dark, quiet space where you began.
The beam sets you down.
Feel the floor beneath you again.
Feel your breath.
Wiggle your fingers and toes.

When you're ready, open your eyes.
Take a moment.

 # PEPPER ASK: After the visualization, take your journal and start jotting down what you just experienced.

- *What was her presence like? Her smile, her energy, her voice?*
- *What was her appearance: clothing, body language, gestures?*
- *What was her home or environment like?*
- *Did she offer you food, drink, or a symbolic gift? What did it represent?*
- *What did she say when you asked: "What do I need to know to move from here to there?"*
- *Did she surprise you in some way?*
- *Did she offer a perspective that feels wiser than your current self?*

Reflection

____

____

____

____

____

____

____

*　　*　　*

The Future Self visualization is powerful, but it's not a one-time trick. Here are 10 extra tips to grow even further into your future self:

1. **Ask in small moments:** "What would she do right now?" Before replying to an email, snapping at your kids, or walking into a meeting—pause. Imagine her presence, and act from there.

2. **Make art about her.** Draw her home, collage her symbols, or create a Pinterest board that reflects her vibe. Seeing her world daily keeps it alive.

3. **Block time to live as she would.** If she has slow Sunday mornings, give yourself two hours this weekend to read, sip coffee, or walk outside. Embody her habits in microdoses.

4. **Eat the breakfast she would choose.** Does she fuel herself with nourishing food or savor a ritual like coffee in a beautiful mug? Recreate it tomorrow morning.

5. **Dress like her for a day.** Wear what she would wear—maybe sharper, bolder, or more relaxed. One Scaleur said putting on red heels (her Future Self's shoes) shifted her confidence for a high-stakes presentation.

6. **Write an email in her tone.** Would she apologize excessively, or would she be clear, kind, and confident? Start shaping your communication the way she would.

7. **Adjust your environment toward hers.** Add one object that reflects her taste—a plant, a piece of art, a candle. Your surroundings shape your state of mind.

8. **Approach relationships as she would.** If she's calmer with conflict, practice pausing before reacting. If she's bolder, speak your truth without shrinking.

9. **Face a dilemma with her by your side.** Visualize standing shoulder-to-shoulder with her, looking at the problem together. Notice how it feels smaller, lighter, less consuming.
10. **Slip into her shoes before important moments.** Before a meeting, call, or presentation, close your eyes and imagine walking into the room as her. Feel her posture, hear her tone, borrow her energy.

Here's another simple but powerful decision tool that draws on your Future Self for wisdom: The 10-Year Test. It's a quick way to cut through doubt and overthinking. When you're standing in front of a decision, ask yourself: *Ten years from now, will I regret not doing this?*

PEPPER TIME 26: THE 10-YEAR TEST

Timing: 3 minutes.

What you'll need: Your journal, a pen, and a quiet space.

What it's about: Overthinking blurs decisions. This test cuts through noise by pulling you out of fear and into perspective. Your Future Self knows the answer—this exercise lets you hear it.

How to do it:

1. **Ask the question straight:** "Ten years from now, will I regret not doing this?"

2. **If the answer is no:** Release it. Let it go without guilt; not every opportunity is yours to take.

If the answer is even a small yes: Don't ignore it. That's your Power Brain speaking. Take the next small step: Book the call, draft the idea, share the thought. If fear shows up, revisit Pepper Time 23: Make Fear Your Compass, and name the fear before acting.

What to expect: Fear thrives in the moment; perspective thrives in the long view. The 10-year lens makes complexity simple—it shows you what truly matters and frees you from perfectionism or other people's opinions.

Your Future Self is your compass, and the 10-Year Test is one of the simplest ways to tune into her voice. Each time you do it, you are rewiring your brain: from fear to perspective, from Judge to Power Brain, from shrinking back to moving forward. Remeber: **The cost of doing nothing is almost always higher than the cost of trying.**

Reflection

____

____

____

____

____

____

*   *   *

By now, you're no longer in the dark. You've seen the Judge and the saboteurs for what they are, faced fear head-on, and learned how to unhook from the trap of praise and criticism and how to communicate with power. You've practiced the tiny resets that interrupt autopilot and rewire your brain in real time, and you've connected with your Future Self.

These are not just ideas. They are tools for your journey:

- Catch the Judge → Reclaim your energy.
- Face fear → It dissolves.
- Unhook from praise & criticism → Find your own center.
- Use tiny actions → Build compound change.
- Communicate with power → Step into presence.
- Visualize your Future Self → Anchor in joy, purpose, and clarity.

This is the rewiring. You've seen the patterns and practiced the shifts. You now hold the tools to rewrite your brain. Awareness cracks the door open, but only consistent action makes the rewiring stick. Now is the stretch, the moment where you stop treating these practices as "nice ideas" and start making them your daily reps until they're your new default. You've already proven you can interrupt the old scripts. Now it's time to hard-wire the new ones so presence, power, and joy become your way of life.

The next chapter will show you how to make it stick.

Chapter 9:

Stretching & Making It Stick

You've made it this far—time to celebrate! Seriously, pause right now. Smile. Do a silly jump. Put your hand on your heart and remind yourself: *I'm here; I'm doing it*. Celebration isn't optional—it's essential because it fuels the momentum that will carry you forward. By now, I hope you've scribbled in the margins, maybe started a journal and collected a few pictures of what your Future Self looks like. Most of all, I hope you've started to feel the shift: You're not just consuming ideas— you're rewiring. This chapter is about how to *make it stick*.

And yes, if you feel a bit overwhelmed or uncomfortable right now—that's exactly where I want you. Because smooth is the enemy of growth. Comfort keeps you stuck in old loops. The best advice I ever received? *Be the 2 percent*. Most people will read, nod, even feel inspired... and then do nothing. The 2 percent implement before it's perfect.

That's what this chapter demands from you. Action. Stretch. Doing what feels uncomfortable—until it doesn't anymore. Action is the most direct path to clarity. Yes, it's a stretch. Yes, it's sometimes messy. But you already have everything you need to build the life you want. You wouldn't even have the dream if you didn't already have what it takes to make it real. Your job is to claim it, break it down into daily reps, and keep showing up.

This chapter will show you how.

Comfortable With Uncomfortable

Here's an uncomfortable truth: You will never feel ready to do the important things you're meant to do. Waiting for "ready" is the nastiest little lie your Judge and saboteurs whisper. Real growth begins before you feel prepared. Progress doesn't happen in the cozy zone of certainty—it starts with a brave decision. If you wait until you feel confident, you'll never move. Confidence comes after action, not before it. The only way forward is to stop overthinking, stop "researching" endlessly, and start experimenting.

Get skin in the game. Value growth and learning over comfort and perfection. Research shows perfection is tied to higher rates of depression, anxiety, eating disorders, and burnout. It doesn't protect you—it paralyzes you. Progress, on the other hand, is messy and imperfect but moves you forward.

I still remember my cringeworthy first workshop. Slides half-baked. Nerves written all over my face. I thought: *This is awful. Who do I think I am?* But you know what? It was better than sitting home editing my deck a hundred more times. Because that "sucky" workshop gave me feedback, confidence, and momentum. Starting small and sucky always beats staying stuck.

Using your Power Brain and deciding what you want is the first step to getting it, and we'll break it down into simple steps. If you don't have something clear and meaningful to work toward, you can experience a host of problems from feeling lost, struggling to prioritize, or failing to produce meaningful results to burning out. You were born with everything you need to answer the call of your soul, and clear goals and solutions will put it all within your grasp. So, in this chapter, we'll make a Pepper Board to make your goals and your path to reaching them even more concrete.

To stretch yourself, you need tactics that anchor you when the Judge yells the loudest. Here are practical ways to make the uncomfortable your training ground:

- **From Passive to Power Brain—Stretching Your Mindset:** This is about moving from autopilot into intentional action. Small steps, not big drama. Plan ahead for obstacles. Ask yourself: *What roadblocks could show up? How can I prepare now to keep momentum later?*
- **Refuse to Be Insulted—Stretching Your Resilience:** Criticism is inevitable. The question is: Will it freeze you, or fuel you? The more you care about what others think, the more they own you. Learn to laugh, let go, and only keep what helps. And never, ever reply when you're triggered.
- **Focus on What You Can Control—Stretching Your Focus:** The shift is simple but powerful. Let go of what isn't yours—traffic, gossip, moods, algorithms—and

pour your energy into what is: your actions, your attitude, your attention. This is the muscle you'll train throughout this chapter.

- **Practice Self-Love as Fuel—Stretching Your Capacity:** The Judge thrives when you're depleted. Without fuel, every stretch feels impossible. Choosing self-love isn't indulgence—it's maintenance. We'll dive deeper in the next chapter, but for now remember: Rest, care, and joy are what keep you strong enough to stretch.
- **Stretch Your Boundaries—Stretching Your Courage:** Every "no" to what drains you is a "yes" to what fuels you. Boundaries aren't barriers—they're breathing room. Start small: Decline one meeting, log off an hour earlier, or speak up once when you'd usually stay silent. Each choice expands the space for your stretch.

Once you decide to stretch, it will feel awkward, strange, even empty at times. There's a space between starting and succeeding where the old habits are gone but the new ones aren't yet solid. It's in this void that growth happens. Growth doesn't announce itself with trumpets. It whispers in the quiet, awkward seasons. If you're in the void right now, don't run from it. Stay. Trust it. This is where your future self is being born.

From Being Okay To Being You

One of the biggest mindset shifts you'll ever make is to stop spending your life on things you cannot control. Your real power lives inside a small circle: your actions, your attitude, and your attention. And here's the paradox: When you accept how small that circle is, your life expands. I call the practice of that acceptance BE OKAY—a muscle you train. It isn't pretending everything is fine or giving up. It's letting what you can't control be "okay enough" so you can move what is yours.

Be okay if people hate the picture you just posted, your flight's delayed, or your neighbor plays loud music once. This isn't passivity; it's precision. It's reclaiming energy that leaks everywhere else and pouring it back into your life. We're hard-wired for control because control feels like safety. So we hover over our kids to force "right" decisions, try to fix our partner's habits, or micromanage friends and teammates. But people will do what they do. Life will throw what it throws. And the more you fight that truth, the more anxious, resentful, and powerless you feel. And yes—people are going to annoy you. But when you allow those moments to hijack your peace, you hand your power to everyone else—and you're left with no time or energy for yourself.

Your body's stress response will still fire. You'll feel irritation or anger. But you can learn to reset before those emotions spiral into suffering. That's what you've been practicing in the earlier chapters. A pause. A Pepper Rep. A breath. A small shift. That's the reset that keeps your emotions from hijacking you. It will take time, but every choice not to feed anger or negativity is another brick in reclaiming your time and energy. BE OKAY is the first step. It pulls you back to your circle—your actions, your attitude, your attention.

I once had a colleague who arrived at the office every morning already in a bad mood because of one irritation or another. By the time he sat at his desk at 9 a.m., his day was ruined. Now imagine if he had redirected his focus. The baby cried? Instead of stewing, he could focus on being present. Traffic was bad?

He could use that half hour to listen to an inspiring podcast or plan his priorities for the day. The radio was full of noise? Switch it off. Put on music or text a kind note to a friend.

Same circumstances, completely different experience. That's what happens when you stop giving power to the circle you don't control and reclaim it for the circle you do. And that small choice changes everything.

Of course, life throws much heavier things than traffic jams. I've lived through seasons of grief stacked on grief: accidents, illnesses, goodbyes I never wanted to say. Those moments will break your heart. Pain is part of being human. But suffering—the ongoing heaviness, the spiral of anxiety—comes when you try to control what you cannot. Healing begins the moment you ask, *What is mine now?* Maybe what's mine is to cry. To rest. To call a friend. To take one honest step. That shift—back to your circle—is what gives you strength to keep walking.

Almost nothing in life is under your full control. Not money, your career, or even your health or relationships—because life is fragile. But there are three things that will always remain fully yours: your actions, your attitude, and your attention. If you hold on to those, you will always have power.

Use this quick reset: the One-Hour Rule. Whenever something hooks you, ask yourself: Will this still matter in an hour? In a week? In a year? If it won't matter in an hour, let it go. If it will matter in a week or a year, take action. That tiny filter alone can save you from spirals of wasted stress.

BE OKAY is the discipline of letting go of what isn't yours. It pulls you back to your circle—your actions, your attitude, your attention. But here's where it deepens: **BE YOU**. Being okay is release. Being you is creation. Together, they're the double engine of real power. When you practice radical okayness, you strip away the noise. But it's only when you choose to be you that something new emerges. That's the moment you stop shrinking to fit other people's expectations and start standing in your own lane. Be You is the pepper move.

- Be you with your values, boundaries, and choices—even when others don't understand.
- Be you when the Judge whispers "not ready," because that voice will always try to stall you with more waiting, more polishing, more preparing.
- Be you when others are loud with certainty, because their confidence doesn't make them right.
- Be you when chaos tempts you to abandon yourself, because storms are the exact moment to double down on your truth.

BE OKAY keeps you steady. BE YOU moves you forward.

And that is more than enough to change your life.

BE OKAY WITH RELATIONSHIPS

Relationships are one of the three pillars of a fulfilling life—alongside performance and well-being. And the truth is, they are all deeply interlinked. Your energy in relationships impacts your performance. Your friendships and family rhythms affect your health and well-being. And your state of mind shapes how you connect with others.

People will always have thoughts about you. **Be okay with their opinion. It's theirs—it doesn't belong to you.** Freeing yourself from this prison unlocks confidence, self-expression, and momentum. Remember: The human brain produces around 70,000 thoughts a day—most random, many irrational, and half outside even our own control. If you can't even fully manage your own mental chatter, why waste your life trying to manage someone else's?

Fear of judgment is one of the biggest sources of self-doubt. Here's how to shift from Be Okay to Be You:

- "I'm not good enough" → For whom?
- "I'm not smart enough" → For whom?
- "They'll be mad at me" → Who, exactly?
- "My parents won't approve" → So?
- "No one will like me" → Who, exactly?
- "What will my friends think?" → Whatever they want.

Don't shrink yourself for anyone. Instead: Be you.

- Be you, and live your life in a way that makes you proud.
- Be you, and make decisions that align with your values.
- Be you, and take risks because your soul wants it.
- Be you, and follow the path your gut is pulling you toward.

Because doing what makes you happy—being brave, taking risks, and following your path—will always matter more than other people's opinions.

Friendships will always play a big role in your life, but adult friendships come and go. You have to be okay with that. People will move away, prioritize new relationships, or simply drift. It just means life is moving. When someone drifts, cheer them on from afar. I've seen my partner reconnect with an old friend after five years as if no time had passed—because the timing aligned and the energy was still there. That's the nature of friendships: They expand, contract, pause, and sometimes restart. Be okay with it. At the end of the day, relationships—just like performance and well-being—circle back to the same truth: You can only control how you show up. And when you live that way, your happiness depends only on you.

Stretch Yourself In Friendships

Building and maintaining strong friendships as an adult requires you to stretch. To put yourself out there, be you, risk being the one who goes first, and accept that not every connection will stick. Here are two ways to practice:

Develop the habit of going first. Be you and be the one who breaks the ice. Compliment someone's nail color, their outfit, even their socks. Ask what they ordered at the café. Smile and say hello to strangers. These tiny actions stretch you out of your comfort zone and send out warmth—and warmth always circles back. Not necessarily from the same person, but from somewhere. Do it without expectation, and watch how much easier life feels.

Create community anywhere. *Be you* and join group classes, events, or circles that interest you. And when you click with someone, take it beyond the class. Friendships don't grow on autopilot—you grow them by making the next move. And remember: *Be okay* with the fact that friends will come and go. Stop expecting permanent invitations. Stop clinging tightly when things shift. Instead, take responsibility for how you show up.

Friendships, like all parts of life, are fluid. People will drift, lives will scatter, and circumstances will change. But the way you show up—curious, open, steady—is always in your control. And that's the stretch: Move from *Be Okay* to *Be You*. Be okay with what you cannot control. Be you in how you choose to show up. That's the shift that transforms not only your friendships but also your performance and well-being.

Our Adult Tantrums

So what happens if you cling to control, refuse to let go, and keep reacting the old way? Refusing to stretch yourself is the grownup version of a tantrum. By now, you've worked hard to reclaim your energy and focus. If you waste it on tantrums—yours or someone else's—you leak power that could have gone into building the life, business, and relationships you want. That's why how you handle the moments when life doesn't go your way matters.

Imagine being eight years old again. Kids don't hide their emotions. When they feel disappointed or frustrated, it bursts out: sulking, stomping, crying. Now fast-forward to adulthood. Do we really outgrow out tantrums? Not exactly. We just rebrand them:

- Child runs away → Adult avoids confrontation.
- Child sulks → Adult gives the silent treatment.
- Child shuts down → Adult acts stoic and cold.
- Child screams → Adult rages and vents.
- Child slams doors → Adult still slams doors.
- Child lies → Adult lies, only more polished.

Different costume. Same script.

Why does this matter? Because if kids aren't allowed to ride out the full wave of their emotions, they never learn how to process them in a healthy way. They grow into emotionally immature adults who take it out on the rest of us. And it is never your job to manage another adult's emotional reaction. That's their work. Hoping someone will "finally change" keeps you trapped in cycles with people who won't. Your power is in deciding how *you* respond.

And yes, sometimes you are the one throwing the tantrum. It shows up in sneaky ways—like comparison. You scroll, see someone else's success, and are suddenly sulking inside: *Why not me?* But comparison doesn't have to crush you—it can stretch you. Jealousy is just a message from your Future Self saying: *You want that life? Good. Go build it.* You don't need to be "special." You need to be consistent, determined, and willing to put one foot in front of the other every day.

- Want financial freedom? It's your responsibility to create it.
- Want a home you love? It's your responsibility to design it.
- Want deep relationships? It's your responsibility to show up for them.

This is where the stretch lives: Instead of throwing tantrums about what you can't control, you redirect that energy into what you can. Little by little, step by step, you build, until one day you wake up and realize you're living the very life you used to feel jealous of. That's the gift of practicing radical okayness. The more you get comfortable with the uncomfortable and stop leaking energy on things you can't control, the more you free up mental space, emotional energy, and time you didn't know you had. And with that freedom, you can finally show up differently—in your well-being, your relationships, and your performance.

Be okay → Be you → Stretch. That's the bridge. That's the work. That's the power.

Stepping Into Your Next Level

The whole point of stretching is to unlock your *next level*. If you do it, you create stability, momentum, and a pathway toward flow. Your default state is happiness, and the stretch is what helps you return to that state again and again. Relationships, well-being, and performance are all integrated. If one rises, the others follow. Master one pillar, and you start rewiring your brain for long-lasting habits across all three.

Let's look at what "next level" means in relationships.

The Commitment Conversation

Every deep romantic relationship eventually arrives at a crossroad: *Where is this going? Are we still on the same page?* It's the moment many people fear—but it's that stretch that takes a relationship to its next level. Honest conversations are the foundation of healthy love. And here's the truth: If the relationship is real, the conversation will strengthen it. Think of this moment as a stretch. Just like pushing your muscles a little further in a workout makes you stronger, leaning into an uncomfortable conversation grows the relationship—if both people are willing to do the work.

The biggest mistake people make at this stage is focusing only on the other person: *Will they step up?* Instead, shift your focus back to yourself. *What do I value? What do I want my time and life to mean?* That's where your power lives. A strong relationship has two things:

- First, both partners want it to work and are willing to do the work.
- Second, the issues don't require either person to give up their dreams or their values.

I learned this firsthand with Tobi. We reached a point where the cracks were showing. It would have been easy to avoid, but instead I pulled the trigger. On a long hike, I chose that moment. Why? Nature has a way of softening the edges, and I wanted the energy to be open, not defensive. I raised the hard topics, asked open questions, and listened deeply—not just to his words, but to his tone, his body language, the small shifts that tell you the real story. I framed it not as *You're the problem*, but as *How can we solve this together?* We tackled one issue at a time instead of drowning in all of them at once.

It wasn't easy moving forward. Some days we crashed. Some days I questioned whether it would last. But because we both cared enough to stay in it, to fight for it, and to grow, we became stronger. Even our arguments changed. What used to take three days to recover from now takes less than five minutes. Progress, not perfection—that's what next level looks like.

But if nothing had changed, if there had been no progress, I would have walked away. Because love isn't about someone's potential. Love the person as they are. If their actions show no willingness to change, that *is* the answer. And you always have a choice. If you stay with someone who doesn't share your hopes or dreams, you will both end up miserable.

And if it ends, what you're feeling is grief. Not just heartbreak, but the unraveling of your nervous system. The loss of routines, inside jokes, familiar songs, even the places that once felt safe. Unlearning is painful—but it's also powerful. You're literally rewiring your brain for what's next. That's why I recommend a hard reset: No contact for at least thirty days. Clear out the triggers—photos, shirts, old messages. Don't stalk on social media. Redecorate your space. Signal to your brain and body: *A new chapter is beginning.*

It will feel brutal. You'll want to give in. It's okay to cry in bed, replay the story, and resist reaching out. Healing isn't linear. But every time you choose to sit with the discomfort instead of running back, you teach your nervous system how to live again without them. That's how you shift back toward your default state: joy, energy, flow.

The hard conversations we had early in our relationship were what saved us. We didn't sweep issues under the rug—we stretched ourselves to face them. We even asked for outside support when needed, because sometimes growth requires more tools than you currently have. And it worked. The time we spent angry shrank, his awareness of when he hurt me sharpened, and the repair became quicker. That's how progress shows up—in small shifts that, over time, change everything.

And it goes beyond relationships. Stretching is the pattern of growth across your whole life. Because when all the parts of your life rise together—when you bring awareness, action, and honesty into each area—you unlock stability, energy, and momentum. That's what the next level is about. It's showing up in your relationships, performance, and well-being every day. And when you raise one pillar, the others rise with it.

We'll explore *flow* more deeply in the next chapter, because flow is the state where stretching becomes natural. But first, let's make your stretch visible and practical—with your Pepper Board.

From Visualization To Pepper Board

My first Pepper Board came to life in 2018, right after I left corporate. I divided it into the three pillars we've been working with: performance, relationships, and well-being. For performance, I wrote down a revenue goal so bold it scared me. Yet within a year, I had hit it. For well-being, I added the Chicago Marathon and a new country I longed to explore. Months later, I crossed the marathon finish line in 4:02 and found myself standing in Malawi, Africa. For relationships, I pictured myself rooted in the US start-up world, so I joined three founder communities and committed to showing up every month.

That single board shaped my entire year. And it didn't stop there. Each year, I created a new Pepper Board and refined my focus. In 2020, for performance, I placed images of books—because I wanted to teach, disrupt, and create something lasting. That year, I launched *Think Big, Scale Fast*. For relationships, I experimented with coaching—not to build a business, but to meet people, expand my network, and see if I enjoyed it. For well-being, I added two new destinations: Japan and St. Martin in the Caribbean. Both became reality.

Over the years, my boards have carried images of countries I'd never seen, companies I never imagined building, Scaleurs I didn't yet know I'd meet, even a family I once thought I'd never have. One by one, they became real. Not perfectly. Not instantly. But consistently enough to prove the process works. Today, I still hang my Pepper Board on the wall. It keeps me honest, and it keeps me stretching when my Judge wants me to shrink.

Your Pepper Board

To build your Pepper Board, simply let your gut lead. Place the things that matter most right in the center or at the top. Group them loosely into the three pillars we've been working with—performance, relationships, and well-being—so your board reflects your *whole* life. Step away, come back, refine. Only glue what feels right. Visualization becomes action. Action becomes habit. Habits become your future.

PEPPER TIME 27: PEPPER BOARD

Timing: Give yourself one week. Don't rush. Spend 15 minutes each day pulling images, symbols, or numbers. Sit with them, step away, return.

What you'll need: Sturdy poster board, glue, and inspiring images, words, phrases, and/or numbers. (You should have some good images saved from earlier experiments.)

What it's about: Clarifying your Future Self and priming your brain for action. This is you saying: *I'm not just imagining—I'm building.*

How to do it:

1. **Start loose.** Place images on your board without glue. Play with arrangement. Put your biggest dreams at the center or top. Follow these steps for each image:
   - Ask: *Why does this matter? Who else benefits if I make it real?* Rate it 1–10 in importance. If it's below 5, it's not your stretch—go deeper.
   - Rate how tough this dream is. Respect the challenge. If millions have done it, so can you. Tried before and failed? Good. That means you're stretching. Don't beat yourself up—adjust your approach.

2. **Use categories.** Anchor around the three pillars we've been working with:
   - Performance (work, creativity, growth)
   - Relationships (love, family, community)
   - Well-being (health, energy, inner calm)

3. **Refine daily.** Step away for 24 hours. Return with fresh eyes. Remove what doesn't feel true. Add what calls to you. On the third draft, commit and glue.

4. **Let your gut decide.** If it doesn't feel right—don't glue it.

5. **Place with intention.** Put it somewhere you'll see daily—your bedroom wall, your wardrobe, even a private digital version if that's safer. The point is consistency: Your brain must absorb it without effort.

6. **Make it active.** This is where the stretch sticks. Pair your Pepper Board with your weekly plan—and trans-

late it into *three daily tasks*. Every time you look at it, ask: *What's one step I can take today toward this?*

- Marathon → Weekly: 35 km. Daily: run 5 km today.
- Book → Weekly: Write 35 pages. Daily: Write 5 pages today.
- Business → Weekly: 25 new leads. Daily: Contact 5 new potential clients.
- Relationships → Weekly: 3 quality connections. Daily: Call or meet 1 friend today.
- Well-being → Weekly: 70 minutes of mindfulness. Daily: 10-minute meditation.

7. **Extra stretch.**

- Horizon: Aim the board at the next 12–18 months.
- Cadence: Quick monthly review—replace images that no longer resonate; celebrate wins.
- Watch-outs: perfectionism (done > perfect), compare-and-despair (your board = your lane).
- Set up your Dream Q&A: Write down questions that challenge you ("What would my Future Self do today?"), and keep them near your board.

What to expect: At first, resistance. Then curiosity. And finally, momentum. Because your Pepper Board isn't just a collage—it's a compass. A daily stretch. A reminder that you're walking toward the life you want, not drifting, not waiting.

Reflection

____

____

____

____

____

____

*   *   *

Making It Stick For Life

Remember:
Your Pepper Board is how you make the stretch stick.
Visualization becomes action.
Action becomes habit.
Habits shape your future.
And your gut is the leader.

It's about the small, daily stretches that compound into a life you're proud of. The images you choose, the reps you practice, the actions you take—all of it is training your brain to return, again and again, to the path that matters most to you. This is how you stop drifting, build momentum, and turn a chapter in a book into a chapter in your life. Because in the end, mastery is about making it stick. And when you do, you'll discover the kind of growth that carries you into every relationship, decision, and dream ahead.

Now that you've learned how to stretch and anchor your growth with habits, it's time to step into the next level: protecting your fuel, so you can sustain your growth without burning out.

"*If you don't prioritize your life, someone else will.* "

— Greg McKeown

Part III - Flow:

Changing The Game From Within

Building is one thing. Sustaining is another. Too many brilliant Scaleurs protect their goals but not their energy—and burn out on the climb. This part is about guarding the fuel that makes everything else possible: your attention, your time, your nervous system, your joy.

You'll set nonnegotiables, spot and seal energy leaks, practice flow on purpose, and upgrade self-love from nice idea to daily policy. Protecting your fire isn't shrinking back; it's how you scale without losing yourself. By the end of this part, you'll know exactly how to keep your growth sustainable, powerful, and deeply aligned.

Chapter 10:

Protecting Your Fuel

When I began writing this chapter, I was pregnant. Then I gave birth. Now I'm typing with a two-month-old laughing beside me and a daughter asking for snacks. Even with all the tools we've practiced—Power Brain, Pepper Reps, Future Self—the Judge still shows up, to-dos still multiply, and life still asks for more. The task is never "done." What can change is how we protect our energy while we do it. This chapter isn't about squeezing more into your calendar. It's about **shifting from time management to energy management**—so you can be present for what matters.

Spotting The Energy Leaks

I've tried every planner on the market, read every time-management book, tested all the systems. No matter how perfect the plan looked—at the end of the day, I felt like I hadn't done enough. Motherhood forced me to shift. I realized my sanity and happiness didn't come from checking off more boxes. They came from having the energy to be present for what mattered. That's when I stopped obsessing over time and started managing my energy.

Energy shapes how we experience time. The same five minutes can feel like stress or joy, depending on the fuel you bring. When I manage energy instead of time, I suddenly have enough space for the things that matter most. The first step? **Find the leaks.** Energy leaks hide in all three pillars of life:

- **Well-being:** When your to-do list never ends, your focus scatters, and even Pepper Reps are hijacked by wandering thoughts. These are signs your fuel tank is leaking.
- **Relationships:** When conversations or interactions leave you drained instead of nourished. Some people lift you. Others siphon your energy like it's their life force. Think of it as a dance with them. The moment you shift your steps—set a boundary, show up differently—the dance itself changes.
- **Performance:** When your brain leaks energy into distractions, Judge chatter, or endless unfinished loops. If your boss's late-night pings keep you wired, that's not just a calendar issue—that's an energy leak waiting to be sealed.

Your energy is your most precious resource. When you protect it, you don't just get more done—you get more life back. Plugging leaks isn't always easy, but it's always worth it. The fuel you reclaim spills into every other part of your life, giving you more presence, joy, and momentum.

PEPPER TIME 28:
IDENTIFY YOUR BIGGEST ENERGY LEAK

Timing: 10 minutes today, 10 minutes tomorrow.

What you'll need: Your journal, a pen, and a quiet space.

What it's about: Spotting the one area draining you most and choosing a first action to plug it.

How to do it:

1. **Choose your pillar.** Write down the 3 pillars of your life, and circle the one that instantly feels heaviest:
    - Performance: career, work, creative output, growth.
    - Relationships: partner, kids, family, friends, colleagues.
    - Well-being: health, rest, spirituality, energy rituals.

2. **Name the drain.** Ask yourself: *What exactly is draining me here?* Don't overthink. Trust your gut and go with your first thought.
    - Performance: "My boss's late-night pings."
    - Relationships: "Evenings feel heavy, no spark."
    - Well-being: "I'm running on empty, no rest rituals."

3. **Take one micro-action this week.** Pick one small step to shift the leak:
    - Performance: Set a *no-ping hour* after 8 p.m., or move random requests into a shared doc.
    - Relationships: Add one daily walk with your partner or kids, phones away.
    - Well-being: Block one nonnegotiable rest ritual: a nap, meditation, or a 10-minute walk outside.

What to expect: Plugging leaks isn't always easy, but it's always worth it. The moment you seal one drain, energy flows back into every other area of your life.

Reflection

____

____

____

____

____

____

____

When you stop leaking fuel, you don't just feel lighter—you reclaim momentum. You invest in your own happiness and shift from drained to energized. And when you see your energy as the precious resource it truly is, you get more done in less time and finally learn what to say no to.

*   *   *

You can even align your energy with your natural rhythms. We already spoke about cycles earlier—your body, your brain, the cosmos all have patterns. Partnering with those rhythms is one of the smartest ways to do less, yet create more. Even a 10 to 20 percent shift in alignment can feel like a miracle. So sync your energy with your rhythms (cycle phases, natural peaks, daily flow). Change the dance with your biggest drainers—whether that's a habit, a person, or your own Judge. The moment you plug just one leak, time itself feels different.

Scattered Focus

Of course, not all leaks come from other people or endless obligations. Some of the biggest drains live right inside your head. Every time your attention drifts during a Pepper Rep, or when you're half-working while half-scrolling, you're leaking energy. That's why we train laser focus. Not to become perfect machines but to strengthen our self-command muscle. Your brain will scatter—because that's what brains do. The skill lies in how quickly you return.

Try it right now: Take one deeper breath than usual. Feel the air moving in, chest expanding, belly rising. Exhale. Notice how many thoughts rush in to hijack your attention. Don't fight or judge them. Just notice—and then gently come back to your breath. That's the muscle. Not avoiding distraction but training your return. (Remember the Sit with It experiment from Chapter 5.) Every rep rewires you.

Most of us overload on to-do lists. Ten things written, three things done, seven things carried over. It's never-ending. I had to flip the game. Instead of chasing tasks, I started chasing energy. I swapped daily lists for weekly lists. Life is messy. Planning in seven-day chunks gave me space for the unexpected and clearer perspective on what really matters. My first priority is always one real action in each of the three main Pepper Board categories (performance, relationships, well-being).

I also stopped writing lists only from the head. Now I ask my body, mind, heart, and cosmos:

Body: Where's my energy this week? Which cycle phase am I in (follicular = brainstorm, ovulation = connect, luteal = detail,

menstrual = rest)? Your body isn't the enemy of productivity—it's the map.

 # Mind: What are my top three priorities that truly move the needle toward who I'm becoming—not just what's urgent? These are the bricks that build your Future Self, not the noise that keeps you busy.

 # Heart: How do I feel now? How do I want to feel by Friday? If my list doesn't shift me toward that state—peace, momentum, joy—then it's leaking energy. Every task should either feed or free your heart.

 # Cosmos: Am I forcing or flowing? Not every closed door means failure. Sometimes the timing isn't right—yet. Trust the stretch. Trust your gut. Flow is alignment.

But even with the best intentions, focus fades. The Judge gets loud. That's why you need anchors. Affirmations plug the leaks caused by spirals and chatter, redirecting your brain toward strength, presence, and possibility. Here's how to use them:

Pick 3 or 4 phrases that resonate with you. Short. Memorable. Fuel for your gut.

- "I'm alright right now."
- "This too shall pass."
- "No one can hurt me now."
- "Things are exactly as they are meant to be."

Write them in your journal, on Post-its, or in your phone where you'll see them daily.

Each morning—or any time the Judge is loud—pause for 1 minute. Read them slowly. Repeat them aloud or silently until you feel the shift.

Your Judge will roll its eyes. That's normal. But keep going. Over time, affirmations become anchors. They train your brain to return faster to calm, focus, and action. The energy you once lost to spirals now fuels your stretch. Scattered focus is one of the sneakiest leaks. When you combine aligned planning with affirmations, you stop pouring energy into noise and start fueling your next level.

Setting Nonnegotiables

Protecting your energy isn't about building walls around your life. It's about building a fire strong enough to keep burning no matter what storms roll in. If energy leaks are the holes in your tank, then **nonnegotiables are the container**—the clear boundaries that stop you from giving away your spark. Gut leadership is about listening to your inner wisdom and making bold choices, even when they're uncomfortable. Boundaries are gut decisions in action. They're how you say: *This is who I am. This is what matters. This is what I will not sacrifice*. Without them, you burn out. With them, you build momentum. Every "no" to what drains you is a louder "yes" to what fuels you.

Earlier chapters stretched you through awareness and habits. Now the stretch is in holding your line. At first, it will feel selfish. Awkward. Even scary. But each time you reinforce a nonnegotiable, you train your brain that you are safe in your truth. That's gut leadership in action—choosing integrity over autopilot. Your nonnegotiables don't need to be dramatic. They just need to be clear. Anchor them in the three pillars:

- **Performance:** "No meetings before 9 a.m." "Slack off at 7 p.m." "Emails answered within 24 hours, never instantly."
- **Relationships:** "Family dinners are phone-free." "I don't explain my choices twice." "No gossip."
- **Well-being:** "One rest ritual a week is sacred." "Move my body 20 minutes daily." "No screens in the bedroom."

Boundaries are not cages—they are fuel. They protect your spark so you can keep showing up stronger.

PEPPER TIME 29: DEFINE YOUR NONNEGOTIABLES

Timing: 20 minutes today.

What you'll need: Your Pepper Board and glue or your journal and a pen.

What it's about: Naming the 3–5 boundaries that will protect your spark.

How to do it:

1. **Review your leaks.** Look back at the biggest drains and leaks you spotted in the last chapter.
2. **Choose one nonnegotiable per pillar.**
   - Performance: career, work, creative output, growth

- Relationships: partner, kids, family, friends, colleagues
- Well-being: health, rest, spirituality, energy rituals

3. **Make it specific and measurable.** Examples:
   - Performance → *No pings after 8 p.m.*
   - Relationships → *One daily walk with my partner, phones away.*
   - Well-being → *Nap or rest ritual once a week.*

4. **Write them down.** Post your three nonnegotiables on your Pepper Board or in your journal.

What to expect: Your Judge will scream; people may push back. But over time, boundaries stop feeling like cages and start feeling like freedom.

Nonnegotiables aren't just about what you hold. They're also about what you release. Most of us carry invisible sandbags: fear, envy, expectations, the weight of what others think. As long as we cling to them, we stay tethered, stuck on the ground. But when you protect your spark with nonnegotiables, you create the conditions for *flow*. Flow only happens when your boundaries hold, your energy is steady, and your gut has the clarity to lead.

Reflection

____

____

____

____

____

*   *   *

Flow On Demand

We've worked on building awareness, strengthening habits, and protecting your fuel. Now we arrive at what all of that was leading toward: flow. The goal of this book has never been to hustle harder. It's to build a life and business you *want*—one that feels aligned, sustainable, and alive. Flow—often described as being "*in the zone*"—is the state that makes that possible.

We've talked about being and doing as two separate worlds. Flow is the best of both: awareness and performance as one. In flow, you're not just checking boxes or grinding through tasks—you're fully present, fully engaged, and often surprised by how effortless it feels. Flow is the state that brings focus, energy, and performance. It's what happens when your thoughts stop pulling in different directions and finally start working together. Instead of noise, you get clarity. Instead of forcing, you glide. Your head, heart, and gut are in sync, moving as one.

Most of us live in constant friction—our brain says one thing, our gut another, our emotions a third. That inner conflict burns energy and slows you down. Flow flips that by cutting through the clutter, quieting distractions, and spotlighting the few moves that really matter. Work feels lighter, faster, more alive. That's why athletes describe being *in the zone* and why creators lose track of time when writing, painting, or building. It's not magic; it's alignment.

And flow is about more than productivity. It's about creating the right conditions so your best self can show up consistently—whether in your business, relationships, or well-being. Your gut is the entry point. When you tune into it, you're anchoring yourself in what feels aligned, what matters, what pulls you forward. That's how you stretch without burning out.

PEPPER TIME 30:
FIND YOUR FLOW

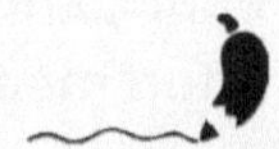

Timing: 15–20 minutes to practice today.

What you'll need: A quiet space and an enjoyable task.

What it's about: Training yourself to slip into flow.

How to do it:

1. **Pick a task you enjoy.** It could be making coffee, playing sudoku, brushing your dog, or cooking dinner. Don't pick something too easy—flow requires just enough stretch to keep your brain engaged.
2. **Raise the challenge slightly.** If you're cooking, try a new recipe. If you're cleaning, see how precisely or quickly you can finish one area. If you're tasting wine, try guessing the grape or writing tasting notes. The goal is to make the task just beyond your current ability—challenging, but not overwhelming.
3. **Clear distractions.** Switch off your phone. Close the door. No multitasking. Flow needs your full attention.
4. **Drop the finish line.** Flow isn't about completion—it's about immersion. Focus on the process itself, not the outcome. Savor the steps as they unfold.

What to expect: Your Judge will try to tell you it's a waste of time. Stay with it. Notice when the chatter quiets and you feel absorbed. That's the doorway to flow. And the more you practice, the easier it gets to step back into it.

Flow is not a luxury. It's alignment. It's where your head, heart, and gut stop fighting and start working together as effort meets ease and your spark expands.

Reflection

____

____

____

____

____

____

____

*   *   *

Self-Love As Policy

We've talked about leaks, nonnegotiables, and flow. None of it holds without one quiet foundation: self-love—the steady, unconditional policy that *no matter what happens today, I am worthy and I am enough*. Back in Chapter 7 we said loving yourself is like Michelangelo "freeing the statue" that already lives inside the marble or brushing years of dust off a Buddha that was always gold underneath. That's the work here: chipping away judgment, doubt, and old expectations until your real self can breathe. With self-love Pepper Reps land deeper, boundaries hold, and flow shows up more often.

Self-love is as simple as remembering that you are as unique as your fingerprints. You don't need to prove your value by doing more or pleasing everyone. It doesn't take hours of meditation to practice this mindset. It takes seconds, A Pepper Rep: a hand on your heart, a breath, a simple phrase repeated—*I am enough. I am worthy. I am already whole.* Do this often, and self-love becomes a daily rhythm. Because the way you treat yourself determines the life you build. Self-love is the spark that makes it all sustainable.

Protecting your fuel is about honoring the truth that your energy is your most precious resource. Time will never feel like enough. Tasks will never be finished. The Judge will never fully go silent. But you can choose how you protect your spark. When you stop leaking energy, set clear nonnegotiables, practice flow, and anchor yourself in self-love, life begins to feel lighter. It's a gut-led decision: deciding from the inside out, building a business and life that runs on alignment instead of depletion.

Take one small action today. Plug one leak. Say one "no." Do one Pepper Rep in self-love. Protect just a little more fuel than yesterday. Then repeat tomorrow. Over time, these tiny choices compound into a fire that keeps burning no matter what storms roll in. Protect your spark, and you'll have the energy to build not just the business you want but the life you're here to live.

The Only Deadline That Matters

Death. You can skip emails, cancel meetings, even dodge your saboteurs for a while—but you cannot escape death. Everything we've been working on—quieting your Judge, building your Pepper Reps, stepping into flow, listening to your gut—leads here. If you don't face death, you'll keep living as if you have unlimited time, stuck in autopilot, forever chasing "someday." But this chapter isn't about dying—it's about living. Death is the mirror that strips away all excuses. It forces you to ask: Am I awake? Am I making conscious choices that will lead me toward the life I want?

Death slammed into me uninvited, tearing the ground out from under my feet. First, it was my mom—suddenly gone in a way that left me breathless and broken. Not long after, it was my aunt. Then my grandparents. Then a close family friend. One by one, the people who had been pillars in my world disappeared, and loss became not a rare event but a relentless presence in my life.

My parents went out cycling one ordinary Sunday morning, something they had done countless times before. The cornfields were high, the roads quiet. A car came too fast around a corner. In seconds, everything changed. She flipped over her bike, and the car struck her. Gone. Just like that. My father rode right behind her. He saw it all. He screamed her name, tried everything in his power to pull her back, to will her to breathe again. But she had already slipped away.

An hour later, my phone rang. My sister's voice cracked open with a scream I can still hear in my bones: *"She's dead!! There's blood everywhere!"* I fainted. My world collapsed. One moment

I had a mother. The next, I didn't. The axis of my life tilted, and nothing would ever be the same.

That moment stripped life down to its rawest essence. Death didn't just take my mom; it ripped away the illusion of certainty. Suddenly, everything I thought I could control—plans, goals, routines—felt fragile. And yet, paradoxically, that experience took away one of my greatest fears: I am no longer afraid to die. Friends shared their own stories of loss with me, many even more shocking than mine. It opened my eyes to something we rarely talk about: Almost everyone you meet is carrying invisible grief: heartbreaks, tragedies, and scars that never fully heal.

Death is the great equalizer. It humbles us, but it also has the power to awaken us.

It's not about controlling the uncontrollable. It's about shifting from fear to presence, from clinging to letting go, from mere survival to finding meaning. Death strips away the noise and makes clear what truly matters—being.

Here are three lessons death teaches—not about dying, but about living:

Lesson 1: Stop Fighting Reality. The first reflex of your Judge when death appears is protest. It's the same voice you've already learned to spot in other areas of life. It fights reality, wastes energy, and feeds fear. But death doesn't negotiate. No amount of *what ifs* or *if onlys* can rewrite the truth. And the more you resist, the more you suffer. The shift happens when you stop fighting what you cannot change and reclaim your energy for what you can. Acceptance is strength and clarity.

It's choosing not to let the Judge chain you to battles you can never win.

Lesson 2: Live Like It's Now. Life is not an endless rehearsal. Yet most of us behave as if we'll always have more time: *Someday I'll rest. Someday I'll travel. Someday I'll tell them how much they mean to me.* But "someday" is an illusion. Losing my mom shattered the lie of infinite tomorrows. It forced me to ask: *What if today is it? What story am I writing right now?* This is where presence and flow come alive. Because life is lived in the exact breath you are taking.

Lesson 3: Hold It Lightly. Everything you love is temporary. One day, you will have to let it all go. That sounds brutal, but it's also liberating. Because if nothing is truly yours to keep, then everything is yours to cherish fully while it's here. The tighter you cling, the more fragile you feel. The looser you hold, the freer you become. Think of it as life on rental. You enjoy the place while you're in it, care for it as best you can, and when the lease ends, you hand back the keys. And you carry with you the moments of joy you lived inside. This is where unconditional love shines through. When my mom died, everything nonessential fell away. What remained was love—pure, unconditional, beyond reason or demand. That's what endures.

Control is an illusion, now is all you ever have, and life is richer when you loosen your grip. We spend so much energy avoiding the topic of death when in truth, facing it is what brings us back to living fully. Every Pepper Rep you've practiced, every stretch, every experiment—it all points here. To presence, love, and living a life you won't regret when the final chapter closes. May death find us awake, grateful, laughing, giving, loving. Because the only deadline that matters is this: Your life is now.

Take one breath, hand on heart. Remember: *I am enough. I choose what matters*. The small reps you've stacked are now a runway. What you've saved in scattered effort is ready to fund your next level.

Turn the page. It's time to use this fuel on purpose—**to answer your calling and step into your Play Big Era.**

Chapter 11:

Your Play Big Era

Play Big isn't just a slogan. It's your *calling*. Earlier, through the gingerbread experiment, you explored what really matters to you. With the Future Self visualization, you saw who you're becoming. With the Pepper Board, you made those priorities visible and actionable. Now it's time to knit it all together—to define your hero's story, your deeper "why," your reason for being here. Because everything is connected.

From the beginning, we've explored why your brain doesn't run well on autopilot or when the Judge is in charge. It needs Pepper—tiny reps that build power, clarity, and alignment. With that fuel, you can do more than survive tasks. You can run your life and business from the inside out, aligned with your calling.

Now, in your Play Big Era, your skills become a story, your experiments become a compass, and your presence, your choices, and your fuel align with your bigger why.

Finding Your Bigger Why

This is the moment where everything we've practiced comes together. You've built the skills, strengthened the muscles, and learned to step into flow. But skills are just the training ground. The deeper question is: **What are you training for?** This is where your hero's journey begins. At some point, it's not about the reps, the habits, or even the flow—it's about the reason behind them. Every hero has a "why," a calling that pulls them forward when comfort would hold them back.

A calling is about aligning your life with your inner compass and doing the work that feels truly yours. It could be raising your children with integrity, creating art that stirs hearts, launching a business that changes lives, or simply choosing to live each day with presence and love. What matters isn't the size of the calling—it's the truth behind it. And every calling begins with resistance. The Judge whispers: *It's too big. Too small. Too selfish. Too unrealistic.* Your hero's journey starts the moment you step in anyway.

This is also when your hidden powers emerge—your Power Brain perspective, your deeper resilience, your capacity to love and lead. And often, when you take that first bold step, life meets you halfway. Doors open where only walls were before. Allies appear. Opportunities surface.

So let's define it clearly: a calling is a longing to address a particular need in the world, to make a contribution for the good, to bring more love into the world. The skills we've built so far are the tools you need to answer your calling. Some callings are big and long-term. Others are small moments that shift lives. What defines a calling is not its duration but the sense of passion and urgency behind it—the pull toward a particular need.

- *I felt called to teach kindergarten and create a safe environment where children could grow.*
- *I felt called to develop a new kind of bodywork that helps people live with vitality.*
- *I felt called to start a tech company that helps women manage their finances with confidence.*

And for me? I felt called to bring women into their Pepper Time—so they stop holding themselves back and finally start building the life and business they truly want right now.

These are very different callings, but each springs from the same source: a genuine longing to serve, create, and love. Following your calling is one of the most fulfilling and courageous ways to play bigger. And this is the heart of your Play Big Era—finally doing what matters.

Stepping Into Your Hero's Path

You've glimpsed your calling. Maybe it's the pull toward coaching, teaching, creating, leading, healing, or building. The form doesn't matter yet—what matters is that you've felt the tug. The question now is: **How do you step into it?**

Every hero reaches this moment. The threshold. The edge of comfort. The moment where you stop imagining and start becoming. And almost instantly, the saboteurs wake up: *Who do you think you are? You're not ready. You'll fail. This is too much.* But the moment you step in, you are no longer who you were. You've entered a new chapter, and with it come new challenges. But this is also where the magic begins. Because in the face of those challenges, you'll discover powers you didn't even know you had.

Heroes grow by stepping into the unknown. Following your calling doesn't just shape what you *do.* It transforms who you *are.* And when you move in alignment with your calling, something else happens: Doors open, allies appear, resources show up. The path reveals itself, one step at a time.

Now it's your turn—step in, try the experiment, and practice what it means to write your next chapter.

PEPPER TIME 31:
WRITE THE NEXT CHAPTER
OF YOUR HERO'S JOURNEY

Timing: 20–30 minutes.

What you'll need: Your journal, a pen, and a quiet space.

What it's about: Recognizing that every chapter of your life—good, hard, random, joyful—has been preparing you for your calling.

How to do it:

1. **Break it down.** Divide your life into chapters (childhood, early career, family, transitions...). Give each chapter a title.

2. **Name the gift.** For each chapter, ask: *What gift did this season give me?* Maybe resilience. Maybe creativity. Maybe empathy. Write it down.

3. **See the story.** Picture yourself in a cinema, popcorn in hand, watching your story play out on the big screen. Feel how each chapter shaped you for the moment you're in now.

4. **Step into now.** When you reach the present, ask: *What is the next chapter my hero is ready to write?* Describe it with color, tone, energy. And here's the pepper twist: Don't write your next chapter timidly. Write it as if you're already the hero, bold and unapologetic. Because the moment you claim it, the journey has already begun.

What to expect: At first, this may feel strange or even emotional. But over time, you'll see that nothing was wasted. Every struggle, joy, and detour prepared you for now.

Reflection

____

____

____

____

____

____

____

*   *   *

 **# PEPPER ASK: Now get specific.**

- *What is still the biggest challenge on your journey?*
- *What do your saboteurs whisper about it?*
- *Who will you become once you've faced them down?*

The Three Buckets Of Life

To fine-tune your calling, always bring it back to the three essential buckets of life. Inside each bucket are the subdomains where your calling can show up:

 # Relationships: How you love, connect, and belong.

- Intimate relationships: the partner(s) you grow with.
- Family & friends: the community you nurture.
- Contribution & impact: how you give back, mentor, or leave a legacy.
- Community & belonging: clubs, groups, cultural ties that give you roots.

 # Performance: How you contribute, create, and build.

- Career: the work you pour your energy into.
- Finances: your relationship to money, security, and abundance.
- Personal growth & learning: your ongoing education, creativity, and skill-building.
- Leadership & influence: how you inspire, guide, and move others.

 # Well-being: How you sustain and expand your energy.

- Wellness: physical vitality, emotional balance, and mental clarity
- Spirituality: connection to purpose, faith, or a larger meaning.
- Play & joy: fun, hobbies, recharging moments.
- Travel & exploration: expanding your horizons, discovering new places, cultures, and perspectives.
- Environment & lifestyle: the spaces you live in, nature, home, and daily rhythms that nourish you.

Each of these subdomains is a place where your calling can take shape. And they don't exist in silos—they feed one another. Strong wellness supports performance. Healthy finances free up energy for joy. Meaningful relationships ground your growth. The danger is spending your life climbing the wrong mountain—pursuing a career to impress, chasing money for validation, staying in relationships that drain you.

Your inner compass already knows your true path. And with the tools you've built, you can keep steering back into alignment. When you do, every bucket syncs with your calling. And the story you write is no longer someone else's script—it's yours.

If you enjoyed the earlier visualizations and want to tune in even closer to your calling, try this next practice. It will help you see how each bucket of your life could unfold when lived in full alignment.

PEPPER TIME 32: THE GALLERY OF YOUR FUTURE BUCKETS

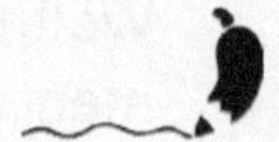

Timing: 20 minutes.

What you'll need: A quiet, comfortable space.

What it's about: Exploring the major life domains (your "buckets") through the eyes of your wiser elder self—so you can see what true fulfillment looks like and feel the pull of your calling more clearly.

How to do it:

1. **Choose your focus.** Decide which five of the subdomains we just discussed you want to explore.
2. **Settle in.** Sit comfortably. Close your eyes. Take a few deeper breaths than usual, feeling the rise and fall of your chest. Let your breath return to its natural rhythm. Gently rub your fingertips together—a Pepper Rep to anchor presence.
3. **Meet your elder self:**
    - Imagine yourself many years into the future.
    - You are healthy in body and mind, radiant, and at peace.
    - Picture the life you're living: where you dwell, what surrounds you, the colors, the textures.
    - Your wiser elder self appears. Notice their eyes, posture, aura. Feel their calm strength.
    - They smile and invite you to walk with them into a gallery.

4. **Enter the gallery:**
   - You step inside. The gallery is quiet, glowing with light.
   - Five large canvases line the walls, each one spotlighting a subdomain of your life lived fully and in alignment.
   - Together, you'll walk from canvas to canvas.
   - Answer the following questions for each canvas:
   - What scene appears here?
   - Who or what is present? Are you in the scene? Someone else?
   - Notice details: objects, symbols, or colors that represent fulfillment in this domain.
   - What emotions fill this canvas?
   - Ask: What truly matters here?

5. **Return & Reflect:**
   - Walk back to the entrance of the gallery.
   - Turn and look at the five canvases shining together. Feel how they form a whole, integrated life.
   - Your elder self embraces you. Feel their wisdom merging into you.
   - Breathe deeply, knowing this wisdom is always accessible.
   - Slowly bring awareness back to your body: your feet on the floor, your breath rising and falling.
   - When you're ready, open your eyes.

What to expect: At first, the canvases may feel vague—just colors, symbols, or emotions. Stay open and trust what comes. Sometimes you'll see what you already knew; sometimes you'll be surprised. Either way, each image is your inner compass showing you what truly matters.

Reflection

____

____

____

____

____

____

____

*   *   *

 **# PEPPER ASK: When you finish, write about what you saw or felt.**

- *What did your elder self show you?*
- *What really matters?*
- *What isn't worth the energy?*
- *What's the next step in your hero's journey?*
- *Have you chosen the right goal, one that truly inspires you?*
- *Does this goal come from your gut and self-respect, or from fear and perfectionism?*

If you feel overwhelmed, remember that you don't have to do it all alone. Find champions and accountability partners. Who in your life will cheer you on and hold you steady? Revisit Pepper

Time 10: your People Tree experiment—you've already mapped them out. See yourself as partnered with a larger force.

Build on your unique strengths and resources. Anchor into what already works for you. Make the supportive choice the default. Use your Pepper Board and your weekly priorities to keep the most aligned actions front and center. Show yourself compassion when you stumble. Progress is built on return. Every time you come back, you get stronger. I want you to live your **full potential.** To create the life and business you dream about—not the one you think you "should" have.

Self-actualization is about alignment. It means fulfilling your deepest human needs and living into the potential that is yours alone.

This is your Play Big Era. Not louder. Not busier. Aligned.

Owning Your Story

As you navigate the challenges of love, work, health, and everything in between, pause and recognize this fundamental truth: A relationship doesn't make you worthy of love. Success doesn't make you worthy of respect. Perfect health doesn't make you worthy of joy. **Your existence does.** You spend your entire life with only one person: you. Which means the most important relationship you will ever have—the one that underpins every other bucket—is the one you have with yourself.

In **relationships,** you've learned to stop making other people the problem and reclaim your power by choosing how you show up. In **performance,** you've realized that impact and achievement only matter when they align with your inner compass. In **well-being,** you've seen that energy, vitality, and peace begin with the way you care for yourself.

You deserve relationships that elevate you, work that inspires you, and a body and mind that feel like home. But the foundation for all of it is how you treat yourself. So respect your own boundaries, show yourself the compassion you easily offer others, and allow yourself to pursue dreams without waiting for someone else's approval.

The love, respect, and care you give yourself sets the standard for every other area of your life. When you stop chasing validation and start honoring yourself, you send a clear message to the world about how you deserve to be treated, how you deserve to work, and how you deserve to live.

PEPPER ASK: So ask yourself:

- *Will I prioritize my own happiness?*
- *Will I pursue my dreams with passion?*
- *Will I set boundaries that protect my peace?*
- *Will I choose relationships that uplift and inspire me?*
- *Will I love myself enough to walk away when something no longer works?*

You are the love of your life. And the story you create—full of meaningful relationships, aligned work, and vibrant well-being—begins and ends with you.

Play Big Or Stay Stuck

Now it's your time to play big. To add that pepper. To design the life you want—relationships that lift you, performance that feels purposeful, well-being that sustains you. The world needs your gift. You are here for a reason.

I know what you might be thinking: *But Jolien, really—I have nothing unique to offer. It's all been done before.*

That's the saboteurs whispering that you're not enough. Here's how you crush it: Start a hype file. Collect every win, every thank-you, every reminder of your impact. Shine your light out, not in. Stop overanalyzing. Put it into the world. Remember the life-changing regrets people confess at the end: *"I wish I'd had the courage to live a life true to myself, not the life others expected of me."* Don't let that be your story.

You've always held the power—you've just been giving it away. Think of the sky: clear one day, stormy the next. You've spent too much energy trying to control the weather, hoping for endless sunshine. But storms don't ruin the sky—they make it magnificent. The same is true for your life. You can't control the weather. But you can choose how it impacts you. That's where your power lives.

Back To Default

One of my biggest goals in writing this book was to help you feel excited again. To reset you back to joy—not as an afterthought, but as a strategy. Because happiness isn't a reward at the finish line. It's the fuel that gets you there. Maybe you've slipped back into old habits at times. Old neural pathways are strong. But every experiment you've done here—every Pepper Rep, every visualization—has built new ones. You've been rewiring your brain toward presence, resilience, and joy. That's what creates lasting change.

Remember: Joy is not a luxury. It's your default state—when you allow it.

"**If you want to go fast, go alone. If you want to go far, go together. **"

— African Proverb

Part IV

The Pepper Revolution

Up to now, this book has been about *you*. But when one Scaleur dares to live boldly, it sparks ripples. When many do, it creates a revolution.

Part 4 is about that revolution. It's where you shift from individual mastery to collective impact. From living aligned to leading aligned. From keeping your pepper to yourself to spreading it like wildfire. By the end of this section, you'll know the GutScaleur Code—the principles that transform personal courage into a movement. You'll learn how to give, how to lift others as you rise, and how to create shifts that go far beyond you.

You'll see that you don't need more time, more degrees, or more permission. What you need is to dare to go all in. Because gut leadership isn't just about building a business or a life—it's about building a legacy.

Chapter 12:

Pepper In The Ass

We live in a world obsessed with "more." More hours. More effort. More proving. Mothers compare lunches on Instagram. Colleagues compare hours at the office. Couples compare their highlight reels. It never ends. But more is not always better. Managing your energy wisely—knowing when to push, when to rest—isn't weakness. It's power. People won't remember the perfect meals, the tidy house, or the endless hustle. They'll remember how they felt when you were really with them.

That's why you need the pepper. Not just to move faster, but to live truer. To give yourself permission to be fully here, fully alive, and aligned with the life only you can build. And that is the doorway to becoming a GutScaleur.

The Gutscaleur Mindset

No real change in the world happens until we first dare to change ourselves. You've already learned how to catch your Judge, flip a sabotaging thought, and strengthen your Power Brain with Pepper Reps. The GutScaleur mindset is about taking those tools and making them your way of being.

Simple? Yes. Easy? No. It takes humility to admit when you're slipping, courage to step again, and self-compassion to keep going. It takes humor when you catch yourself back in old habits, and patience as you rewire, one rep at a time. Your brain is always running programs in the background. You've trained yourself to notice when a program is destructive. The GutScaleur twist is this: Don't just interrupt the thought—*upgrade the whole operating system.*

When a thought says, *"I already know this,"* don't shut down. Pause, take a breath, and drop into your gut. Ask: *"What's the deeper layer here? How can I live this more fully?"* When a thought says, *"This won't work for me,"* notice it for what it is— the Judge trying to protect you. Then check in with your gut: *"What would make this work for me?"*

Every time you flip a thought, you strengthen your Power Brain, open space for your gut to speak, and train yourself to see opportunities instead of dead ends. That's the GutScaleur mindset: curiosity, courage, and alignment in action.

What It Means To Be A Gutscaleur

You know the tools. But tools alone don't shift your life or business. A GutScaleur is someone who **lives by them daily**—someone who refuses to just collect insights and instead turns them into aligned action. At its core, a GutScaleur is someone who takes **100%** responsibility for their life and business. No outsourcing. No waiting. No blaming circumstances, bosses, or parents. They know that leadership starts with the one person they'll spend every day of their life with: themselves.

A GutScaleur chooses alignment over excuses, even when it's uncomfortable. A GutScaleur turns obstacles into experiments instead of dead ends. The setback of a launch that flopped becomes fuel for a sharper offer. The fight with a partner becomes a lab for practicing boundaries and love. Most of all, a GutScaleur knows the difference between reasons and results. Reasons sound logical: *The market isn't ready.* But reasons don't move you forward. Results do. And GutScaleurs are ruthless about choosing results.

GutScaleurs follow a few simple but powerful rules. They try before they deny: Instead of dismissing an idea or experiment, they test it. That's how innovation happens—through messy reps, not polished plans. They lean into the stretch: Discomfort isn't danger—it's the signal of growth. A GutScaleur dares to launch the program before it feels perfect, to say no when it would be easier to people-please, to pitch the client that scares them. They rise with their tribe.

And courage multiplies when shared, so GutScaleurs don't isolate or play lone-wolf heroes—they build circles of accountability, generosity, and boldness. They know movements are born in communities, not in silos. And they lead from their gut, not their ego. Ego chases approval, applause, or external validation. Gut leadership listens inward, acts in alignment, and dares to go all in. A GutScaleur builds a business not just to impress but to serve. They scale not by burning themselves out but by fueling others along the way.

That's the identity. That's the practice. And when you live it, you don't just build a business—you build a legacy. You don't just scale numbers—you scale impact, joy, and meaning.

Busting The Big Three Excuses

Many of my Scaleurs who start coaching with me hit the same three walls. GutScaleurs don't pretend these excuses don't exist—they just refuse to stay stuck there.

The first is *"I don't have time."* But if it matters, you make time. If it doesn't, you make an excuse. I once worked with a client who said she had no time to launch her side business. We found she was scrolling two hours every evening. She gave herself pepper—set a timer, cut the scroll, and used that window to draft her first offer. Within weeks she had paying clients. The time was always there. The choice was the shift.

The second is *"I don't have the money."* Resources are built, not handed over. You can find side gigs, spend less, sell what you don't need, seek grants, or ask for help. GutScaleurs get creative because they know lack is often perspective, not reality.

\# The third is *"I don't know how."* Not knowing is neutral—it's just the starting line. Believing you can't learn? That's the trap. GutScaleurs flip it into: *"How can I figure this out?"*

The Pepper Choice

At the end of the day, the most powerful words in the universe are the ones you say to yourself. Every thought, every reaction, every day is a choice. GutScaleurs choose courage over excuses. They choose gift goals over should goals. They choose pepper—not just to go faster, but to live truer. And once you start choosing like this consistently, you stop seeing yourself as someone *trying* and start seeing yourself as someone *becoming*.

That's the GutScaleur identity.

It begins with being—the quiet power of observing your thoughts, choosing presence, and refusing to live on autopilot. From there comes action—the tools you've practiced to rewrite your brain, silence the Judge, and listen to your gut. Once you act from that place, flow becomes possible. That's when you stop forcing and start aligning, when your choices feel lighter because they match who you truly are.

Flow isn't just about productivity—it's about joy. And when you stay long enough in alignment, you rediscover your default state: happiness, the unconditional joy of being fully alive. And here's the final step: When you touch that joy, you can't help but share it. True fulfillment comes when you give—from your presence, your talents, your love, your leadership. Once you've chosen pepper for yourself, the question becomes: What will you do with it?

The answer is simple. You give.

Giving To Grow

GutScaleurs shift into useful thoughts quickly when life throws them off course. They don't waste energy cursing the problem. They move. They call a meeting, gather facts, and get going. That shift into useful thinking is one of the biggest neural drivers of happiness—and one of the best-kept secrets to lasting success.

And here's the twist: The most powerful way to create useful thoughts is through giving. Fear shrinks your world to survival—my deadlines, my stress, my problems. But giving flips your attention outward: *How can I contribute? How can I help? What can I create that lasts beyond me?* Giving is the bridge that turns private growth into public impact.

Think about the three main pillars of life we've been building all along:

 # In Relationships, giving means love without conditions. When I became a mother, a flood of unconditional love rushed through me. Not *"I love you because..."*—but *"I love you. Full stop."* That love taught me the essence of giving: no demand, no transaction, just presence. And presence is the greatest gift we can offer. A mother who puts down her phone at the dinner table to give her child full attention gives more than time—she gives security, connection, and joy. When you extend that same love to a partner, a colleague, or even a stranger—a smile, a compliment, a word of appreciation—you don't just lift them, you expand yourself.

In Performance, giving means creating with purpose. The entrepreneurs and leaders we admire most aren't remembered for their revenue numbers but because they gave dignity, opportunity, or possibility to others. Think of a leader who takes time to mentor a junior colleague instead of hoarding knowledge. Or a founder who builds a product around what customers truly need, not just what looks good on a pitch deck. These choices may not always look like the fastest way to profit, but they're the ones that create trust, loyalty, and legacy. Performance-giving shifts the question from *"How do I get more?"* to *"How do I give more?"*—and ironically, when you give this way, success follows anyway.

In Well-Being, giving begins with yourself. Conditional self-love says: *"I'll rest when I earn it. I'll love myself when I succeed. I'll be kind once I've proved enough."* But true well-being starts when you give yourself what you'd freely give a loved one: warmth, safety, rest. An entrepreneur who gives herself permission to pause is fueling her own courage and creativity, which in turn fuels everyone she leads. Neuroscience shows that when you feel safe, your brain literally rewires—stress hormones drop, creativity rises, resilience strengthens. And sometimes giving means letting go: of the hustle myth, of the clutter, of the toxic client. Letting go is its own kind of generosity—one that creates space for better things to flow in.

The best part is that giving doesn't deplete you—it expands you. More stuff makes us anxious. More status leaves us restless. But giving almost always leaves us richer inside. I've seen it countless times: the client who donates to a cause and rediscovers her passion. The founder who shifts from *"How do I get more?"* to *"How do I give more?"* and finds that the clients come anyway. The mother who gives her child presence at the dinner table and finds herself nourished, too.

That's why I've made this my mission: to help one million Scaleurs build the life and business they love. But not just to thrive alone. I want them to light up their families, their clients, their teams, and their communities. I want them to fall back in love with themselves, their work, and the world. Because giving isn't a sacrifice—it's the smartest thing you can ever choose to do.

That's why *Give* is the final loop. Everything we've built so far—remembering your default state of joy (part 1), rewiring your brain and gut to work for you instead of against you (part 2), and stepping into alignment and flow (part 3)—was leading here. Because growth is meant to ripple outward. When you give, you multiply. Give love, and it grows in the people around you. Give energy, and it expands into the spaces you touch. Give courage, and you create permission for others to rise.

This is where your pepper-boldness shifts from *me* to *we*. From building a life and business you love to shaping the culture around you. From chasing "more" to creating what matters. Giving isn't the end of your journey—it's the point where your personal transformation becomes a revolution.

Every extra thing—whether a shirt in your closet, a client who drains you, or a belief you've outgrown—takes up space you could use for joy. If nothing is ever really yours to keep, what can you release today? What can you give that would multiply—not just for someone else, but for you too?

From Solo Rebellion To Collective Rise

My mission has always been clear: one million Scaleurs happy and loving. Not perfect. Not always "on." Just alive, present, and building lives and businesses they love. Because when we prioritize happiness—not as a reward, but as a daily choice—we stop waiting for someday and start living now. And when you change your thoughts, actions, and presence, you change your world and touch others. Your little world—your family, your team, your circle—is where the ripple begins. Make that world better, and you've already changed the bigger one.

In a nutshell:

- Make happiness your strategy—not the afterthought.
- Invest in your joy and presence like they're your most valuable assets.
- Tell people. Share it. Happiness grows when it's spoken out loud.

I've lost count of how many Scaleurs I've worked with who circle back to me—sometimes weeks later, sometimes years. They send photos of their Pepper Boards becoming reality. They write about conversations they never thought they'd have, dreams they never thought they'd chase, and goals that once felt impossible now sitting in their calendars. Proof that awareness plus action creates a thriving trinity of brain, body, and spirit. Because the more you visualize, the more you practice, the more you dare—the more your life starts to align. And as it aligns, it multiplies.

Momentum compounds. You attract more, achieve more, and *become* more each year that you live truer. And yes, Scaleurs tell me, "You changed my life." But no. I gave them the tools. They changed it. They were the ones who showed up, rewrote the stories, stretched beyond the Judge, and chose pepper over autopilot. It was their courage, consistency, and belief that made the shift.

So imagine looking back at the ripple you started today in five, ten, and twenty years. Imagine the business you built, the love you cultivated, the impact you created—not by waiting, but by daring to live it now. That's the power of pepper. That's the revolution. I'm proud every time participants tell me they've discovered that they are, in fact, already enough to go after what they want. And most of all, that they see themselves as part of something bigger—a global network of leaders creating a shift.

That's why I built this movement. Because I got tired of meeting women with brilliant ideas, powerful messages, and stories that could change lives who were staying silent out of self-doubt. The world doesn't need quieter dreams. It needs louder courage.

So, here we are. You've done the inner work. You've practiced the reps. You've chosen pepper. And now, it's no longer just about you. It's about us. This is where individual rebellion becomes collective rise. Where your spark joins others and together we create a culture of courage, joy, and contribution. That's the revolution: not waiting for permission or shrinking back into "fine," but choosing to rise—boldly, unapologetically, together.

Chapter 13:

Daring To Go All In

Back in the preface, I asked you a question: *What would be the most inspiring change you want to create in your life this year?* That wasn't just a warm-up. That was your compass. Every experiment, every Pepper Rep, every gut check, every shift we've made together was pointing you here, to this choice.

You've walked through the lies of the Judge, stretched through discomfort, rewired your brain, and felt your gut pulling you back to truth. You've chosen bold pepper moves and tasted flow, joy, and unconditional love. You've seen how giving multiplies. You've even stared death in the eye and realized time is too precious to waste. All of it was leading here, to this final dare.

Ask yourself: If all the energy and time you've spent resisting reality—wanting lines to move faster, wanting people to text you back, wanting your boss to recognize your worth, wanting people to like you, wanting your family to support your choices—if all those thoughts, feelings, and precious hours were redirected toward something that truly mattered, where would you be? Who would you be? What would you have built?

What's the cost of not daring to go all in? Think of the people you never introduced yourself to. The career you wanted to pursue but shelved. The music, the stand-up, the book you never wrote. The photo you didn't post. The trip you never planned. The truth you never said. The love you never risked. Can you afford that price? I know I can't.

We all tell ourselves stories about why others succeed: They were born rich, they're prettier, luckier, smarter, more connected. That's a cop-out. The real difference between you and them is that at some point, they stopped waiting. They stopped letting the weather outside dictate their sky inside. They dared. They stretched. And every stretch made them stronger.

STOP!

Stop wasting your brain space on the million tiny things that don't matter. It's time to use every second of your day for all the amazing things you know you're capable of.

Stop letting the fear of what people might think paralyze you. It's time to go after your dreams boldly, relentlessly, unapologetically.

Stop tiptoeing around everyone else's emotions. It's time to fiercely protect your own peace.

Stop letting other people's success devastate you. It's time to get to work.

Stop trying to change people who don't want to change. Let adults be adults.

Stop trying to rescue everyone. Let them heal the way they need to.

Stop wasting your time begging for love. Choose the love you deserve.

This is your moment to reclaim your power. You can have the life you've always wanted. You can be a millionaire. You can have the love story you dream of. You can build a career that excites and fulfills you.

The question is: Do YOU dare to go all in? Do you dare to put that pepper in your ass and make it happen?

The whole point of pepper is to remind you that you are responsible. For your happiness. For the energy you bring. For how you show up. For telling the truth even when it's hard. For waking up every day and moving toward what matters. No one else owes you anything, but you owe yourself everything.

And if you're not where you want to be, here's the good news: The second you decide differently, everything changes. The world will always do what it does. People will gossip, doubt, succeed, fail, cheer, or criticize. But you? You will remain unshaken. You get to decide what you think, what you say, and how you live. That's the pepper. That's the shift. That's your liberation.

DARE

Now that we're here, I want to welcome you into your *Play Big Era*.

Dare to get started.

Dare to take a risk.

Dare to write the book.

Dare to speak the truth.

Dare to get in the best shape of your life.

Dare to apply for the dream job.

Dare to stop pouring love into people who don't want it.

Dare to build the life that makes you proud. The one that makes you happy. The one where your energy fuels presence, joy, and impact.

You've always had the power. Now, it's time to put the pepper where it belongs and take it back.

Because the world needs you fully awake, fully bold, fully you. So here's my invitation: Stop waiting. Start now. Keep coming back to the experiments. Keep practicing the reps. Keep choosing pepper. Keep daring. Whatever dream you see for yourself, however wild, impossible, or "too much" it feels—I see it for you. And until you believe it yourself, let me believe it for you. This is the beginning of your *Play Big Era*.

It's time.

Pepper time.

Let's play.

Afterword :

Pepper Time

What would your life look like if you lived more loyal to your dreams and less influenced by your fears?

For me, daring to answer that question changed everything. What began as a side spark—something small, a hobby, an experiment—grew into companies, teams, a global community, a movement. A movement of GutScaleurs who stopped waiting for permission and started adding pepper, trusting their gut, and playing big on their own terms.

I dared to go all in. And that meant daring across all three buckets:

- I went all in on my **performance,** starting and scaling companies, raising funds, leading teams, even when fear screamed louder than my confidence and critics lined up with their opinions.
- I went all in on my **relationships,** becoming a wife and a mother of two, showing up not perfectly but

fully—choosing presence over comparison, love over judgment.

- And I went all in on my **well-being,** giving myself permission to rest, ask for help, travel with my family to new countries every year, and let joy be a compass instead of an afterthought.

Was I scared? Absolutely. Did I get criticized? A hundred percent. But going all in doesn't mean waiting until the fear disappears or the noise quiets. It means moving anyway—choosing courage over excuses, pepper over autopilot, your truth over their expectations.

And here's the rawest part: I wrote this book while pregnant, growing a baby and these words at the same time. Two parallel acts of creation—one kicking inside me, the other pouring out of me. People asked if motherhood would change my work. If ambition and presence could coexist. If I could still put pepper in my ass and be a loving mom.

My answer? Yes. It changed everything. And no, it didn't take anything away. I am both. I am the mother who delights in baby giggles and sleepless nights and the entrepreneur who lights up building visions with her team. I am fiercely in love with my kids, and I am fiercely in love with my work. And I refuse to believe that one cancels the other.

Motherhood demanded a new kind of daring. Trusting my gut about when and how to ramp work back up. Giving myself permission to ask for help. Challenging that inner critic that whispered, *"You're a bad mom because you put your kid in daycare."* I had panic moments thinking I couldn't finish this book with a newborn. But then I discovered something liberating: There was no conflict between being a loving, present mom and doing my work. Both had space. Both mattered. Both were me.

We don't hear enough of these stories—the ones where women thrive in both. Where they say, "I feel good about how it all fits together." Too often, we only hear exhaustion and sacrifice. But you don't have to lose yourself to love your family.

So here's the truth I've lived: You are in charge. Always have been. When you stop handing your power away and go all in, your dreams don't stay pinned on vision boards. They materialize and ripple outward—into your family, your business, your community, your world. And when the Judge creeps back in (because it will), when autopilot sneaks up, when fear whispers again—come back. Come back to the experiments and the Pepper Times. To your reps, your gut, and your pepper. Again and again.

This book has been about daring to live fully. Daring to play big in your performance, your relationships, and your well-being. Daring to be loyal to your dreams instead of obedient to your fears.

So wherever you are—whether at a desk, in a boardroom, in your kitchen, or rocking a baby to sleep—this is your moment. Don't shrink. Don't wait. Don't hand your joy over to judgment. Put the pepper in your ass.

Because what's good for you is good for everyone you touch.

Appendix A:

Sensory Pepper Reps

Your fastest way back to presence isn't by thinking differently—it's by sensing differently. Your body is always here, always now, and your senses are the anchors that can pull you out of autopilot in seconds. That's the power of Sensory Pepper Reps. Each one uses a simple sense—sight, sound, touch, breath, taste, or body awareness—as a reset switch. They take as little as ten seconds or as long as you want. You can do them anywhere: on a Zoom call, walking down the hall, before hitting "send," even while brushing your teeth.

Think of these reps as **hardware hacks for your nervous system.** Mindset work is like rewriting your software: It changes the stories you run. But Sensory Reps work directly on the hardware, calming and recalibrating your body in real time. Do them often, and they become your default—anchors that bring you back to calm, focus, and presence whenever life tries to knock you off course.

THE VISUAL PEPPER REP: REALLY SEEING

Most of us look without truly seeing. We rush past the details right in front of us, lost in thought, projecting old stories onto people and places. The Visual Rep interrupts that.

Here's how: Pick a color. Find one object in your space that has that color. Study it. Notice its shades, edges, reflections, and textures. When your mind wanders—and it will—gently return to looking. After twenty to thirty seconds, pick a new color and repeat.

What happens? The noise in your head quiets. Your vision sharpens. You see what's actually here, not just what you expect. In conversations, this makes you listen more deeply. Before a big meeting, it drops you into presence. Out on a walk, it makes the world come alive.

THE AUDITORY PEPPER REP: CHOOSING WHAT YOU HEAR

Your nervous system is always scanning sounds in the background—traffic, notifications, someone's voice. Subconsciously, those sounds shape whether you feel tense or safe. The Auditory Rep trains you to choose where to focus your hearing.

Here's how: Close your eyes if you like. Find the farthest sound you can hear—a bird, the refrigerator's hum, a distant car. Then shift to the nearest sound—maybe your breath or your clothes moving. Go back and forth once more, far to near. If thoughts carry you away, return to listening.

The effect is instant. Your system calms down, your focus sharpens, and you're no longer at the mercy of noise. Try it in a meeting by tuning into the timbre of someone's voice instead of racing ahead to your reply. Or listen to a single instrument in a song instead of the whole track. On a walk, follow the rustle of leaves. Even in stillness, notice the faint hum of your room. Each time you do, you teach your brain: Focus is my choice.

THE TACTILE PEPPER REP:
BACK IN YOUR BODY

When stress hits, you tend to leave your body and live in your head. The Tactile Rep pulls you back through touch.

Here's how: Rub your fingertips together and feel the ridges and texture. Slide the fingers of one hand slowly across the other, noticing every shift in pressure and temperature. Hold a mug of coffee or tea and feel its warmth spread. Wiggle your toes inside your shoes and see how many you can sense.

The effect is grounding. Suddenly you're here again, not spinning in thought. Touch sends a direct safety signal to your nervous system. Do this before diving into a big task, before a conflict, or anytime you feel scattered. It anchors you back in the present moment—safe, steady, and able to choose.

THE BREATH PEPPER REP: THE UNIVERSAL RESET

If you only remember one rep, let it be this: breath. Your breath is the one reset always with you, everywhere, anytime.

Here's how: Take three to five slow breaths, deeper than usual. Notice your chest or belly rise and fall. When thoughts pop in, gently label them "thinking" and return to your breath.

You can experiment, too:

- **Box breathing:** Inhale for 4, hold for 4, exhale for 4, hold for 4.
- **Sigh breathing:** Inhale fully, then release with a long audible sigh.
- **Mini-break breath:** Take one deep, intentional breath every time you switch tasks.

Breath Reps work in as little as ten seconds. Do them while washing your hands, in the first minute of a meeting, or before opening an important email. The effect is immediate: calmer nerves, clearer focus, and a little more space between you and your reaction.

THE FOOD & DRINK PEPPER REP: SAVOR THE FIRST BITE

Most people eat and drink on autopilot—scrolling, rushing, barely tasting. The Food & Drink Rep makes your first sip or bite a mindful anchor.

Here's how: Notice the color, smell, and texture. Take one sip or bite. Let it sit in your mouth. Feel the temperature, the weight, the flavor as it shifts. Chew slowly or gently move the liquid with your tongue, track how the taste evolves, then swallow with full attention.

It takes less than a minute, but it changes everything. You feel more satisfied with less, your body's hunger and fullness cues get clearer, and even a simple snack becomes a reset. Your morning coffee centers you. Dinner with family becomes presence, not distraction.

THE TENSION PEPPER REP: RELEASING THE GRIP

We get so used to carrying tension that we stop noticing it. The tight jaw, the hunched shoulders, the stiff belly—they become invisible. The Tension Rep teaches you to notice and soften before the pressure breaks you.

Here's how: Close your eyes. Take a slow breath. Scan your body from head to toe: jaw, shoulders, chest, belly, hips, legs. Pick one tight spot. Stay with it for twenty to thirty seconds. On each exhale, soften it by 2 percent. If it doesn't soften, gently create a squeeze for five seconds, then release and feel the rebound.

The effect is visible: Your face softens, your breath drops lower, and suddenly you feel more space inside. Do this at your desk, in traffic, or lying in bed at night. Each time you release tension, you're training your nervous system to reset instead of snap.

When in doubt, always come back to breath. It's the simplest, most universal rep—and it pairs with everything. Every sip, every walk, every pause can be layered with one conscious breath. That one act, repeated, rewires your system toward calm and presence.

Love Pepper Reps

THE LOVE OTHERS
PEPPER REP

When someone snaps, criticizes, or judges us, we often see only the sharp edge. We react with irritation, defensiveness, or anger. But behind their words is usually their Judge—hammering them even harder than they hammer you. Fear of rejection. Fear of not being enough. Fear of failing. This rep trains you to look beyond the plaster and connect with the Pepper Self underneath.

How to do it:

- Pause when you feel triggered. Close your eyes if you can, and take one grounding breath.
- Recall the person who irritated or judged you. Notice your body's reaction: tight chest, clenched jaw, shallow breath.
- Say silently: *"Their Judge is punishing them harder than their words punish me."*
- To soften further, picture them as their five-year-old self—wide-eyed, hopeful, vulnerable. See their small hands, their smile, their innocence.
- Whisper inwardly: *"I see your fear. I see your Pepper Self under the plaster. May you feel love."*

Anchors: Use this rep when a colleague interrupts, when your partner snaps, when a stranger is rude. Even a single breath-and-reframe can shift irritation into compassion.

What to expect: The anger may not vanish instantly, but it will loosen. You'll feel steadier, less hooked, more human. Sometimes, this opens connection. Other times, it simply gives you peace. Either way, you've reclaimed your power.

THE LOVE YOUR BODY
PEPPER REP

Your Judge loves to attack your body. Over years, that script becomes so normal that you forget the truth: Your body is not a project. It's your lifelong partner. It breathes for you, carries you, heals for you, and shows up every single day. This rep rewires the relationship: from criticism to gratitude.

How to do it:

- Stand in front of a mirror, or simply pause wherever you are.
- Take one deeper breath and soften your gaze. Instead of zooming in on "flaws," let your eyes see the whole of you.
- Place a hand on your chest, belly, or another area that feels tense. Hold for a few breaths.
- Say out loud or silently: *"This body has carried me here. It owes me nothing. I owe it care."*
- Name one loving truth: *"Thank you, legs, for walking me. Thank you, lungs, for breathing. Thank you, skin, for protecting me."*
- If the Judge interrupts—*"You should look better"*—name it: *"That's plaster talking."* Then return to gratitude.
- For a deeper rep: wrap your arms around yourself in a hug. Feel your warmth, your pulse. Whisper: *"This is home."*

Anchors: Start with micro-moments: In the shower, thank your body for carrying you. At night, place a hand on your heart and whisper appreciation before sleep. In stressful moments, breathe into one tense area and thank it for working hard.

What to expect: At first, it may feel awkward. But repetition softens the harshness. Soon, you'll choose healthy food, rest, and movement—not out of guilt, but because love makes care natural.

THE LOVE YOUR LIFE
PEPPER REP

Life isn't neutral—it's either autopilot or presence. The Judge trains you to focus on lack: *What's missing? What's wrong?* But joy is already here if you pay attention. This rep shifts you from complaint to gratitude—not the thin *"I should be grateful"* but the full-bodied appreciation that fills your chest and calms your breath.

How to do it:

- Pause once today—morning, evening, or mid-chaos. Take one slow inhale and exhale.
- Choose one ordinary thing: a cup of tea, the chair beneath you, the sound of birds, your child's laugh.
- Tell yourself: *"This is not small. This is life supporting me right now."*
- Let the details come alive: warmth of the cup, strength of the chair, melody of the birds, sparkle in a child's eye.
- Optional: Run through a list—family, friends, health, work, small pleasures. With each, take one breath of appreciation.

Anchors: Pause for ten seconds before your first sip of coffee, before your first bite of food, or when you climb into bed, and express gratitude. At night, list three small wins or gifts from the day.

What to expect: At first, the Judge may argue that what you have isn't enough. Ignore it. With practice, gratitude shifts your state. You feel more resourced, more alive, less trapped in scarcity. Over time, joy stops being an afterthought and becomes your baseline.

About Me

Just before the launch of this book, I gave birth to our son George — a calm, peaceful baby who seemed perfectly fine.

Until the diagnosis.

Out of nowhere, our world collapsed.

Only 0.01% of babies are born with a profound, bilateral hearing loss.

George was one of them.

We didn't know if he even had an auditory nerve.
We didn't know what his future would look like.
We didn't know how much he would be able to hear, learn, or connect.

Today, George is wearing his first hearing aids.
We are learning, adapting, and discovering a new way of experiencing sound, connection, and growth — together.

And what once felt like fear...
is slowly becoming strength. Life has never spared me from challenges.

Abuse. Loss. Miscarriages. And now this.

But here's what I've learned:

Life doesn't ask for permission before it throws roadblocks — big and small — in your path.

What *is* a choice, is how you respond.

I gathered my energy.

I started again — this time even deeper.

Exploring alternative therapies.
Listening to my body.
Trusting my gut.

Adding the pepper back into my life.

This book was born from that place.

Because this book is not about avoiding pain.

It's about moving through life with the right energy — even when things are uncertain.

It's about continuing — consciously, courageously, and with joy.

I'm Jolien Demeyer.

A **capacity trainer** and founder of **GutScaleurs**.

I help ambitious founders — especially women — expand their internal capacity so they can lead, decide, and grow at their next level.

Because success is not limited by strategy.

It's limited by what your nervous system can hold.

I walked away from a successful corporate career to build a deeply rewarding life — on my own terms.

Today, I'm a gut-driven entrepreneur and coach, supporting **Scaleurs** — entrepreneurs who want to scale not just their business, but their life.

I help them pursue what truly lights them up, make it real, and make it stick.

Over the years, I've launched and built multiple businesses:

- Marketing Scaleurs, a US-based marketing agency I successfully sold
- MyCataleya, a travel and real-estate venture in Florida
- Jelloow, an AI-powered data intelligence company

All of them were built on logic, strategy, and spreadsheets.

But life taught me:

Logic alone is not enough.

Through personal challenges, I shifted from only listening to the brain...

to also listening to the body and the gut.

I trained in polyvagal theory, somatic experiencing, and brain science —

and began rewiring my entire approach to leadership and growth.

That's how GutScaleurs was born.

Today, I'm on a mission to help one million Scaleurs build a life and business they love — and spread that energy outward.

Because when you expand your capacity, everything expands with you.

Pepper Time is the foundation of that work.

A way to retrain your system — in small, daily moments —

to move from knowing… to doing.

From stable… to fully alive.

From stuck… to activated.

Gut Leadership is at the heart of everything I do.

Not choosing between head or heart —

but integrating mind, body, and intuition to lead from within.

Originally from Belgium, I've lived in Chicago and Düsseldorf, and now call Switzerland home — where I live with my husband Tobi and our two children.

You're not stuck.

You're under-seasoned.

It's Pepper Time.

Jolien

Notes

Notes

Notes

Notes

Notes